APPRECIATING PEOPLE

by
Miriam Adahan

Jerusalem – 1988

Readers who cannot find this book in their local bookstores can order it from Yehudis Karbal, 6309 N. Whipple, Chicago, Ill. 60659, or from the author, Miriam Adahan, 1316/2, Ramot 03, Jerusalem, Israel, 97725, Telephone: 02-868-201.

First published 1988 • ISBN 0-87306-485-2

Copyright © 1988 by Miriam Adahan

Third Printing, 1990

Published by Feldheim Publishers Ltd. in conjunction with
Gefen Publishing House Ltd.

Distributed by

Feldheim Publishers Ltd.   Philipp Feldheim Inc.
POB 6525 / Jerusalem, Israel   200 Airport Executive Park
Printed in Israel   Spring Valley, NY 10977

Typesetting by Gefen Publishing House Ltd.

DEDICATION

I DEDICATE THIS BOOK TO MY MOTHER, ANNE DANN LUBORKSY, WHO TAUGHT ME THE MEANING OF TOLERANCE.
AND TO ALL MY GROWTH-ORIENTED FRIENDS AND E.M.E.T.T. MEMBERS, WHO HAVE ENRICHED MY LIFE SO GREATLY AND INSPIRED ME WITH THEIR DEVOTION TO TORAH AND MITZVOTH.

THE BA'AL SHEM TOV SAID THAT THE EXTENT TO WHICH WE LOVE G-D IS SEEN EXACTLY IN THE EXTENT TO WHICH WE LOVE MAN. MAY THIS BOOK INCREASE BOTH LOVE OF G-D AND LOVE OF MAN.

Table of Contents

APPRECIATING PEOPLE

ACKNOWLEDGMENTS
First, I want to express my great appreciation to Rabbi Zelig Pliskin for his on-going encouragement and wisdom. Pam Novak and Happy Ehrlich-Klein devoted many hours of painstaking editorial work and vital corrections. My thanks to those who first looked this manuscript over and offered encouragement, including Rivka Freidman, Tamar Wittenberg, Batya Dilman and Mark Schaffel, and to Rita Halevy for her initial proof-reading. Nechama Moldofsky, of Toronto, wrote enthusiastic letters in which she has shared many helpful insights which I have incorporated into this book. I am indebted to all the many EMETT members and friends who have shared their thoughts with me and verified my belief in the importance of this work.

NOTES ON THE SECOND EDITION
I thank my dear brother, Moshe Dann, who made valuable comments on this second edition. My special thanks to Tzvia Erlich-Klein, who has the editorial brilliance and patience for the meticulous work which was necessary to improve this edition.

Due to various time pressures, the first edition was put out quite hurriedly, in less than two weeks. In the rush, many mistakes were not caught and the lay-out left much to be desired. This was a great embarrassment to me, and I apologize to readers. It is hoped that this edition will be more readable.

To those who read the first edition and wondered why I did not give equal space to each of the eight modes, this is because I have emphasized those types who are most likely to read this kind of book or who find it most difficult to understand themselves.

Many readers complained that, even after reading the entire book, they still could not type themselves, or could not type the people around them. This is a common response. Please do not agonize over who is the "real you." Keep in mind that you are a complex variety of many traits. Some situations and people bring out certain traits, while other situations and people bring out other traits. Some bring out the best in you, some the worst. Furthermore, at different periods in your life, you may be trying to perfect different skills or aspects of yourself. It may take six months or a year of integrating this material in order for you to see your innermost tendencies.

INTRODUCTION
Pain carves dimensions in our psyches which would not otherwise be there. The word "Jew" comes from *hod* — to be appreciative. The source of our strength as a people, and also as individuals, has been our gratefulness to G-d, especially in times of pain. And so, I want to thank Hashem for the many painful events I have experienced because, in retrospect, I can see that they were important learning experiences which led me to be a more compassionate, understanding person: loneliness and rejection, years of struggling with colitis, anorexia, depression, and PSI (see *Raising Children To Care* for explanation).... These losses and disappointments have become as meaningful as the many more obvious gifts with which G-d has blessed me.

The classification system described in this book has helped me to accept myself and has liberated me from my unrealistic demands of myself and others, thus enabling me to be a more loving person. I hope it can do the same for others.

I thank Hashem for caring family members, caring friends, for a poetic soul which both soars and suffers, for four wonderful children who are the joy of my life, for my loving husband, without whose support I would not be able to continue my work, and for the great *bracha* of being able to live in the Holy City of Jerusalem, whose atmosphere and people are a continual inspiration.

LOVE AND KNOWLEDGE

To love someone is to want to know them. When we love a child, for example, we are intimately involved in his or her life. We are concerned about his tangible, physical needs: Has he eaten enough? Has he brushed his teeth? Do his clothes fit? Is he warm enough? In addition, we are also concerned about his intangible, emotional and spiritual needs: How does he feel about his teachers? Are they nice or mean? Is he being challenged intellectually? Is he getting along with his peers? What are his hopes and dreams, his likes and dislikes, his fears and worries? We are there for him and involved with him. We respect his individuality. This is what it means to know and love someone.

Unfortunately, surprisingly few people feel they have ever been really "known" by anyone, and, therefore, have never felt truly loved. In fact, many people feel that they do not know how to love themselves, or know how to sustain a loving relationship with others. In many ways, we remain a mystery to ourselves. And the people around us remain even more of a mystery to us.

The differences between us could be an inspiraton for greater self-awareness and self-improvement. Instead, relationships are very often a source of pain rather than joy. We seek understanding and cooperation and, instead, are often met with antagonism and indifference. We want to have others meet our needs and standards, but, find, instead, that they have their own equally important but opposite demands. The lack of understanding engenders fear, despair, and hatred. Instead of reaching out, we hold back, lash out angrily, or turn off in cold indifference. Instead of nurturing, we criticize. Instead of forgiving, we hang on to resentments. Instead of appreciating what people are, we demand that they change to fit our needs and expectations.

One of the goals of this book is to help you avoid the tendency to retreat in hostility or dominate in anger when your needs are not being met. This book will give you a key for understanding your own and others' motivations and needs, thereby enabling you to be more tolerant and, in many cases, more loving as well. **Remember, this book only provides a key; you then have to open the door and get to know each person as an individual human being.**

HOW THIS BOOK CAME TO BE

Obviously, understanding ourselves is important, for we are told, "Knowledge of self is knowledge of G-d." (*Sefer Ha'Ikarim*) This process of self-knowledge begins by naming ourselves.

It is said that when Adam, the first man, gave names to all the animals, he understood his unique position in the world. The process of seeing what he was not, enabled him to know what he was. In addition, by naming the animals, he saw that he encompassed within himself characteristics of everything he was naming. It also made him long for a mate who would both be similar to him ("bone of my bones") and be different enough to spur him to greater growth and awareness ("opposite but equal helpmate") (*Bereshith* 2:20).

Four years ago, a Jerusalem Rav gave me the book, *Please Understand Me*, by David Keirsey and Marilyn Bates. No other book on psychology had ever fascinated and inspired me the way this book did. I wanted to share it with everyone. However, I realized that many, like myself, who lack Keirsey's scholarly, analytical grasp of complex ideas, might find his terminology rather exasperating and difficult to grasp at first. Thus, I came up with my own terminology which made it easier for the general public to quickly translate the main concepts into a useful reality.

Keirsey's system was briefly described in my last book, *Raising Children To Care*. My EMETT students and friends were delighted with their new awareness. Like myself, they too were having countless "Aha!" responses. It was like lights going on in our heads. We were all suddenly understanding ourselves and the people around us in a way we never had before. People told me how much more accepting and forgiving they were of others. People now had a language with which to define and validate their likes and dislikes. Almost everyone said that they were now more accepting and loving of others and that they had automatically changed their communication tactics with certain people. Obviously, we were on to something quite wonderful.

The four types of children described in my book comprised a simplified version of the sixteen types described by Briggs, Myers, Keirsey and Bates. I gave them names of my own which could be easily remembered and which avoided Keirsey's difficult terminology. The four types represent four different motivating factors. While we all must have some of the traits in each category in order to function effectively in the world, the predominance of one mode over the other emerges as a unique personality type. These four types are:

1. The **AMO**: The name stands for *Autonomy, Adventure, Action and the Manipulation of Objects* in the environment. This type of individual reminded me of a lively "ammunition depot" — action-oriented, freedom-loving, fun-loving, optimistic, tending toward insubordination, individualistic, and hungering for mastery of instruments, tools, and the physical world in general.

2. The **DOS**: This name stood for *Duty, Obedience, Organization, Strictness and Service.* Those who work with computers know that they will not run unless you first put in the DOS, or the Disc Operating System, which provides the structure for the whole system. In the same way, a person who is dominant in this characteristic will tend to be responsible, reliable, obedient, organized, frugal, traditional, concerned about keeping laws, and maintaining order and stability in the physical environment.

These two solid, "earth-bound" types are in contrast to the following two more complex, meta-physical, ethereal types:

3. The **KIP**. KIP stands for *Knowledge and Intellectual Proficiency.* This word has no objective meaning. "K" is given

first to emphasize that the hunger for knowledge about the meta-physical world is the main motivating force for this type of individual. This scholarly, philosophically inclined KIP prefers to relate to the world in an objective, impersonal manner.

4. The **LT**. LT stands for *Love and Truth*. This highly sensitive, empathic, poetic, psychologically insightful type is motivated by a drive for emotional intimacy and self-transcendence. The LT prefers to relate to the world in a subjective, personal manner.

I received a great deal of positive feedback from parents on this information, especially those who could now understand their overly sensitive LTs and their exuberant AMOs. However, while simplicity was gained, depth was lost. My terms did not really convey the depth of these four differences in terms of essential motivations and needs. Therefore, I have decided to return to the original terminology to provide a greater depth of understanding.

POSSIBLE OBJECTIONS

Inevitably, there will be those who will find reasons to reject or invalidate the classifications described in this work.

To those who object on grounds that it is not based solely on Torah, I hope that such readers will realize that anything which helps us to be more aware and understanding *is* in the spirit of Torah. Torah teaches us the importance of understanding ourselves and understanding others' uniqueness and their unique needs. We are bidden to give to people according to their needs, not according to what we think they should need. We cannot do that if we do not understand who they are.

Just as we use the inventions (like telephones, airplanes and computers) and the medical advances of non-Jews, and elevate them for a higher purpose, so too can we use this system in the proper spirit of Yiddishkeit — i.e., to make us more loving and understanding human beings. It would be unfortunate for the Orthodox world not to have access to this valuable information.

To those who say that this work is too simplistic, I heartily agree that it does not, in any way, aim to explain all human behavior, only certain basic motivating factors and basic patterns which tend to remain more or less constant.

To those who object that this system is too complex, I can say that I sympathize and agree that the initials used are definitely cumbersome at first. Since each term contains a wealth of information, it does take time to digest it all. Trying to remember all the initials and what they stand for is going to be frustrating at times. It is completely normal if, at any point in your reading, you think, "This is all too much! These initials give me a big headache! I give up!"

But wait! If you patiently struggle through this material and apply this new language in your daily life, you will eventually have a valuable tool for understanding and appreciating people.

SEEING AND APPRECIATING MORE THAN YOU HAVE SEEN BEFORE

It is a fact of life that we do not "see" what we cannot name. For example, the Eskimos have 28 words for "snow." We have only one. This means that when we see snow, we see snow in a limited way, whereas the Eskimo sees a wondrous variety of conditions and factors of which we would not even be aware.

Likewise, when we were little, we learned the color "blue." As we grew older, we learned to distinguish various shades of blue and gave them names, such as aquamarine and turquoise. Before we had specific names for these shades, all we saw was "blue." But as we grew, we "saw" more than we saw before. If you are an artist, then you see a spectrum of blues that no one else "sees." In the same way, a musician "hears" more than a non-musician, even when both listen to the same music. In other words, people perceive events differently, depending on their conditioning, training and innate talents.

The same is true when it comes to understanding people. We know that every person is unique. We realize that we get along with some and not with others. But what do we really "see"? To what extent do we appreciate the source of these differences or the meaning reflected in our behavior? G-d obviously meant for these enormous differences to exist. He has obligated us to love each other despite them, and to appreciate everything He has created, including the people He brings into our lives. The more we understand people, the more we can appreciate them, instead of being angry and resentful that they see the world differently than we do.

As you read about various personality types, you will notice that this information is not really new to you. You have already noticed all eight modes of thinking and behaving in the people around you. For example, you have noticed that some people are *istanis* (the word used by *Chazal* to describe a very finicky, meticulous type of person). You have already noticed that some people are very independent, adventuresome and impulsive, and others more conservative, restrained, and traditional. Some people seem very sensitive or "spiritual," while others are more matter-of-fact and materialistic.

What will be new to you is your understanding of the motivating factors underlying these differences. Because you now have names by which to define what you are seeing, you will now see a variety and richness in human beings that you never saw before. This classification system will enable you to "see" more deeply into people's motivations and needs. This will help you to relate more effectively to others and also help you to appreciate who and what you are.

PEOPLE ARE MORE THAN THEIR LABELS

"Just as there are no two faces which are the same, so too are there no two people who think alike." (*Berachot* 5:9)

Before proceeding with an explanation of this typology, I want to emphasize that classifications can only provide a general description of a person's predispositions, never a description of the person himself. Keep in mind that:

A. Classifications are always somewhat unfair because when you classify a person, you have, in a sense, negated him. Every human being is completely unique. Any "group" definition automatically obliterates that uniqueness to some degree. People are far too complex to fit into any simple category. No typology can ever encompass or explain the vastness and complexity of any single person. When you classify someone, the danger is that all you see is the label, not the individual. Throughout our history, that has often been the first step to the oppression of the Jewish people.

Classifications are destructive if they cause you to feel that you now have the right to ignore, dismiss or hate whole groups of people. The first step in the dehumanization process is to see a person as a number or a collective name. Then the person becomes an "it," no longer an individual human being. Depending on your personal views, the words "secular," "religious," "leftist," "rightist," can all become excuses to treat others inhumanely.

The typology described here is in no way meant to box people into any rigid category. Rather, **it is a way of describing and understanding the various motivations which cause people to adopt certain attitudes and strive for certain goals**. It is a way of explaining why different people are attracted to or excited by certain ideas, events and people, and are put off by others. This system cannot, of course, explain all of the reasons why people act the way they do, why some people are refined and loving, and others are coarse and cruel.

B. Classifications are destructive if they cause you to deny others' potential for growth. Once you classify yourself or another person, you may become discouraged, giving up hope of the possibility for change. This is tragic, for man is a being of unlimited potential. For example, if you label someone as mean or cold, you might not even notice the times he is nice and helpful. Or, you may discount the positive acts as insignificant or as exceptions to the rule, thus further polarizing the person into a negative box, not only in your own mind, but often in the other person's mind as well. Call a person "stupid" or "lazy" often enough, and the person will come to believe that he is his label.

The Talmud (*Erchin* 15b) equates *lashon hara* with murder.

Nothing in this book is meant to give permission to put people down with negative labels.

C. No classification system can ever take into account the hundreds of factors governing human behavior, such as: level of intelligence; the effects of religious and cultural conditioning; hormonal imbalances or neurological defects; the influence of siblings, teachers, peers; birth order; poverty or affluence; lack of parental nurturing, etc.

D. Beware of self-fulfilling prophecies. You may read a list of characteristics and think, "It says here that this certain type has trouble following through. So now I have a good excuse to be lazy, procrastinate and give up quickly!" On the contrary! Knowing your type also makes you aware of your possible weaknesses, which then makes you even more responsible for improving them.

APPRECIATING PEOPLE

Most of my classes are focused on the importance of creating a safe, nurturing, loving environment in the home. As often happens, I got a call the day after a class from a woman who said sadly,

"What you said about the importance of creating a nurturing environment is fine. But all I've ever had in my life is criticism. How can I be loving to my children when I never experienced being loved? I don't even know where to start. Since becoming Observant, I realize that according to Jewish thinking, we're supposed to love ourselves. But the truth is that I don't think well of myself. Deep down, I don't really feel that I have any value."

Her voice reflected the pain caused by years of rejection. As we talked, I knew that part of her low self-esteem was the result of not accepting — or even knowing — herself and her basic nature. She was in an environment in which she felt like a fish out of water. But she blamed herself for not being able to fit in, instead of recognizing that she was trying to be something she was not, trying to compete with women whose talents and predispositions were far different than her own. It would take great effort to chisel away at the wall of self-deprecation which had built up over a lifetime.

If you have a poor self-image or any other destructive beliefs, realize that it takes as much of a struggle to restructure one's own psyche as it does to restructure a body which is out of shape. Hopefully, this work will help you recognize and internalize a heart-felt convinction of yourself as a being of value who has something unique to offer the world.

I hope that this book will help others to create a nurturing environment in their hearts and homes. We *can* learn to love. We *can* become more appreciative of ourselves and of others. The "prison" we make for ourselves with our unrealistic demands and resentments has no bars and no locks in reality. It is always open. We just have to be loving and tolerant, instead of hateful and self-deprecating.

In terms of the typology described in the following pages, I am an I-N-F-P. [These initials will soon become clear to you.] As is typical for this personality type, my mission in life is an idealistic one: I hope this book will enhance people's ability to get along with each other, to better appreciate themselves as well as their fellowmen, and to enhance our ability to put into practice the fundamental principle of Judaism:

"Love your fellowman as yourself." (*Vayikra* 19:18)

I welcome any insights which readers might like to share with me as they apply this typology to their own lives. I am always happy to hear if my books have been helpful to others. Please write to me at: 1316/2, Ramot 03, Jerusalem. Israel 97725.

CHAPTER I: UNDERSTANDING OUR DIFFERENCES

"Wisdom is the consciousness of self." (Rambam, *Guide for the Perplexed*, 1).

Throughout history, those interested in human nature have tried to formulate various classification systems (also known as "typologies") by which to categorize, and thereby understand, some of the different motivating factors which produce such a rich variety of behavior in people.

Categories abound throughout Jewish writings. In Hebrew, temperament is referred to as *mezeg*, which means a blending of various properties within each individual. One system categorizes people according to the properties connected to their *mazal*, or birth sign. Another sees people as being strong or weak in one of the ten *Sefiroth*: *chochmah* (wisdom), *binah* (understanding), *da'ath* (knowledge), *chesed* (unlimited kindness), *gevurah* (severity, self-restraint), *tifereth* (compassion), *netzach* (conquering), *hod* (humble appreciation of one's position), *yesod* (foundation) and *malchuth* (the actualization of potential.) On Sukkoth, we talk about the Four Species, which are meant to represent the various levels within the nation of Israel: the *etrog* (those who have both Torah wisdom and good deeds); the *lulav* (those who have Torah, but are lacking good deeds); the *hadas* (those who have good deeds, but lack Torah); and the *arava* (those who are lacking both good deeds and Torah).

Another system sees people as composed of various passions: Fire (anger and pride); Water (the appetite for sensual pleasures); Air (the appetite for frivolous, time-wasting activities such as idle talk, shopping, card playing); and Earth (the tendency toward melancholia and inertia) (Rambam, *Hilchoth Yesodai Hatorah* 4:2 and *Likutai Amarim*, Ch. 1).

The Rambam (*Hilchoth Deoth* 1:1) describes the major categories found in the general population:

"Every human being is characterized by numerous moral dispositions which differ from each other and are exceedingly divergent. (1) One man is choleric, always angry; another sedate, never angry..., or only rarely so. (2) One is haughty to excess; another humble in the extreme. (3) One is a sensualist whose lusts are never sufficiently gratified; another is so pure in soul that he does not even long for the few things that our physical natures require. (4) One is so greedy that all the money in the world would not satisfy him.... Another so curbs his desires that he is content with very little, even with that which is insufficient, and does not exert himself to obtain that which he really needs. (5) One is stingy and will suffer extreme hunger for the sake of saving, and does not spend the smallest coin without a pang, while another deliberately and wantonly squanders all his property. (6) There are the hilarious and the melancholy..., (7) the cruel and the kind-hearted, (8) the timid and the stout-hearted, and so forth." (Numbers are this author's)

The Rambam states that while some of these traits are acquired through habit (either good habits or bad), many are *innate*, i.e., Divinely-determined, intrinsic aspects of the person's very being which form a kind of "governing principle" within the person's nature.

A popular belief holds that "Anyone can be anything he wants if he just tries hard enough." This is true in terms of character traits [*middoth*]. While effort is, certainly, a crucial factor in determining success, our inborn tendencies and talents determine, to a great extent, whether or not we want to involve ourselves in certain activities in the first place. Lack of a satisfying outlet in one's Divinely-determined area of interest and expertise can have a depressing effect on one's entire being, so that one does not even accomplish much in those areas where accomplishment is possible. Thus, it is crucial to understand yourself in order to know where to put your energies.

A CATEGORY IS NEITHER A CONDEMNATION NOR AN EXCUSE FOR BAD HABITS

Our forefather, Yaakov, upon blessing his sons, recognized innate differences in their personalities. He admonished them to be cognizant of those differences in order to be aware of the negative tendencies which had to be restrained. Yet in order to be able to develop their potential strengths to the fullest, they had to recognize their weaknesses (*Bereshith* Ch. 49).

It is important - and often difficult - to distinguish the innate essence of a person from acquired habits and "moral dispositions" (*middoth*). While innate nature cannot be changed, we are all capable of achieving moral excellence.

In a sense, we are all handicapped in some way. An awareness of our shortcomings or predispositions is not an excuse to give in to them. Our purpose here on earth is to improve ourselves. To do so, we have to know what is innate nature (i.e., what must be accepted) as well as what can be changed.

"Awareness of your inner tendencies is crucial in order to have greater control over your behavior." (Rabbi Yerucham Levovitz, as quoted in *Growth Through Torah*, Rabbi Zelig Pliskin, p. 272)

A BEGINNING

One helpful way of starting this process of self-awareness is to understand our innate talents or predispositions according to a system which was first proposed very briefly by Swiss psychiatrist Carl Jung, and developed by Katharine Briggs, her daughter

Isabel Briggs Myers, and David Keirsey and Marilyn Bates. **It is based on eight basic differences in innermost motivations, the way we perceive people, ideas and events, and the way we form conclusions and judgments.** This typology has many similarities to the above-mentioned categories of the Rambam.

Obviously, these eight are a small number in comparison to the innumerable factors which are involved in the psychology of a human being. However, an awareness of these differences in mental activity provides a foundation and a framework for understanding people, their unique needs, and their motivations and values.

HOW PERSONALITY TYPOLOGY CAN HELP

Love implies understanding. Lack of understanding often leads to anger, fear, and shame, all of which inhibit open communication and loving relationships. If used wisely, this typology can be helpful in a number of ways:

1. **To increase self-awareness.**

Those who become familiar with this typology often exclaim, "If only I had understood myself, I would have made such different choices in my life! I would not have wasted so many years putting myself down for not being or doing what I am incapable of being or doing. I would have been more accepting of myself in some areas and I would have pushed myself in others. If only I had understood my nature, I would have developed my innate talents and not felt so inadequate or guilty for not being able to live up to my own impossible standards or trying to live up to standards set by others who had no idea of who I really was."

This particular typology will provide you with at least a partial explanation as to why you feel so uncomfortable with certain people and so frustrated and out of place doing certain activities. It will provide you with definitions and concepts with which to express and validate your own needs and feelings, to assertively stand up for your rights, and to express your individuality.

2. **To arouse greater understanding of and compassion for others.**

This typology does not provide a detailed description of any particular individual, but rather provides a general framework for understanding major differences in human behavior. This will enable you to more easily establish rapport with others and to communicate more effectively, especially with people who have a different way of perceiving life. It will also give you guidance in your efforts to help others grow in harmony with their particular talents and needs. It will help you differentiate between realistic demands placed on others and the unrealistic ones which may have alienated them, making you and them resentful and bitter.

This typology has helped many people to forgive those whose lack of acceptance and understanding caused them pain in the past, particularly parents and children who did not appreciate or respect each others' individuality. It helps explain why communication with certain people was so difficult, if not impossible.

Example: "Here I am, thirty years old, and only now, after understanding the different types, do I realize that my father did love me, after all. He wasn't a verbal person. He was comfortable with things, not with people. I thought he didn't care. But now I realize that, even though he couldn't show his love the way I wanted him to - by talking and sharing ideas and feelings with me - he did love me in his own way, like by taking us on trips and buying things.... I see now that he did his best."

Example: "Now I understand why my mother favored my younger brother. Because the two of them are so similar, they had a natural affinity for each other which would have made me feel left out no matter what, just as I am closer to one of my daughters than another. Nobody is purposely hurting anyone. I feel like a load of guilt, shame, and anger has been taken off my shoulders."

3. **To help us have more realistic expectations of our children**.

We are told, "Educate a child according to his particular way" (*Mishlai* 22:6) But a parent's personal agenda for how he or she wants the child to be gets in the way of seeing who the child is. In other words, because you want so much for a child to be a certain way, you might hope he has talents which do not exist in reality, and then consider that he is stubborn and lazy for not displaying what you think he has. Once you understand your child's essential nature, you can help him to capitalize on his strengths and compensate for his weaknesses. You will no longer try to force square pegs into round holes, destroying the child's spirit in the process. This is especially true of the shy introverts, the exuberant, tool-oriented "AMO" (Or "Sensing-Thinking" in our new terminology) children who often have difficulty in school, and the hypersensitive "LT" (or "Intuitive-Feeling" type as referred to here).

By appreciating and encouraging each child's own preferences, you can make each child feel loved and special, and thereby avoid the damage caused by favoritism of one child over another.

Example: "I was ashamed to admit that I loved my second son more than the first. The second is very quiet and sensitive, like myself. The first is more wild and earthy. I used to favor the second. Now I realize that I can build a relationship with the first by entering his world more, doing physical activities with him and helping him awaken greater sensitivity to people by spending more time communicating with him."

When you have a greater understanding of your children's individual natures, you will no longer feel guilty for those traits over which you have no control. You will soon see why you needn't feel guilty about the fact that some children are more introverted, some more extraverted, some more scholarly, and some less so, some more obedient and orderly, and others more resistant to authority. Hopefully, you can exert a more forceful influence in those areas where you do have some control and let go and be more accepting in others.

4. For pre-marital and marital counselling.

Example: "I'm twenty-four and have not been able to find the right girl, mostly because I've been going out with very strict, severe types because I thought that's what would be good for me. Being a man, I never wanted to acknowledge the strength of my feelings or my fun-loving side. But after reading this manuscript, I see that I do have strong needs for emotional communication and for a more easy-going approach. Now that I know the types, I have a much more honest and realistic picture of what I want in a wife. It's a big relief to feel O.K. about myself."

Example: "After reading this manuscript, I realized that I don't want to marry a girl who will make a lot of emotional demands on me. I want someone who will be very strong and independent and will be a good manager so that I can go off to learn and not worry about whether or not she will be able to hold up under the stresses of a large family."

Statistically, marital happiness is far greater when couples have similar styles of perception and/or complementary traits which provide balance. People do not consciously marry extreme opposites in order to live in misery for the rest of their lives, lacking understanding or empathy. The fact that they often do marry opposites is due, in part, to an innate, healthy hunger for completion and balance. On the other hand, they are often sorely disappointed because people often marry blindly, with the naive expectation that despite their differences, the other person is really very much like himself, underneath it all. They think that these differences are only superficial, and will not get in the way of closeness.

Those who have unfulfilling marriages often read about this typology and sadly think, "If only I had known what to look for in a spouse! I would perhaps have made a different choice." Or, "If only I had known what my own needs really were, I would have worked to satisfy them on my own instead of demanding that he/she fulfill them for me. I would have been more accepting and understanding. I would have tried other ways to get through instead of being so critical and demanding. I would have focused on his/her strengths and our similarities instead of being so resentful of our differences."

By helping people realize the profound implications of various differences, they will be less likely to have unrealistic expectations, such as:

* "Since we feel the same way about things, we will always communicate smoothly and easily. We won't have any major

conflicts after we marry. Any conflicts we do have will be quickly and easily resolved."

* "Since we love each other, childhood abuse and traumas will soon be healed and forgotten and, therefore, will have no effect on our relationship."

* "Since everyone is basically the same, people can be easily 'molded' - i.e., with gentle nudging or constructive criticism, one can turn domineering, lazy, or cold people into easy-going, responsible or warm ones."

A person who is aware of profound underlying differences in character and motivation between people can more objectively evaluate a prospective spouse. It will alert singles to possible areas of conflict which may arise, so that they will see and give significance to those "warning signals" which are so quickly overlooked or dismissed as "nothing" before marriage.

For those already married, an understanding of the types will bring about greater appreciation, compassion and forgiveness. You will be less likely to take people's irritating habits personally if you understand their unconscious motivations and drives.

5. **To provide a guide for people in the helping professions**.

This typology can help therapists to be more understanding of their clients' needs and motivations. Even experts may not realize that therapy or advice which is good for a person with one mode of thinking can be very unsuited — even destructive — to someone with a different mode. For example, an emotionally aloof therapist who tries to get a highly emotional, depressed patient to become even more introspective and aware of feelings might make the situation far worse. Highly emotional people must be encouraged to use cognitive tools (such as are provided in *EMETT*) to become more calmly objective and to break the pattern of excessive self-preoccupation by engaging in confidence-building, outer-directed activities. A Rav, in directing a young man to a yeshiva, can take into account his emotional needs as well as his intellectual ones. For example, some young men need a need a warm, personal approach. Others are happier in a different kind of environment.

In sum, understanding how people think will, hopefully, help you become more tolerant, more loving, and more accepting of the wondrous variety of people in your midst.

As you read through the next few chapters, it will be helpful for you to glance once in a while at the CHARTS in the back of the book. These charts will help you to keep things simplified in your own mind and keep you from getting overwhelmed and lost in the amount of information packed into these next few chapters.

CHAPTER II: EIGHT WAYS OF DEALING WITH LIFE AND PEOPLE

We all know of people with musical or mechanical talents. There are also more subtle talents, such as the talent to be organized or to grasp complex philosophical abstractions. We are going to look at these talents as they exist in pairs, in contrast to one another. These pairs *compete* within us for attention and dominance.

As you look at the descriptions of these various pairs of traits, you might think, "I don't fit in anywhere. I have many qualities in each category. I'm not one or the other." This is a healthy attitude, for you could not function effectively unless you were able to use the attributes from each of the eight modes. However, if you were to chart your responses to people and events, you would find that you have a general preference for, or feel more comfortable with, one mode of behavior than the opposite.

Just as you prefer to use your right or left hand, so too will you tend to prefer one mode over the other. However, you do not completely ignore your non-dominant hand. Both are essential for smooth functioning, as is each and every mode which will be discussed.

Also, although you may lack two or three of the traits in a particular category, you may still have dominance in that category. No one can fit perfectly into any system.

Notice that each mode has its own "meta needs." These are higher, spiritual, emotional, intellectual needs (as opposed to physical survival needs for air, food and shelter) which must be satisfied in order to make you feel "well-nourished" emotionally, intellectually or spiritually. Someone who is not getting his "meta needs" fulfilled may feel chronically depressed or angry.

Each mode is like a whole "society," with its own language, values and goals. It will take time for you to become acquainted with these different cultures. Since each mode of behavior can only be understood in relation to the others, you have to read the entire book to really understand any part of it fully. Thus, the reader should not expect to grasp all the aspects involved in this typology from the first reading. Instead, read the entire description once for general comprehension. Then go back and read it again, for specific applications and greater depth of understanding.

Remember, *no value judgment is placed on any of these modes. Each mode is equally valid, useful and necessary for healthy functioning.* We must know how to use them all, at the right time and place, depending on the circumstances.

As you read, keep our goal in mind: acceptance of who you are, and who others are.

PAIR 1: EXTRAVERSION ("E") V. INTROVERSION ("I")

Introversion means, literally, to look within. Extraversion means, literally, to look out. You cannot be focused on your inner and outer worlds simultaneously. How much you prefer to be with people as opposed to how much you prefer to pursue solitary activities is a major factor in determining the percentage of extraversion and introversion in a person's personality.

In order to understand this better, you might think of yourself as having two sets of eyes. Your "extraverted eyes" are focused on the outer world, on outer circumstances, demands, appearances and images. Your "introverted eyes" are focused on your inner reactions - your thoughts, inner needs, fears, hopes, worries, dreams, etc. If you are using your "introverted eyes" when you should be focusing on your outer world, you will bump into doors, mismatch your socks, forget why you opened that drawer or where you put something just ten seconds ago, or even forget where you are at times. It is not that you are selfish, stupid, lazy, or senile (though one may be any of these) but rather that you forget to switch from one set of eyes to the other.

People who have an innate tendency toward introversion or extraversion have very different needs and talents stemming from this preference. Remember, "innate" means Divinely-determined. Therefore, there is no reason to feel guilty or ashamed for the tendency in either direction, or to get angry at those who have a strong preference either way. This holds for each pair of traits.

EXTRAVERTED TYPES (E)

This trait is dominant in 75% of the American population. [This percentage and all others are taken from *Please Understand Me,* and do not necessarily reflect the Jewish population].

The more extraversion ("E") in a person's make-up, the more outgoing and *ex*tensive he will be as opposed to the "I" (introvert) who is more *in*tensive and introspective. Dominant "E"s (extraverts) tend to be relaxed and confident in social gatherings. They are more likely to be people of action and practical achievement. "E"s strike up conversations easily with people, including strangers. They feel more relaxed and confident in social situations than introverts do. "E"s plunge readily into adventures and into new and untried experiences, while "I"s are more hesitant. "E"s act in response to objective, external conditions, as opposed to internal wants and needs. The "E" "meta needs" are for action and social interaction.

When the need for action, variety and social interaction are not met, the "E" becomes restless and hungers for stimulation. If the isolation goes on for long, he may become quite depressed and even physically ill. For example, the typical home-maker, who seems to have everything, yet is depressed, is not mentally ill. She is probably starved for challenging activities which will involve excitement and social or intellectual stimulation.

INTRODUCED TYPES "I")

This trait is dominant in 25% of the U.S. population.

Introverts ("I"s) are people of ideas and abstract interests. The more introversion in a person's make-up, the more reserved, contemplative, and self-conscious he will be. Consequently, the more awkward and uncomfortable he is in social situations, especially noisy, unstructured ones.

Of course, there is a broad range of introversion and extraversion. There are introverts who almost hate being with people and extraverts who cannot bear to be alone. Most people, however, are more balanced combinations of both traits.

Introverts are more interested in internal reactions than external happenings, becoming so engrossed in those internal responses that they pay little or no attention to the outer world. "I"s can more easily shut out the external environment in order to concentrate on their own interests. The "meta needs" of the "I" are for reflection, depth of understanding and solitude.

Example: "I need space for myself. I don't care how small the little cubicle is, but it has to have walls around it so that I can call that little space my own."

Example: "When I am writing or teaching, I am mainly in an introverted state. After, I have to consciously force myself out of that state in order to drive safely and get the next meal fixed and on the table. When I'm in my introverted state, thinking about ideas for my next book or how best to help my students learn, I hardly notice the jumble in the house. But when I'm in my extraverted state, the disorder bothers me very much."

Although introverts can be just as talkative as others, they can suddenly be impenetrable and uncommunicative.

Introverts are also more territorial than "E"s. They like private space, private places, private talks with others, or pursuing solitary activities. They do not mind being alone. Introverts feel most alone when they are in a crowd. They then feel isolated and disconnected. They may feel the need to withdraw in order to "reconnect" to themselves.

Example: "My only introverted child always disliked having a lot of guests in the house when he was small. He would get upset and angry, and calm down only after they left. It used to embarrass me terribly. Now I understand why."

Introverts - and the extraverts around them - may think they "should" be more extraverted and sociable, and wonder what is wrong with them that they lack the social ease of "E"s.

Example: "It was Friday night, and after *kiddush* my husband sort of withdrew into himself, as he often does. For years, this made me furious. But now that I understand the types, I have stopped condemning him for withdrawing. I just tell myself that as an introvert, this is his need, and that he will eventually come out of himself again after his batteries have recharged. By the next morning, he is ready to interact with me and the children again."

Example: "As an introvert, I don't enjoy having more than one or two guests over at a time. I prefer one or two Sabbaths a month without any guests at all. My wife, an extravert, likes to have lots of guests. The more the merrier. For the sake of peace, we had to work out a compromise. Two weekends with guests; two without."

Example: "When one of the women on our block had to move to another city, her friends wanted to give her a surprise party. But knowing that she is an introvert, I told them that it would be better to let her know about it ahead of time so that she could prepare herself emotionally for having to face a crowd, even a crowd of friends."

INTENSIVE V. EXTENSIVE: Introverts ("I") are more interested in internal reactions and depth, while "E"s seek breadth and are more focused on external surroundings. While the extravert ("E") seeks interaction, the "I" seeks more intense, concentrated activity. While the extraverts expend their energies without concern, the introverts tend to want to conserve theirs for some internal goal. "I"s worry more about losing their energy or not having enough, and what will happen when their energy runs out. "I"s often tire more easily.

Interestingly, extraverts can be depressed but not realize it because they tend to be less introspective and more active.

Introverts can think they are depressed, simply because they are more introspective and contemplative, when, in reality, they are doing quite well.

SOCIABILITY: Extraversion and introversion have nothing to do with liking people. Both introverts and extraverts can be equally warm, friendly and likeable, or the opposite - cold, calculating and mean. However, extraverts do tend to be more sociable. They don't like being alone for long and get their "batteries" charged up by being with people. Introverts feel "recharged" and replenished by being alone for a period of time.

No matter how much a person likes another, he will feel drained or depleted after a while and want to get away. This happens sooner with an introvert than an extravert. Socializing depletes the introvert and energizes the extravet.

Many introverts *look* introverted: i.e, they look shy, reserved, and uncomfortable in social situations. However, other introverts look like extraverts: just as dynamic and outgoing as "E"s. This can make them seem, superficially, to be extraverted "E"s, rather than introverted "I"s. The difference between the real "E" and the "I" who merely seems like one is that, inwardly, the "I" wishes he were alone or with a small group.

"I" mothers become emotionally depleted after being around their children sooner than "E" mothers. This is a difficult problem if the mother has no help in the home and many young children. In addition, female introverts tend not to validate their need to withdraw and feel guilty for doing so.

Introverts tend to prefer small groups, structured situations or one-to-one interactions.

Example: "After I had my baby, the very act of talking to people would exhaust me. I kept hoping no one would visit, or if they did, that they would stay a very short time. But my extraverted neighbor in the next bed had company all the time and loved it. Now I understand why she could take it and I couldn't."

Example: "Before I understood these types, I was always *schlepping* my introverted daughter to social events in the hope that she would become more outgoing. It was hard for me, an extravert, to understand that she was very happy with just one or two close friends, or being by herself, just studying or reading. I was even more worried about her younger sister, who is a social butterfly and doesn't care much about school at all. I kept telling the second one that she wouldn't amount to anything if she spent all her time socializing. Now I see that all that criticism was for nothing. We now have a much better relationship. I wish I had been more accepting before."

Example: "I'm quite introverted. When making vacation plans with my sister, an extravert, we often have a conflict. I prefer a small park with few people where I can easily keep track of my children, and go home after a few hours. The less noise and commotion, the better I feel. However, she likes a noisy amusement park with lots of people and a whole-day affair. I used to always give in to her because I didn't understand myself or my needs. Now that I understand myself better, I can more easily stand up for myself and express my likes and dislikes without feeling that something is wrong with me."

Introverts need people just as much as extraverts:

Example: "I'm an introvert, but I very much need close friends. My children had been sick for almost a week. By Thursday afternoon, I was so depressed that I just wanted to sit and cry. I felt so disconnected, so alone. Then a good friend came to visit unexpectedly. I became so full of life that I felt like a different person. It was like I got a shot of vitality. I felt alive again."

DIFFERENT TIME-SPACE REALITY. The introvert is often in a different time-space reality than the extravert. The adult who looks at you absent-mindedly when you are trying to get his attention, or the child who sits staring dreamily into space instead of getting dressed or doing his homework, is probably not being purposely obnoxious or defiant. Rather, he is probably in a whole different time-space dimension than you are at the moment. Instead of getting angry, use some non-hostile techniques to bring the person back to an externally-oriented reality: e.g., a touch on the shoulder, a five-minute warning that something needs to be done soon, or some other transition signal.

CHILDHOOD: Introverted children tend to hold back when faced with something or someone new. They also may seem less intellectualy capable than they actually are because they are slower to respond, tending to reflect on ideas or objects instead of responding quickly like the extraverts. They tend to be more self-doubting, have more trouble adjusting to a new school or new situations, and do not verbalize as quickly as the extraverts do.

PROBLEMS IN RELATIONSHIPS: Obviously, a more extraverted partner may feel rejected if the introverted one needs a lot of time alone. When introverts need to withdraw - whether it be for the purpose of studying, being creative, or just to get away from the noise and confusion - it is often helpful for them to tell loved ones in the environment, "I'm not rejecting you. I just need to recharge my batteries by being alone."

Another problem is that introverts tend to bottle up their intense, passionate emotions and then explode positively in a burst of creativity, or negatively in a burst of anger at someone. Extraverts are more likely to unload their emotions little by little, so that there is less of a build-up.

As in all the four pairs of traits, balance is essential for a healthy personality. It is thus quite common for very balanced people to feel split 50% — 50%. Extremes are far easier to identify: the extreme introvert is impractical and inattentive to the outer environment; the extreme extravert is overly attentive to external appearances and quite unaware of his inner world.

Keep in mind that no one is all one thing or another. We are speaking here of percentages, i.e., how intensive ("I") or extensive ("E") your relationships are, and to what extent you need to be alone in order to replenish your energies after having been with people.

REVIEW:
WHEN YOU THINK "I" (INTROVERT), THINK:
likes quiet
likes to concentrate (dislikes intrusions and interruptions)
is intensive rather than extensive
has trouble remembering names and faces
works contentedly alone
may have problems communicating freely

WHEN YOU THINK "E" (EXTRAVERT), THINK
likes variety and action
plunges readily into new and untried experiences
good at interacting with a lot of people
communicates freely
often acts quickly, without thinking

CHAPTER III: SENSATION ("S") V. INTUITION ("N")

This pair has to do with whether you prefer to focus on practical, tangible, sensory objects, or in the intangible, non-sensory realm. This pair of preferences is confusing at first because the words "sensing" and "intuitive" have little meaning to most people, and are difficult to grasp even with an explanation. In addition, you have to keep in mind that the initial "N" stands for "intuition," since "I" has already been used to indicate introversion.

In order to keep yourself from getting confused, you might want to stop right now and repeat to yourself a few times: "'N' means intuition. 'I' means introversion." Another way of remembering is to think of "N" as referring to *non*-sensory realities, i.e., beyond the grasp of the physical senses.

Obviously, we all use our five senses (touch, sight, etc.) to gather information. However, people who gather information mainly by way of their physical senses are called "S"s — "Sensing types." Those who rely mainly on insight, instinctive knowledge, perception, and inspiration are called "N"s — "Intuitive types."

SENSING TYPES
This trait is dominant in 75% of the U.S. population.
The major thing to remember about Sensing types ("S"s) is that

they are basically concerned with what can be experienced through the senses (seen, heard, touched, bought, sold, etc.) They have acute powers of observation and memory for facts and details. The more "S" in a person's make-up, the more grounded, down-to-earth, and common-sense oriented he is. "S"s enjoy working with things: instruments, tools, nature, etc. They are not in close communication with their unconscious, nor are they likely to care much about their unconscious motivations. They enjoy working with their hands, whether their field is medicine, engineering, building, baking, banking, gardening, etc.) They also enjoy gathering solid facts and figures (historical facts, financial data, the facts of a person's life, etc.) The "meta need" of "S"s is for involvement in and mastery of the concrete, physical world.

"S"s are usually more accurate in observing and noticing details because they see what actually exists, whereas the "N"s are "seeing" possibilities or simply not "connecting" to what is going on in the real world.

"S"s trust what they have experienced, and are, therefore, more likely to be suspicious of other people's reports, whether verbal or written, while "N"s will be curious about the possibilities and are likely to investigate. "S"s enjoy exactitude and accuracy, often at the expense of imagination and ingenuity; "N"s often have little patience for routine details, often at the expense of exactitude and accuracy.

QUALITY: The quality of a person's sensing ability ranges across a vast continuum. At the highest level, the Sensing type is a master of the physical world, capable of dealing with almost any emergency in the physical environment, able to wheel-and-deal, and possessing mastery of body, instruments, and tools. A high level "S" might be a surgeon, lawyer, or homemaker who beautifully manages a large family and the multitude of skills necessary to do so. At the other end of the continuum is the person whose life and thoughts are immersed in this physical reality at the most simple level, managing to somehow get through the day with a minimum of skills.

INTUITIVE TYPES ("N")

Intuitives ("N"s) are dominant in 25% of the U.S. population.
"N"s have the same five physical senses as "S"s, but they have
an added, "extra-sensory" dimension which makes abstract
intangibles as real to them as the tangible world is to the "S"s.
The "real" world of the "N" is the realm of ideas, spirit,
philosophy, fantasy, meanings, inner relationships, symbols,
imagination and probabilities. Intuitives have a quick grasp of
complex material related to their field of interest, though they
may be very slow in other areas.

If you go to an inspiring lecture and feel that you are
transported out of this mundane, physical reality, you are in the
realm of the intuitive. Afterwards, you may even feel that you
then have to "pull yourself back down" to ordinary existence.
That "other world" is the world of the intuitive.

Very dominant "N"s are concerned with existential questions
about the meaning and purpose of life even in early childhood.
They are more intellectually and academically inclined than the
practical, down - to - earth "S"s.

"S"s dislike having to deal with intangibles (i.e., the "N" world
of ideas, theories, and possibilities) because their sense of security
is based on *concrete* proof that their opinions are true and correct.
When one is dealing with theories and probabilities, one does not
have the same sense of assurance that there is no other right
opinion or conclusion. "S"s feel that their security is undermined
when dealing with the world of the "N", for that world cannot
provide the same assurance of the absolute rightness of their
beliefs. Thus, when an "S" states an opinion, he is usually positive
that it is the only opinion possible.

QUALITY: The quality of the "N"s inspiration and intuition
ranges across a vast continuum. At the highest level, there are the
the brilliant scholars, poets, and literary geniuses. At the other
end are the types who want to escape from the world, who walk
around in a daze, and who think that their ideas are brilliant and
their words profound, but who are only imagining profundity and
brilliance where it does not exist.

SPECIAL NEEDS: The "meta needs" of "N"s are for knowledge, inspiration, elevation, and transcendence. "N"s crave the ecstatic "Aha" experience of discovering new insights and *chidushim* in Torah, or expanding their awareness of life and people. When this form of spiritual nourishment is missing, life seems dull, flat, even meaningless to the "N". To intuitives, inspiration is, literally, the breath of life. It is like oxygen to them. They feel most alive and happy when they are in an inspired state, especially when they can be innovative or creative.

This is a serious problem for "N"s who are forced by circumstances to be immersed in an "S" world, such as highly creative, intelligent people who must work at mundane jobs or "N" mothers of young children who have no creative outlet or intellectual stimulation, or people married to spouses who find it boring to talk about ideals, ideas, or meanings.

Example: "When I finally started taking classes for a degree after being home with the children for so many years, I felt like a part of me had been 'fasting' since my first child was born. I simply had not been getting the creative nourishment which I needed."

"S"s usually cannot understand the "meta-needs" of the "N". For example, they will tell "N" young mothers to be happy with their "S" lives. For the "N", that is like telling them to be happy with a diet of bread and water. The person may survive, but will certainly not find the meals very satisfying. Because most "S"s do not give significance to the importance of this "N" dimension, they often add the pain of criticism, either implied or direct, to the "N"s' already painful state.

COMMUNICATION: "S"s and "N"s talk a different language. "S"s tend to take things literally, while "N"s talk figuratively, involving symbols and deeper meanings in what they say. The two often feel that they "just can't get through" to each other. Because "S"s are more grounded in physical reality, they may seem more sure of themselves and the stand they have taken. The "N" may get defensive and self-doubting, wondering if the reason he cannot get through to the "S" is because the "S" is

really right, since he is so adamant about his views. Unless the
"N" can define his position in concrete, factual terms for the "S",
he will not be able to communicate his wishes or opinions.

The tempo at which each type grasps the other's reality is quite
different. The "S" usually takes longer to "wake up" to the need
to relate to abstract concepts or non-visible emotional needs. The
"N" usually takes longer to see the need to relate to practical,
sensible life skills and goals. The "waking up" process may take
many years. Thus, many "S"s suddenly get "turned on" to Torah
in their thirties and forties, after having been very rebellious
about learning during their formative years. And many "N"s get
very practical and down-to-earth in their forties, as they begin to
marry off their children and are saddled with huge expenses.

MAJOR DIFFERENCES: Some people like to think of
dominant "S"s as "earthlings," and the dominant "N"s as
"extra-terrestrials." The reason is clear:

* "S"s are better at dealing with the physical; "N" with the
metaphysical.

* "S"s see things more simply; "N"s live in a more complex,
multi-dimensional and multi-faceted world.

* "S"s are more concerned with visible needs: physical health,
food, clothing, furnishings, etc.; "N"s focus mainly on intangible
needs (emotional, intellectual, spiritual) and dislike routine
chores or any activity which requires sustained concentration on
external sensing.

* "S"s focus on the actual; "N"s focus on ideas, dreams,
theories, hunches, and possibilities.

* "S"s are concerned with being practical and sensible, with
how the information can be used, applied and practiced; "N"s
enjoy amassing knowledge for its own sake, whether it is useful or
not.

* "S"s are more concerned with the here-and-now, and with
external form and function; "N"s *hear* overtones, *see* between the
lines, *feel* unexpressed needs.

* "S"s are less in touch with unconscious motivations, less

concerned about inspiration, less innovative or ingenious, yet may have artistic genius and be far better at dealing with the physical world; intuitives ("N") are, by nature, initiators, originators, and inventors. ·

* "S"s are patient with routine details, are impatient with complex situations, are usually good with precision work, and take longer to reach conclusions because they take a step-by- step approach; "N"s reach conclusions quickly, are impatient with routine details and dislike taking time for precision activities which seem unnecessary to them, but are patient with complex situations.

No wonder the sparks often fly in relationships between "S"s and "N"s. Their interests, perceptions and values are so different.

RELIGION: In terms of religion, "S"s have to constantly work to elevate themselves above the material world, while "N"s have to bring the spiritual down into physical reality. "S"s are motivated by the connection they feel with their heritage through those concrete, sense objects which are an intrinsic part of the Jewish way of life, such as certain books, head coverings, candles, *tzizith*, etc. "N"s (Intuitives) are inspired by the deeper meaning and the mystical implications which they find significant in those objects and in the more abstract, philosophical aspects of religion.

SENSE OF EXPECTANTCY: Another important aspect of "N"s is that they live with a sense of anticipation: "Whatever is, could be better." "Something great is just around the corner, waiting to happen." This enthusiastic expectancy exists because they live in the realm of ideas and possibilities. They are forever wondering, "How can I improve myself, my relationships and the world in general?" This dissatisfaction and restlessness can be very positive if it incites the person to be creative and make significant changes in his life. But it is a destructive force if the person just sits around daydreaming instead of doing something constructive with his ideas, or uses his imagination to brood obsessively about all the possible disasters which might occur in the future. The tendency to brood is increased if the "N" is also a meditative "I" (Introvert).

DIFFICULTY FITTING IN: "N"s often seem like "non-standard" people, and often feel ashamed and defensive, as if there is something wrong with themselves. If they do not understand their special qualities, they agonize over their failure to "fit in" and be like the "S"s in their environment. They would be happier, however, if they would devote their time to developing their own special talents, and avoid comparing themselves to "S"s. On the other hand, "N"s do have to engage in "grounding," "S" activities. Otherwise, they become dreamy and impractical, unable to function or manage everyday matters.

Extreme "N"s tend to feel disoriented, overwhelmed and confused when forced to deal with the "S" world for any length of time.

Example: "I never felt that I belonged anywhere. It even seemed strange and uncomfortable to me that I was in this world — somehow trapped in a body. I could walk out on the street and wonder where I am, which reality I belonged to. I was just fine when I was teaching. I managed beautifully. But then I'd feel so disoriented when I was out of my element. Now that I understand the types, I realize that when I must be in an 'S' reality, like when I go shopping or have to deal with certain people, I have to switch my thinking and pay more attention to physical realities and use Sensing skills, like patience for routine details and step-by-step procedures. Now I don't let myself get so spaced out."

If the "N" is also an introvert, then the ethereal quality is reinforced.

AN "N" IN AN "S" WORLD: "N"s sometimes have trouble doing things which come easily to "S"s:

Example: "As an 'N', I find it hard to motivate myself to prepare for the holidays because it means that almost all of my time is devoted to 'S' activities: cooking, baking, cleaning, shopping, etc. As a creative person, I feel like I'm losing my identity if I don't have time to write or study. It's not that I can't do 'S' activities, but after about an hour or two, I start to get very bored and uncomfortable."

Example: "I had the instructions for a new appliance sitting on my desk for six weeks. I kept trying to figure out how to get the accessories on, but the diagram just didn't make sense to me. Then I asked my 'S' son, who is only nine, to look at the diagram. He didn't even have to read what was written. He knew instantly exactly how to work all the parts."

The following conversation was overheard at a Jerusalem busstop:

Grandmother ("S"): "My children in America are always telling me to write more. But when I look at a piece of paper, I freeze. I just can't write. It's like pulling teeth. Give me a pair of knitting needles and I'm in seventh heaven. I've always been good with my hands. But I've never gone in for intellectual things."

Grandmother ("N"): "I wish I could make things for my grandchildren, but I've never been successful with sewing or knitting. But I write them stories that they love. It's easier for me to write ten pages than to knit one row."

Example: "Our house is difficult to find. When talking to an 'S', I give minimum directions. They always find us somehow. But when talking to an 'N', I have to make my directions much more specific. Even then, they tend to get lost."

Example: "My oldest daughter is a strong 'S' (Sensing Type). She can walk into the kitchen and clean up in five minutes, whereas it might take me an hour. She's also more adept at baking, sewing, and organizing. I'm a strong 'N' (Intuitive type). It's far more difficult for me to bring myself down into physical reality. I know, intellectually, that things have to be shined, cleaned, organized, folded, ironed, etc., and I'll do it because it is necessary for a calm environment. But it's an effort to get myself down into the physical reality and do it and I get very bored after a short time. I'll spend five or ten minutes making a meal whereas my 'S' daughter will make a whole gourmet spread. She wants me to be more attentive to 'S' physical details, such as fancy food and dress, for example. I try to please her, but these things just don't interest me all that much. I do have enough 'S' to enjoy nature and sports with her, but my deepest satisfactions come from sharing ideas and feelings with others - teaching and learning."

This is not to say that all "N's are completely incompetent in the physical world. There are many "N" artists, doctors, dentists, and craftsmen. However, they are quite different from "S" artists, doctors, dentists and craftsmen. The "N" artisans use their bodies and their instruments in order to reach levels of inspiration and elevation which they could not reach without that particular means of expression. Thus, just as introverts can seem like extraverts, and vice versa, so too can "N"s seem, superficially, to be like "S"s and vice versa.

Example: "I'm an 'N' dancer. When I first advertised to teach, I got mostly 'S's, which did not satisfy my need to connect spiritually to others. So I put up new fliers stating that the class would work on intuitive movement and spiritual elevation through dance. Then I got more 'N's like myself."

Example: "Most of the teachers of learning disabled children in our clinic are 'S's. They connect to the children in a different way than I do. It's hard to explain what I do. All I know is that I used to feel very left out because I couldn't talk about this other 'N' dimension with them. Like, I work a lot on intuition instead of just relying on the tests. Many times, I feel that a child has a lot more potential than what the tests show. I can usually rely on my hunches about a child and I'll fight for him and believe in him even when others say that the prognosis is poor."

"N"s often engage in "S" activities in order to "ground" themselves and provide some balance and relief from their usual abstract endeavors. Thus, one might find "N" teachers, scholars, scientists or psychologists working in the garden on weekends, fixing things around the house, cooking special meals, taking an exercise class or working on some artistic creation. These activities are important to them, but are not the focal point of their existence, as they would be for the "S".

Imagination is an "N" quality. Yet many "S"s are very imaginative and creative. There are creative "S" artists, engineers, builders, and businessmen. However, their imagination is directed toward tangible, *sense realities* involving fabrics, tools, food, building materials, etc. or figuring out how to be more efficient and organized in the home or office. On the other hand, the creativity of the intuitives is directed toward the realm of ideas, theories and possibilities. Some people are skilled in both worlds, such as a novelist, who must have a deep understanding of people and a vivid imagination ("N"), plus acute powers of observation ("S").

Obviously, healthy "N"s are also concerned with their appearance and the beauty of their physical environment. However, "N"s, especially introverted "N"s, will not give such matters the same priority that "S"s do.

Example: "My 'S' wife is always telling me to keep my shoes shined and my hat brushed. I don't know why, but I just don't *see* what she sees. I look at my shoes and don't even see that they need shining. It doesn't occur to me until she has pointed it out."

Example: "I am very organized in my mind and in the realm of ideas. But when it comes to the kitchen, I have far more difficulty managing all the endless details. On the other hand, when I asked an 'S' friend whose house is always spotless and orderly to take notes for me at a lecture, I was surprised that they came out in a jumble, without any clear organization."

Example: "My 'S' husband can come into the kitchen after I've cleaned and tell me that it's still a mess. I have to ask him to point things out to me that still need to be done. It's not that I don't want to see them. It took me a long time to get him to realize that I am not deliberately avoiding certain jobs. I just don't *see* what he sees."

Some people are equally good at both "S" and "N" modes, able to function beautifully in either.

CHILDHOOD: The "N" child may be difficult to handle because he seems to have such a strong sense of being his own person, which some adults find quite objectionable. Adults may get angry because he may not be attentive to present realities. Seeing that faraway look in his eyes, the adults may yell at him to pay attention. If this happens often enough, the child's self-esteem will be damaged, even to the point of stopping his creative processes by filling him with a fear of failure and rejection.

Because intuitives are quicker to grasp abstract symbols, they have a big advantage in school, where this ability is necessary for reading and math. For example, in learning to read, the intuitive child immediately grasps that the "B" is a symbol for a certain sound and that the number "3" has to do with "threeness." The sensing ("S") child has to first translate these symbols into something which can be sensed, such as by making a "B" out of clay, and counting three pencils on his table. Thus, the sensing child may be slower to catch on in school, even though he is just as intelligent as the "N".

On the other hand, "S" children are quicker to grasp information requiring physical coordination (music, dance, athletics), and organizing the environment, working with tools, crafts, etc. "N"s often feel awkward and clumsy when dealing with artistic or mechanical objects, or even learning dance steps.

RELATIONSHIPS: Since "N"s (Intuitives) have an extra-sensory dimension which is difficult, if not impossible, for non-"N"s to grasp, "N"s can understand the world of the Sensing types, but "S"s can never really understand the world of the Intuitive types. This can be a major problem in marriage, especially if one is an NF (Intuitive-Feeling) and feels very deprived of the strong bond of intimacy which these types crave. NTs (Intuitive-Thinking) may not be so upset with an "S" partner, since they do not have the same hunger for emotional closeness. However, the lack of intellectual rapport may be distressing to some "T"s.

Nevertheless, many "N"s marry "S"s because they feel that the "S" will take care of the "real world" and provide the practical, "grounding" influence which they need. It is only afterwards that they experience the loneliness which comes from not being able to share their "N" dimension.

There are two types of Intuitive:

INTUITIVE-THINKING (NT): The ability to grasp complex intellectual matters, such as those involved in physics, philosophy, psychology, and science, in an impersonal, dispassionate manner.

INTUITIVE-FEELING (NF): The ability to grasp complex intellectual and psychological matters, especially concerning psychology, in a warm and personable manner.

In addition, either the NT or the NF can be introverted ("I") or extraverted ("E"). Both have the "N" qualities of creative inspiration and an intuitive grasp of difficult ideas. The extraverted intuitive is more comfortable with self-expression and is more outer-directed than the introverted intuitive.

PROBLEMS IN RELATIONSHIPS: The "N" and the "S" often simply fail to "connect" to each other. The "N" connects by sharing ideas, dreams, thoughts and feelings, while the "S" connects through touch, or by sharing physical adventures, trips, talking about concrete plans, sensible goals, buying and selling, getting the best deals, organization and upkeep of the physical environment and concrete physical needs (food, clothing, money, shelter, etc.) In addition, the introverted "N" is doubly immersed in an intangible world and may not be able to share the depth of his introspective insights with an "S".

REVIEW:
WHEN YOU THINK "S" (SENSING) THINK:
likes an established way of doing things
acutely aware of external environment
reaches conclusions in a step-by-step procedure
patient with routine details and precision work
good at observing actualities
enjoys dealing with sensory objects
may be unaware of inner meanings, deeper feelings, unseen needs
bored and uncomfortable with "deep" discussions

WHEN YOU THINK "N" (INTUITIVE) THINK:
craves inspiration; faces life expectantly
imaginative at the expense of observation
hopeful at the expense of being realistic
restlessly inventive, innovative and original
independently indifferent to what others say and do
dislikes doing the same thing repeatedly
works in bursts of energy powered by enthusiasm, with slack
periods in between
reaches conclusions quickly
dislikes taking time for precision work
patient with complicated situations
enjoys deep discussions

[If you are excited about this book and are already thinking about all the possibilities you see in yourself and others as you read these definitions, then it means you are an "N" or are an "S" with a strong "N" component to your personality. Other types may not be sympathetic to or find relevancy in the terminology, emotional orientation, or emphasis on psychology in this system.]

CHAPTER IV: THINKING ("T") V. FEELING ("F")

This pair has to do with how you make your judgments: personal and subjective ("F"), or impersonal and logical ("T"). You can consider yourself an "F" if, when you have to make a decision, are you more likely to choose on the basis of your personal feelings and subjective values (i.e., whether you like or dislike the person, idea, or item). If you prefer to make your decisions on the basis of objective facts and rational analysis, or some other objective criterion, you are a "T". Obviously, we all need both modes at various times. What you feel most comfortable with is what determines your dominance.

Everybody thinks and everybody feels. But you cannot be "T" — i.e., dispassionately objective and impersonal — and, at the same time, be "F", i.e. warmly subjective and personal. You can use the "T" mode one minute and the "F" mode the next, but each time you react to a person or event, you have to choose one mode or the other.

When you are in a Thinking mode, you must be impervious to sentiment so that you can make a cold, rational decision without your feelings getting in the way of logic. When you are in a Feeling mode, you have to allow yourself to be open to and affected by emotion.

"Man must know that his intellect and his heart are two distinct entities" (Rav Eliyahu Lopian, *Lev Eliyahu*, p. 71).
These two "entities" talk different languages and have different uses. Both are equally important. However, people who generally prefer one mode to the other have quite different needs and motivations.
Do not confuse "Thinking" and "Feeling" with being considerate and caring. Both types can be equally loving — or equally cruel.

THINKING TYPES: "T"
Sixty percent of the American male population, and 40 of the female population is dominant in this trait.
"Thinking" is the talent for making choices based on impersonal facts and figures. Dominant "T"s (Thinking types) observe the world in an emotionally objective and detached manner. Intellectual curiosity, the ability to analyze information and organize facts and ideas into a logical sequence, and to relate impersonally, are all aspects of this talent.
The major concern of "T"s is facts, not feelings. "T"s tend to be skeptical of anything which cannot be proven with facts. If you cannot prove what you are saying, your opinion is likely to be rejected.

Because "T"s are less affected by others' feelings, they have less difficulty saying "No," and holding on to their own ideas and opinions no matter what others think. In addition, "T"s generally have difficulty giving compliments, listening to people's personal problems, or giving positive feedback, as these are emotional needs which "T"s may not notice or value.
The "meta needs" of the "T" are for information, facts, and logic.

QUALITY: Thinking ranges from the highest levels of visionary brilliance and erudition to the lowest level, in which the "T" merely thinks he is thinking rationally, when, in reality, his ideas and conclusions may be totally irrational and invalid. This second type mouthes ideas he has heard from someone else but has not really internalized, or states thoughts which make sense to him, but to no one else.

Thus, just because a person is a strong "T" does not mean that he is intelligent or that his thinking is of a high quality. Quality thinking is only as good as the intelligence of the person, the facts which he starts out with, and the logic employed to put those facts together.

Some Thinking types are very dry, cold, dispassionate, stone-faced and stony-hearted, while others are dynamic, passionate, moody, or hot-tempered. Both types are considered "T"s because: a) they prefer to work with things or ideas rather than people, b) are more comfortable with impersonal, objective judgments, and c) attempt to persuade people with an appeal to logic rather than an appeal to emotions.

To get the attention of a "T", it is helpful to use words like: objective, logic, laws, firmness, analysis, categories, standards, critique.

Very dominant "T"s are less bothered by having to live or work in a hostile environment or even protracted combat situations, whether that involves law-suits or actual war. They have less difficulty giving orders, making demands, firing workers, or being critical (constructive or otherwise).

Many "T"s have difficulty "making time" for relationships, or seeing the importance of emotional intimacy.

Although healthy "T"s are very devoted to their families, they do also tend to be critical, and must be sensitized by non-hostile feedback early in the relationship. The emotionally deprived "T", whose Feeling side is underdeveloped, may truly not understand why others are upset by their criticism, since they will not be sensitive to others' emotions, and may be quite impervious to change.

There are two types of "T"s:

SENSING-THINKING (ST): Impersonal and analytically oriented and preferring to deal with things in the concrete, sensory world, such as tools, instruments, mechanical devices, concrete facts, and whatever else can be seen, heard, touched, etc.

INTUITIVE-THINKING (NT): Impersonal and analytically oriented and preferring to deal with things in the meta-physical world: ideas, theories, philosophies, and pure science, etc.

Principals who hire STs to work with young children should make sure that they are patient, able to give praise, and can display warmth and affection. Otherwise the children's emotional needs will be neglected.

FEELING TYPES: "F"

Sixty percent of the American female population and 40% of the male population is dominant in this trait.

In the context used in this book, "Feeling" is the ability to make choices based on personal feelings and subjective values. "F"s are tender-hearted, less logical, more sympathetic. They "bond" differently than the "T"s, getting emotionally involved with people more quickly and taking things more personally. They also show their feelings more easily.

In contrast to the imperviousness of the "T", "F"s are more "porous," automatically absorbing people's emotions (both the positive and the negative). "F"s are usually less critical than "T"s and are more willing to "bend" a little, as they take extenuating circumstances into account. "F"s are good at persuading, teaching and winning people over because they consider the personal impact of their words on others.

The "meta need" of the "F" is for close relationships and the expression of feelings. Even a few minutes of true concern and sharing, or a few words of appreciation and affection, are often enough to "revive" a saddened or ill-tempered "F". Without these moments of contact, "F"s feel that their spirits, and their relationships, wither.

LOWER SELF-ESTEEM: "F"s tend to have higher "highs" and lower "lows." Since most cultures value a stoic, unemotional approach to life as a sign of strength, wisdom, maturity, and sanity, many dominant "F"s think of themselves as less "together," weaker, less intelligent and less stable in comparison to the more cool-headed "T"s. They may feel defensive, self-doubting, inhibited, and patronized in the presence of a strong "T".

Many "F"s are ashamed of their strong feelings, thinking that they should not have them, or that they should be able to control, quickly "overcome," or easily suppress them. Furthermore, "F"s are more apt to see rejection where it does not exist, to sense it where it is only vaguely implied, and to be more devastated, for longer periods of time, by the rejection, whether it is real or imagined.

FUZZY BOUNDARIES: "F"s also "merge" spontaneously and unconsciously with others, sometimes losing their boundaries, as seen in the following example:

Example: "My father was a brilliant 'T', but he also had a strong "F" side. Whenever he would talk to someone, he would unwittingly take on their mannerisms, and even their accents. People thought he was doing this on purpose, but my father didn't even realize it was happening. When someone would point it out, he would be so surprised that he was doing this."

QUALITY: Anyone, "F" or "T", with a highly developed "F" side will be sensitive to and care about others' feelings. Anyone, "F" or "T", with an undeveloped Feeling side, will only be concerned with his own hurts and desires. Thus, "F"s can be very insensitive to others, while "T"s can be very thoughtful and compassionate. It all depends on the extent to which the Feeling function has been developed.

POSSIBLE CONFUSION: As with all four pairs of preferences, it may be difficult to identify a person's dominance. You cannot always tell an "F" from a "T", especially if the "F" is male or the "T" is female. Men are encouraged by society to maintain strict control over their emotions, so it is not always easy for anyone to detect the warmth and compassion which may actually exist. In the pursuit of a goal requiring "F" charm, warmth and friendliness, "T"s can usually act like "F"s. However, they cannot sustain this behavior for long, and will revert to their "T" modality once their goal has been achieved. For example, many men are temporarily self-revealing during courtship. But since self-disclosure is difficult for most men, they usually do not continue to do so to the same degree ·after marriage.

Both "T"s and "F"s can react with the same degree of emotional intensity. Both types can be coldly logical and objective or explosively angry and intensely loving. In addition, "F"s may be so overwhelmed with emotion, so fatigued, or overloaded with demands that they become numb and dumb, seemingly devoid of all feeling, with a flat, expressionless face, and a depression of the whole emotional system. Or, under pressure, they can become cruel and aggressive.

"T"s on the other hand, can be quite emotional, making it seem that they are Feelers. For example, when "T"s talk about their particular areas of interest, they can show profound feelings. Many "T"s are impassioned speakers. Also, either type can have very strong feelings for themselves and their own honor and interests, but be oblivious to the needs and desires of others.

You cannot judge a person's type from one interaction. We are all warm and friendly to certain people and restrained in the presence of others. As with all the pairs of traits, the person's overall pattern must be taken into consideration.

LEGITIMATE V. EXCESSIVE EMOTIONALISM: "T"s often complain that "F"s are being excessively dramatic, while the "F" experiences his responses as being perfectly appropriate and legitimate. This is because "F"s may experience events more intensely and for longer periods of time. That emotional intensity can be annoying to others, especially if the "F" is long-winded and keeps repeating the same complaint over and over again. In truth, "F"s often do exaggerate the importance of minor strains in the relationship because such incidents have such great importance to them. On the other hand, "T"s often minimize the significance of even major events. Thus, "F"s often complain that "T"s don't take their feelings seriously or respond appropriately to emotional pain and human suffering.

Some "F"s feel that the only way to have a relationship or to get people's attention is to be very emotional. They may be reluctant to be calm and rational because they fear that if they are, no one will listen or that they will have no way of connecting to others. They need to experience that others will care and pay attention even if they are calm, confident, and capable. Likewise, "T"s may think that people will look down on them if they show deep feelings. They need to experience that they will still be respected even if they reveal their feelings of love, hurt, inadequacy or loneliness.

RANGE OF FEELINGS: There is a broad continuum of Feeling types. Some are very emotional, crying or exploding at the drop of a hat. Other "F"s are more easy-going and even-tempered. Whatever one's nature, it must be accepted, not condemned.

Example: "It was the last day of nursery school. All the children came marching in with their little crowns on. When I saw my son, tears started rolling down my cheeks, despite my attempt to hold them back. I always cry at ceremonies. I used to be so embarrassed, thinking something was really wrong with me when I'd look around and see that no one else was crying. Now I understand that I must accept myself as a person whose emotions are very strong and always bubbling just beneath the surface. I find that since I've stopped condemning myself for being like this, the intensity of the emotions fades faster and I recover much more quickly than before."

COMBINATIONS: There are two kinds of Feeling types:

SENSING-FEELING (SF): SFs are care-givers: warm, friendly, nurturing, and highly responsive to their own and others' visible needs (food, clothing, the environment, etc.)

INTUITIVE-FEELING (NF): NFs are also warm, friendly, and nurturing, but have the added "N" dimension: linguisitcally skilled, psychologically insightful, and highly sensitive to their own and others' invisible needs, such as the need for praise, autonomy, and creativity. NFs often have a more delicate nature, and may lack the resilience of SFs, who tend to bounce back more quickly, even from major blows.

In addition, the "F" can be either introverted or extraverted.

Introverted "F"s, while just as emotional as extraverted "F"s may have difficulty expressing their feelings to others, partly because of the intensity of their emotions, and also because they do not react as quickly as extraverts do to outer cues. They often have a delay in reaction time, experiencing only later the full impact of how hurt they've been by what someone said, or thinking of just the "right thing" to say when there's no longer anyone to say it to.

People often get confused between the SF and NF. One difference is that SFs usually dislike in-depth psychological analyses, and soon get impatient and bored with "deep" conversations.

Example: "My father, an SF, was a very good, generous man, but was also very practical, direct and no-nonsense. We never had any in-depth discussions about personal matters, but I always knew he cared deeply about me. As an NF, I would have preferred more depth of understanding and more complete communication. I always felt the lack, like I wasn't really being understood."

Example: "I think my SF neighbor, who has many children, has an easier time of things because she doesn't get so emotionally involved in their emotional or physical aches and pains. She is perfectly content if everyone is healthy and the house is running smoothly. As an NF (Intuitive-Feeling type) I get more wrapped up in what my children are thinking and feeling, and in satisfying their deeper needs, such as for creativity and emotional closeness. That requires far more time with them. When one of her children falls down, the first words out of her mouth are, 'Nothing happened,' even before she knows if there has been any damage. I, on the other hand, tend to overreact, and expect the worse and react more strongly. Once, the two of us took our children to an amusement park and put them on one of the rides. I didn't realize it was going to be so scary for them. I looked up and saw our children's faces frozen in terror. My neighbor was laughing about it. But tears were rolling down my cheeks. I totally identified with their feelings. I used to feel so inferior to her. Now I realize that we simply have different ways of relating. One isn't better than the other."

NEED TO CONNECT: "F"s have a strong, innate drive to relate. Introverted "F"s like one or two close friends, and may be happy "connecting" through writing. Many "F" children, if unable to make that contact in a positive way with a parent or teacher, get depressed, adopt irritating habits, run away from home or school, and show other signs of disturbance.

Example: "My 'T' son really disliked a particularly strict teacher, but he was able to get through the year. However, my nine year old 'F' son was just devastated by the criticism. I thought that because the older one managed, that the younger one would too. But his spirit was crushed. He stopped learning, wouldn't open a book, and was very depressed. I had to switch him to a different school where the rebbe was known to be very warm. I see that it's very important for my 'F' children to connect emotionally to their teachers, or else they really suffer."

A person who has a difficult, complex problem is likely to want the special, empathic quality of the NF:

Example: "We were having marital problems. Most of the people I consulted gave me simplistic solutions, usually starting with the words, 'Why don't you just....' Then I went to a well-known Rebbe. When I told him what was going on, he actually had tears in his eyes. I could feel that he understood the situation completely, that he really cared about me, and really felt my pain. Just knowing that someone understood made me feel better. That made me much more amenable to accepting his advice than when I got those flippant, pat-answers that implied that the problem could be solved so easily."

Parents of very strong "F" children can help them develop a bit of "elephant skin" so that they do not take everything to heart so quickly, and teach them to discriminate between those situations which call for a strong emotional response, and those which should be handled with indifference or calm assertiveness. However, being "F"s, it should be expected that such children will be much more pained by criticism and rejection.

TRANSITIONS: Because of their more pervasive emotional response, "F"s often have more trouble with transitions, whether they be major events (such as a birth, death, job change, a move to a new home, or a "life passage") or even minor ones like jet lag, a change in schedule, or from sleeping to waking or vice versa.

NEED TO PLEASE: Because "F"s need people more than "T"s, "F"s are more interested in pleasing others, living up to their expectations, doing whatever is necessary to bring harmony into relationships, and to avoid being criticized or snubbed. In contrast, the greater the pecentage of "T" in a person's nature, the less the need for emotional intimacy and the less concern there is with being liked or disliked.

TO ENGAGE OR DISENGAGE: Everybody has feelings, both "T"s and "F"s. The major difference between the two is that "T"s can disengage more quickly from their feelings, and are better able to control their feelings in order to obtain a specific goal, such as making an impression or gaining some desired object.

When Feeling types become emotional, they have a much more obvious bodily response: the hands become moist, color flushes or drains from the face, the body trembles, the heart beats faster, etc. However, when the "T" becomes emotional, the same bodily reactions may not be as evident, and, therefore, not as noticed by others, or even by the "T" himself, unless the "T" is a hot-tempered type.

Thus, "T"s may seem stony-hearted, cold, heartless, almost inhuman. If the feeling function really does remain undeveloped, then this may be true. However, it is as false to think of "T"s as unfeeling as it is to assume that "F"s are incapable of logic just because they are so emotional.

Remember, "Thinking" and "Feeling" have nothing to do with *middoth*. "T"s and "F"s can be equally manipulative and coniving, using their emotions to persuade and manipulate others.

They can also display the highest levels of concern and caring.
Example: "My husband has a truely scientific, analytical 'T'

mentality. When I tell him about a personal problem, he first considers it mentally. Then, he decides whether or not to experience what I'm feeling. If he allows himself to feel, then the information goes back up to his head. Then, maybe he'll say something about what I've just said. If not, he simply does not answer. I don't have a normal conversation with him like I do with an 'F'. But I do know that I can trust him totally to come up with the best possible solution and that he will consider whatever I say very carefully and not be swayed by feelings as I am."

Example: "My 'T' lawyer can be very dramatic, even explosive, then calm down in a second, depending on who he's talking to or what the situation requires. It's quite amazing to watch him in action, using whatever emotion is useful in any given situation, then coming back to his basically detached, logical self."

Because "T"s are able to more readily disengage from their emotions, they can choose more rationally whether or not to allow themselves to feel. "F"s don't usually have that choice. By the time "F"s become aware of their desire not to get attached or upset, it's too late — they have already become emotionally involved. If they want to detach, they must go through a conscious disengagement process by switching to "T" mode logic. For the "T", the problem is the opposite; i.e., to take the time to consciously get emotionally involved.

When upset, "T"s can more easily divert their attention and immerse themselves in other matters without the undercurrent of srong emotionalism which the "F" feels.

Example: "A 'T' friend, who also has a strong 'F' part, had a miscarriage at the same time I did. She felt bad, of course, and we sympathized together. But then she just went on with her life, while I felt so bereft and found it much harder to function and get myself back together. The grief just *schlepped* on and on. It's not that she didn't care. She did. The initial blow was probably just as strong with her. But she doesn't have to wage this tremendous struggle with so many intense feelings. She was able to disengage more quickly. Even when something good happens, I'm so excited that I have more difficulty functioning. I used to feel ashamed for having strong emotions. Now that I understand this system, I don't condemn my feelings. I let them be, and I go on with my life. I'm far more functional without those condemnations."

Example: "There have been rumors that my husband's company may go out of business. My husband, a 'T', says that they are just rumors and not to pay attention to them, that we'll deal with the problem when the time comes. He has this ability to divert his attention and put the whole thing 'on hold.' But me, I haven't stopped feeling tense since I heard about the possibility. My stomach is in knots and I feel insecure no matter how much try to think positively."

LOGIC V. FEELING: The major difference between the "F" and the "T" is simply that the "F" makes choices on the basis of feeling, while the "T" makes choices on the basis of impersonal logic.

Example: "We were looking at houses to buy and I found the perfect one, right size and location and everything. But my husband said that it was beyond our budget and couldn't even be considered. I felt that because I liked it so much, that things just had to work out somehow. He wasn't distracted by such feelings. He was considering the facts and figures."

"T" is the proper mode to use when one is dealing with things or ideas. But this impersonal approach is often disastrous when dealing with people, for feeling is the bridge between one human being and another. Maturity demands that one be able to use both "T" and "F" modes at the appropriate time. Sometimes it is necessary to switch off our feelings, becoming impervious to our own inner drama or other people's emotions. Other situations demand that we make contact with others in a warm and sympathetic manner. As with all the modes, balance is essential.

Ultimately, it is the uplifting ideas in Torah which pull the "F"'s out of their excessive emotionalism by giving meaning, purpose and direction to life. These ideas make sense out of our pain and disappointments, thereby helping overcome depression and bitterness. Likewise, it is the obligation to love others, no matter who or what they are, that keeps the "T" from becoming cold and indifferent.

WRONG THINKING, WRONG FEELING: Thinking types assume, "Because I thought it, it must be true." Feelers assume, "Because I felt it, it must be true." Both can be completely wrong. For example:

False feeling: "I felt so inadequate, but everyone assured me that I had done a wonderful job."

False assumption: "I was sure he was being so quiet because he didn't like me. When I asked, he said he was just tired and very preoccupied with other matters."

Feeling types assume that a strong emotional response means that there must be something to get upset about. This is not necessarily true. Often, the event is a triviality which should be ignored or handled dispassionately. In contrast, "T"'s may think that because they do not feel strongly about something, that there is nothing to get upset about. This, too, is often untrue. The "T" must often work to "engage" or arouse his feelings in order to experience the importance or seriousness of what is happening. "F"'s often think that the "T" is "right" because the "T" is being so calm and rational. This, too, may be wrong.

PROBLEMS IN RELATIONSHIPS: "T"'s and "F"'s can be equally caring or uncaring. However, the two types have different ways of showing that they care. For example, "T"'s tend to be more sensitive to and angry about slights to their sense of honor or their belongings, while "F"'s are more sensitive to and angry about slights to their feelings of essential worth or even the smallest dimunition in the degree of closeness. "F"'s need praise, reassurance and positive feedback. But "T"'s often see such needs as unnecessary and childish and a sign of weakness.

Extreme, unbalanced "T"'s can be just as difficult as extreme, unbalanced "F"'s:

Example: "I come from a very warm, demonstrative family. Thus, it was quite a shock to meet my spouse's relatives. To them, 'niceness' means that they offer food and talk about the weather or current events. But they never asked me about me as a person.

On visits, I would feel like I was invisible, or, at best, a piece of furniture. I used to withdraw in hurt silence. But now that I realize that they are 'T's with very little 'F', I understand that I have to relate to them by talking about their interests and not expect a personal relationship. They are very nice, good people, but they just don't relate the way I do."

Example: "A certain relative is so overly responsive to her children's feelings that they end up whining and making demands all the time. She is a real martyr type, doing everything for them, and never allowing them to be self-sufficient. I realize that she, herself, had such a deprived background that she is probably trying to make up for it through her children, but I worry about how they are going to make it in the world."

"F"s connect to others by sharing feelings. However, many "T"s do not experience a strong need for an emotionally intimate relationship. If the "T" is an ST (Sensing-Thinking), he wants to "connect" mainly through touch or by doing things together (e.g., shopping, eating, going on trips). If the "T" is an NT (Intuitive-Thinking), the connection is mainly through learning together and sharing ideas. It the "T" is also an "I", there is usually even less of an interaction.

"T"s may think they are "connecting" just because they are talking, no matter what they are talking about. Being an "F" or a "T" has nothing to do with being talkative. "T"s, especially extraverted ones, can be just as talkative as "F"s when speaking about particular interests. But "F"s, especially NFs, may be wholly unsatisfied by that level of communication, and may feel that the "T" does not really care, because the converstion is basically superficial or meaningless.

"F"s may get very angry or depressed at not having a personal, emotional bond with others, yet may also feel defensive and guilty about wanting that contact.

Since "F"s feel most comfortable when dealing with people and "T"s when dealing with things, it it inevitable that "T"s will sometimes be emotionally oblivious, treating people like things. It is just as likely that the "F" will sometimes over-react emotionally to any hint of rejection. Both can become very angry if they think the other person is doing this deliberately.

A vicious cycle then begins: when upset, an "F" lessens anxiety by sharing feelings, by talking it out — over and over again if necessary. But a "T" feels safest when *not* connecting emotionally. Under pressure to relate, "T"s lessen anxiety by withdrawing even more, leaving the "F" feeling doubly rejected, guilty and desperate. Over time, "F"s and "T"s can polarize into opposite positions, and often end up not sharing at all. The problem can be partially avoided if the "F" will make the environment safe for the "T" by avoiding all condemnations and using the "T"s' language at first, in order to get the conversation started. Unfortunatley, instead of being more accepting, these two types often try angrily and desperately to get the other to be more like him/herself.

Example: "I have only the highest praise for my husband, a very intelligent NT. But one thing always bothered me, which was that it was difficult for me to ask him to help me with the children. Even when I do finally get up the courage to ask, I quickly back down if he shows the least bit of hesitation. Since he understands this typology, I asked him one day. 'Can you help me analyze why it is so difficult for me to ask you for help?' So he went through all the reasons, according to my particular constellation of characteristics. Then he said, 'If you want to ask for help, you have to be very direct about precisely what you want. He told me what words would be most effective. I tried his words the next day and it worked! And I know why: I didn't criticize him; I hooked into his 'T' mode by asking him to analyze the problem; and I let him feel that it was his decision and that he was in control."

When trying to explain feelings to a "T", the "F" often complains, "It's always such an *effort* to make myself understood. I know he cares, but he gets so impatient. He complains that I'm over-reacting, over-emotional, or not being reasonable or rational. The worst part is that when I try to explain what I feel is missing, he/she doesn't understand what I'm talking about when I use words like 'closeness' or 'relationship'!"

If the "F" is continuously emotionalizing everything, the "T" may think, "Boy, if that's what it means to be emotional — all this drama and hysteria — I don't want any part of that world. I don't want to feel at all!" And the "F" can think, "Well, if I have to become cold and detached in order to get him to listen, then I won't relate at all."

Healthy "T"s are very caring and concerned about others. Unfortunately, this is less true for "T"s who were raised in an emotionally deprived environment, i.e., where there was a great deal of verbal or physical abuse. Having had no opportunity to experience a close, loving relationship early in life, they will usually find it very difficult to establish any feeling of connectedness with others. In fact, the very idea that other people have feelings may be an abstraction which is difficult for emotionally deprived "T"s to grasp. Because their feelings were never taken into consideration, they never learned to do so to others. Thus, a broken leg which can be seen or a fever which can be felt may arouse some emotion on their part. But more "abstract" hurts, such as the hurt feelings which result from their indifference or criticism may not be experienced as having any real significance or validity. Indeed, "T"s may smirk, smile blandly, or get angry if a person expresses pain over their insensitivity.

Example: "As an 'F', the worst thing is my spouse's indifference. I'd rather that my spouse be angry than cold. I think I sometimes actually provoke a confrontation so that I can get some expression of involvement, and maybe even to avoid having to experience feeling so unimportant and insignificant."

In order to have a satisfying relationship, both partners must be very patient and willing to modify their behavior for the sake of the other. For example, when relating to an "F", the "T" must allow time for the emotions to rise and fall, while remaining sympathetic and understanding. Once the emotional intensity has begun to fade, then the "T" can appeal to reason and logic. Likewise, if an "F" wants to get through to the "T", he must remember *not* to respond angrily to the initial coldness or disinterest, but to patiently allow the "T" time to engage the feelings and then find a non-hostile way of arousing sensitivity.

While there is no perfect solution to this gap between "T"s and "F"s, coping mechanisms will be discussed in later chapters.

REVIEW:
WHEN YOU THINK OF "T" (THINKING), THINK:
decides on the basis of facts and logic
values logic above sentiment
impersonal, more interested in things than human relationships
more truthful than tactful
can get along without harmony
may hurt people without realizing it
firm-minded
finds it relatively easy to reprimand and punish when necessary
stronger in executive ability than social arts
likely to question conclusions
brief and businesslike
good at organizing facts and ideas into a logical sequence
tends to suppress, undervalue and ignore feeling
intellectually critical

WHEN YOU THINK OF "F" (FEELING), THINK:
values harmony
aware of other people's feelings
tries to live up to others' expectations
takes extenuating circumstances into account
enjoys pleasing others
dislikes telling people unpleasant things
values sentiment above logic
more tactful than truthful
stronger in social arts than executive ability
naturally friendly; difficulty being brief and business-like
may ramble and repeat his/herself
may have difficulty organizing thoughts
may suppress, undervalue and ignore logic

CHAPTER V: PERCEIVING ("P") V. JUDGING ("J")

This pair of preferences is divided equally (50-50) in the American population.

This fourth and final pair is difficult to grasp at first because the terms are not used in the way we are used to seeing them used. The P-J (Perceiving-Judging) mode has to do with whether you prefer to keep your options open, waiting to the last minute to make a decision ("P"), or whether you prefer to have closure as soon as possible, by making decisions, formulating rules, setting boundaries, and devising schedules and structures ("J").

To "perceive," in terms of this typology, means to take information in. When you are "perceiving" ("P"), you are becoming aware, being open to new information and experiences. When you are "judging" ("J"), you are forming conclusions or judgments about what you are experiencing, making decisions, taking a stand, deciding on a direction.

You cannot be perceiving ("P") and judging ("J") simultaneously. In any given circumstance, you must choose one or the other. When you stop taking in new information ("P"), you can then take a stand ("J"). Obviously, even a strong "P" (Perceiving type) has to come to conclusions at some point and make a decision. He cannot go on endlessly collecting data. And a strong "J" (Judging type) is sometimes forced by circumstances to allow new information to enter his consciousness.

PERCEIVING TYPES ("P")

The best way to conceptualize the "P" personality is to think of the word "options." The "P" feels best when collecting data and considering options, as opposed to making a final decision. The "P"s' most essential desire is to be free, not to be tied down, obligated, or restricted. This is central to an understanding of this type. "P"s tend to be flexible, open-minded, adaptable and impulsive. They tend to have a "live and let live" attitude and are more likely to consider the validity of other points of view. They like to think of themselves as "free spirits," even if they live within the boundaries of a strict external environment.

"P"s are natural performers. Even introverted "P"s will often find some way to get public attention with either positive or negative acts. This performing urge also enables "P"s to take on different personalities. Parents of "P" children may find those children "trying on" a variety of persona as they move through adolescence into adulthood. Some "P"s have trouble coming to a fixed, settled idea of who they really are, just as they have trouble coming to fixed and settled decisions, schedules and commitments. There always seem to be so many choices, and so many pros and cons to each choice.

The "meta need" for "P"s is for awareness, autonomy, and freedom to consider options.

COMBINATIONS: There are various types of "P"s, all of whom tend to be independent-minded, impulsive, and craving action and variety.

SENSING-PERCEIVING (SP): Emotionally healthy SPs have a drive to excel in the physical world, working with things and people, as opposed to abstract ideas.

There are two types of SPs:

A. STPs (Sensing-Thinking-Perceiving) prefer working with things (e.g. concrete facts, money, tools, crafts, instruments, machines)

B. SFPs (Sensing-Feeling- Perceiving) need to interact with people, and are warm and friendly.

INTUITIVE-PERCEIVING (NP): Healthy NPs have a drive to excel in the realm of abstract knowledge, such as philosophy, science or psychology. Like all "N"s, they are creative and original. They crave the "eureka" experience of coming up with new insights or information. There are two types of NPs:

A. NTPs (Intuitive-Thinking-Perceiving) enjoy working with abstract theories, philosophies and ideas, in an impersonal approach.

B. NFPs (Intuitive-Feeling-Perceiving) need to work with people, using their abstract theories, philosophies and ideas, in a warm, personal, empathetic approach.

In addition, any of the above combinations can be either introverted or extraverted.

QUALITY: As always when dealing with types, the quality of a "P" ranges over a vast continuum. The "P" can be a person who uses his pioneering spirit, spontaneity and sense of individuality to "break-ground" either in spiritual ("N") or material ("S") realms. High level NPs can be brilliant Torah scholars, innovative businessmen (SP), creative artists (NP or SP), or fiery idealists who help the oppressed and the needy (NFP).

At the other extreme, the "P" can be an impulsive, violent, hedonistic, unstable individual, wildly running after immediate pleasures and wreaking a path of destruction in his wake. There are all kinds of "P"s. The difference is in their level of intelligence, their *middoth*, and how they use, or misuse, their innate talents.

INDECISION: Often, "P"s finally come to a decision when, out of sheer frustration, they impulsively make a move, despite the feeling that they really do not have all the information they need. However, even then, they may agonize over the decision, modifying it or brooding regretfully over the choice. Thus, "P"s often feel uneasy after they make a decision because a) they never feel that they had enough information to make their evaluation process complete, and b) they feel confined and restricted by the decision.

The procrastination of the "P" may be due to laziness, or may actually have a deeper source, i.e., in their hope that if they wait long enough new data will turn up which will make their decision more sound in their eyes and will not cause them to feel uncomfortable or inadequate.

The "waffling" of some "P" can be very exasperating to others.

Example: "A certain friend is so good at seeing other people's points of view and agreeing with people that we never know if she's agreeing just to agree or if that's what she really believes. I can never be sure what she really thinks. She keeps changing her opinions depending on who she's with."

Example: "I'm a strong 'P'. It's hard for me to come up with firm rules and regulations and, even when I do, it's hard for me to stick to them. For example, I'll make a firm rule for the kids like 'No more eating in the living room.' But then I'll forget, or people will drop by, or I'm too tired to fight with them, or I'll start questioning whether or not I really want to stand firm on this issue, and before I know it, the rule is out the window. I'll say, 'No, absolutely no, you absolutely cannot have that or go there,' and then the next thing I know, I begin to see the other side and I'm not so sure, and suddenly I'm all confused and questioning my decision. I just don't follow through. My neighbors complained about them not being in control. Their principals complain about them. And my husband keeps complaining why I'm not on top of things. And I ended up condemning myself from morning to night. Since reading about the types, I realize that I have to start small, with some simple rule each and every day, something I feel I can live with, like making sure they put their laundry in the bin. It's like I have to go on a diet to reduce my 'P' and gain 'J'. I can't change our basic natures, but I can certainly work to be more disciplined wherever I can do so, and not give up completely, though that is very tempting."

CURIOSITY: "P"'s have a strong curiosity hunger. They want to know about everything pertaining to their particular area of interest. This hunger shows up very early in life, as they take watches apart, want to know all about your thoughts and feelings, or explore nature, and understand how their bodies work.

Example: "I told my four year old 'P' son that if he did a certain thing, he would get a big punishment. Then he went right ahead and did it. I asked him, 'Why did you do that when I said you would get punished?' He said, 'I was curious about what the punishment was.'"

INDIVIDUALISM: "P"s treasure their sense of individuality, unlike "J"s, who are more willing to give up their sense of separateness and take on the identity of the group to which they belong. "P" wives are more likely to want to relate as equals with their husbands, whereas "J"s tend to adopt a parent-child or child-parent position. "P"s often prefer to be their own boss and to be in control of their own lives, even at an early age.

Example: "I'm a strong 'J' and had pretty good control over my children, all except my youngest, a girl aged twelve. She simply does not see herself as subordinate to me. She wants to come and go as she pleases, eat when she likes and what she likes. She has a strong sense of herself as her own, independent being. I don't always know how far to go in letting her make her own choices, or when to get tough and how much of a battle I should put forth in getting her to respect my wishes. If I'm too strict, she gets withdrawn and depressed or else hostile and rebellious. She is a tremendous challenge. As a parent, I know she must be guided firmly and disciplined strongly when necessary. But she must also have a certain degree of freedom."

Example: "I became an Observant Jew as a teenager. I had to defy friends and family to do so. So I guess I shouldn't be surprised that my children also have such strong, independent spirits and are not as obedient as I would like them to be."

"P"s are so individualistic that even if they belong to a rigid system or have to wear a uniform, for example, they will find some way of expressing their individuality, such as by wearing the regulation hat at a different angle than everyone else, or by some other small "touch" which symbolizes their sense of uniqueness. They are the ones who start new fads and have the courage to go against the crowd to do so.

Example: "If a saleslady says to buy something because

'Everybody's wearing it,' then I know that that's the very thing I don't want. I have to be different."

The "P" need to preserve a sense of independence and autonomy can be an admirable trait if it urges them to oppose an authority figure who is a tyrant or an incompetent person whose regulations and opinions should be not be followed. Throughout history, we, as a people, have often stood up defiantly to oppressors even under threat of death. We have preserved our laws under overwhelming odds. However, that same defiant attitude is disastrous if it leads the "P" to defy parents and teachers or break *halachoth*, which maintain sanity, morality and stability.

FLEXIBILITY: "P"s have a *flexible* approach to rules and regulations. For "P"s, plans, structures and rules are to be used when practical and ignored or discarded when they no longer serve a purpose. "P"s are likely to look for loopholes and to try to avoid established procedures and laws, especially if they make no sense from a practical or logical point of view. They're the types who first started the practice of sleeping next to their sick children in hospitals, in defiance of hospital orders, and who are likely to defy established hierarchies and procedures if they think those procedures are silly or unnecessary.

CHILDHOOD: As children, "P"s are more playful, mischievous, and naughty than the obedient "J"s. "P" children have to be reminded to get dressed, do their chores, do their homework, and keep their things in order. If forced to comply, they do so reluctantly, because they don't see the need for all these rules and regulations and also because they don't like to be controlled by outside forces. Parents of "P"s must patiently repeat over and over again what the rules and regulations are — and that those rules and regulations are still in effect since yesterday — or since five minutes ago, since the "P" is always testing the limits. On the other hand, if there is some pleasure or reward involved, such as going on a trip or doing a craft project, they can be very organized and orderly. If a parent or teacher can make work fun, the "P" will do it with enthusiasm.

"P"s are always ready for new conquests and adventures.

Example: "My 'P'daughter lost her contact lens at the same time that her class was going on a trip to Tzfat. We didn't have money for both the lens and the trip. I thought it would be far more practical for her to get the lens, but there was no question in her mind: Tzfat, of course! Thanks to my understanding of the types, I didn't argue or condemn her for her decision. I accept her strong need for variety and excitement."

All types of "P"s may find that their energies can become scattered in many directions because they become easily excited by new ideas or adventures, thus losing interest in their old endeavors. Their initial enthusiasm for a project or relationship may suddenly fade once the newness — and the excitement — wear off.

IMPULSIVITY: The biggest problem for the "P"s is their high level of impulsivity. Whether it's blurting out an answer in the classroom before the teacher calls on them, or buying something on impulse, they want what they want when they want it. They feel most alive when they are acting spontaneously. If they do not restrain their impulses and direct them in positive ways, the results can be a break-down of morality, and a lack of reliability, dependability and integrity.

PLEASURE V. DUTY: For "P"s, it is important that life be pleasurable, in contrast to "J"s, for whom it is enough to know that they are doing their duty, doing the right thing. "P"s need something exciting to look forward to. The "P" must often wage an inner battle between the gratification of some immediate impulse and the need to delay gratification for the sake of a higher ideal. The "J" has other battles to wage.

JUDGING TYPES "J"

The major motivating drive of the "J" is for closure. To that end, "J"s tend to be organized and decisive. ["P"s can be just as organized and decisive, but then the motivation is different.] Talented "J"s have high level executive and managerial skills. They are self-disciplined, exacting, dependable and trustworthy.

They are known for their great integrity. They have a reverence for traditions. They tend to do things the way they have always been done, and maintain traditional customs, systems, institutions and laws. Every normal person has a drive to maintain order, structure and predictability in order to provide a sense of stability. The "J" has a stronger, innate drive to do so.

At the highest level, "J"s quickly and easily formulate laws, plans procedures and schedules. They do not balk at following set rules. They tend to be attracted to professions which require order, structure, and meticulous attention to laws and details.

As much as the "P"s want to be free, the "J" wants to be bound by firm structures, wants to be good and to do the right thing. In contrast to the "P"s, who feel uneasy after making a decision, "J"s feel relieved, sure that whatever decision they made was the right one.

Do not confuse "J" with being critical or judgmental. It would be best to associate the "J" with "judicious," i.e., wise decisions, integrity and fairness. As for the the tendency to be hyper-critical, that is something which all people, regardless of type, must avoid if they wish to achieve a high level of spirituality.

Because Judging types are happiest when things are settled and decided, they often seem more mature and more sure of themselves than "P"s.

While "J"s are product-oriented and concerned with doing what is right, "P"s enjoy just being active and being involved in the process of doing, and care less about the final outcome.

"J"s like knowing their place, and feel safe living in an authoritarian social system, heirarchy, or bureaucracy.

Unlike the "P"s, who relate fraternally, "J"s are either authoritarian or obedient. Some people are "J" in their relationship with people, but "P" in their need for autonomy and freedom. The same is true in any of the pairs of traits, where an individual can be one way in some situations and the opposite mode in others.

In contrast to the "P", who is sometimes too flexible and not strict enough, "J"s may cling to various laws and self-made rules and regulations even when they are no longer constructive or necessary. Doing something even one time may make the "J" feel committed to keep doing it. For the "J", customs, schedules, and rules take on a "holy" status, even those that have no basis in Torah.

DIFFERENCE IN THINKING: "J"s can approach almost any subject differently than "P"s.

Example: "When my 'J' daughter got married, she wanted furniture in the same antique design which her favorite grandmother had. My 'P' daughter, of course, wanted something very modern and original. It was the same with them in school. The 'J' daughter always wrote papers according to an outline which she worked out ahead of time. The 'P' daughter used to write the outline after she had finished the paper, much to the consternation of her teachers. She would say, 'But I don't know what I want to say until after I've written down what I want to say!' Thankfully, they are both pretty balanced so that the 'P' always finishes her projects and is responsible, and the 'J' is tolerant and capable of having fun."

ADVANTAGES AND DISADVANTAGES: When adaptability and spontaneity are necessary, the "P"s have an advantage. But when schedules and systems need to be formulated and followed, or something needs to be done according to a set procedure, the "J"s have the upper hand. Not all "J"s are good managers and get things organized to their satisfaction. If the "J" cannot figure out a system and a method for doing something, it might be left undone, leaving the "J" feeling terribly ashamed and guilty about not being more together.

Example: "When I had my first baby, everything fell apart. I couldn't figure out when to do what or what to do. As a 'J', I need to have a set time to do things. I finally sat down with a 'J' neighbor and made a list of what to do when. The only problem was that my baby had no set sleeping pattern, so I sometimes got all confused and didn't do anything all morning. The 'P's all told me to feed her on demand. The 'J's told me to get her on a schedule as fast as possible. I had to go with the 'J' advice for the sake of my mental health, while my 'P' friend with a new baby went with the 'P' advice for the sake of her mental health."

WORK ETHIC: Another essential difference between "P"s and "J"s is that "P"s have a play ethic, while "J"s have a work ethic. It is much harder for the "J" to take time for pleasurable activities. Even as children "J"s want very much to be good, to do the right thing, while "P"s are more concerned with expressing themselves or having a good time.

Example: "I divide my children between the 'P-bodies' and the 'J-bodies.' The 'P-bodies' are definitely more restless, more demanding of excitement and variety, and more difficult to manage."

INHIBITION: Judging types are more inhibited than Perceiving types. "J"s have trouble saying "Yes" to their impulses, while Perceiving types have trouble saying "No" to theirs. "J"s are more serious than "P"s. Typical "J" statements are: "You can never be too careful." "Look before you leap." "Save for the future." "P"s say: "He who hesitates is lost." "Live fully in the present." "Don't plan. Just let things happen."

Thus, "P"s might feel stifled in the very same atmosphere in which "J"s thrive.

QUALITY: As with all the other modes, there is a broad range of "J" capability. At the highest level, the "J" can be the manager of a school, hospital, or be in a high governmental position. At the other end of the continuum, the "J" can be quite befuddled and unable to cope with even minimal demands.

At the highest level, the "J" is a truly wise, judicious person whose judgments are sound, trustworthy, and humane. At the other end of the continuum, the "J" is a person whose judgments are irrational, arbitrary, and even inhumane, but who sticks to them no matter how much pain and inconvenience they cause to others.

Unintegrated "J"s are often obsessive-compulsives who torture themselves and terrify everyone in the environment with their petty perfectionism over unimportant details and self-produced rituals. Others almost paralyze themselves into a state of dysfunction with their excessive guilt and anxiety over not being able to be perfectly good and right at all times. Unless they have the approval of an authority figure, they are afraid to make even the most minor decision. Thus, insecure "J"s often do not manage well, are not able to make decisions, and fail to get their minds or their homes organized.

POSSIBLE CONFUSION: As with all the pairs, it is easy to get confused as to what someone is since every healthy person, whether "P" or "J" naturally wants to be trustworthy and reliable and to function effectively in the world. You may have to know a person quite well to determine his innermost motivations.

Also, the impulsivity of the "P" should not be confused with the quick decision-making tendencies of the "J". The "J" acts in order to attain closure and a feeling of safety. The "P" acts in order to discharge energy or because of his hunger for action.

Example: "When I first looked at the types, I thought that I was more 'J' than 'P' because I'm a very meticulous, organized person. But I like variety and action and am also quite independent. I guess I must be a strong combination of both, which is a good sign of mental health."

PARENTAL: The "J" likes to control and manage. This includes giving advice about what others should and should not do. This parental approach of the "J" has the advantage of giving others a sense of security by providing strict limits, consistent policies, and set schedules.

The disadvantage of this parental approach is that some people, "P"s in particular, may feel patronized and wholly inadequate in the presence of the "J". While some people like to have their lives managed by others, many others become hostile and rebellious.

Example: "When I was first learning about Orthodoxy, I needed the 'J' parental approach. I needed to be told what to do and led like a child. But as I grew in Torah learning and became more secure, I needed to strike out on my own, as I am essentially a 'P'. As I changed, it was hard for them to accept that I was no longer in the position of a child. I began to feel distant from those early 'parental' figures."

Example: "I had been leading a small support group for mothers of learning-disabled children along the lines of EMETT. We had been doing very well. There was a lot of enthusiasm and growth. Then a woman moved into our community who had experience leading such groups. At first, I was really happy to have her expertise. But she was very 'J' and wanted everything to be run strictly according to the rules she had learned as a social worker. She made me feel like everything I was doing was wrong. I know she didn't mean to do this on purpose, but her presence made me feel totally inadequate. I just can't function if I have to always be thinking of whether or not what I'm doing is right or wrong. I just can't go strictly according to the rules. As a 'P', my spirit soars best when I can be spontaneous. If I feel that someone is observing me critically, I just close up completely and go dead inside. Thankfully, I could define the problem in terms of differences in mode, instead of condemning myself for not being able to get along with everyone or condemning her for the way she acted. She would be very good for a different kind of group. So I told her honestly that for the sake of my mental health, I would prefer that she start her own group."

Example: "I was asked to work on a project with a very nice 'P'. But after a few days, I realized that this person didn't have enough 'J' dependability. I just couldn't rely on him to show up on time or complete the work I asked for. I decided that for the sake of my mental health, I would have to find someone else."

COMBINATIONS: The "J" can combine with other modes in various ways:

SENSING-JUDGING (SJ): Healthy SJs have a drive to apply their managerial and organizational skills in the concrete, physical world, such as the practical application of *halacha*, the formulation of household rules and schedules, banking, systems analysis, medicine, school systems. There are two kinds of SJs:

A. STJs (Sensing-Thinking-Judging) are people who prefer to

work with things (facts, budgets, systems analysis, etc.) and take an impersonal approach to people and problems.

B. SFJs (Sensing-Feeling-Judging) are care-givers who need to work with people and apply their managerial and organizational talents in a warm and personal manner.

INTUITIVE-JUDGING (NJ): Healthy NJs have a drive to apply their managerial and organizational skills in the world of philosophy, science, psychology, grammar, etc. NJs are often excellent and exacting teachers, and enjoy formulating principles, theories, and laws. There are two kinds of NJs:

A. The NTJ (Intuitive-Thinking-Judging), who adopts an impersonal approach to his subject matter.

B. The NFJ (Intuitive-Feeling-Judging), whose approach is warm and personal.

In addition, any of these types can be either introverted ("I") or extraverted ("E").

Example: "I'm an NJ, which means that I'm a very organized teacher. But when it comes to SJ organization in the kitchen, I'm not very efficient. I used feel terribly inadequate about my lack of efficiency, because I am quite a perfectionist. But now that I realize that many people are not as equally organized in the 'S' world as in the 'N' world, I've stopped condemning myself. Amazingly, since I'm more accepting of myself, I've begun to function more effectively in the kitchen too!"

Example: "I went to an STJ dentist who had been highly recommended. But I couldn't relate to him, partly because, as an introvert and a 'T', it was difficult for him to provide any feedback about what was going on. I need this contact and feedback to reassure me and lessen my anxiety. So I found an SFJ dentist who is friendly and sensitive to my needs and just as meticulous about his work."

CHILDHOOD: The organizational and managerial skills of the "J" usually show up early in life.

Example: "My five year old 'J' invited a friend over. As soon as the little guest came in, my son took him to the toy shelf and explained, 'These are the toys. You can take down one at a time.

When you are finished playing, you have to put it back before you can take another toy.' Although I myself am a strong 'J', I've never said anything like that to him. I don't know where he got it from, but he stated that rule with so much assurance and confidence, just like an adult."

Whether this child was imitating a teacher or another adult, the fact is that stating rules and setting limits came easily and naturally to him, which is not true for "P" children, who are always testing the limits and pushing to see if they can go just a bit beyond them.

Example: "My 'J' daughter first started running a camp for small children at the age of eleven. It amazed me to see how well she had everything organized by the time the children arrived each day. She also has a lot of 'P' in her personality, so there was a great deal of fun and excitement, with new projects each day."

CONSERVATISM: "J"s feel comfortable when they conform to standards and do things in a socially acceptable, conventional, conservative manner.

Example: "When I got sick, I approached my 'J' doctor with the suggestion that perhaps some alternative forms of medicine would help - perhaps acupuncture, vitamins, herbal remedies, or natural diet. He just scoffed. I understand that he feels safest taking the conservative approach of the conservative medical establishment. But I needed a more open-minded approach, so I found a 'P' M.D. who is also a nutritionist."

In the extreme, "J"s can have an automatic, irrational suspiciousness and hostility to anything new or different.

PERSEVERENCE: "J"s may persevere with blind devotion to a person or cause long after they should have let go. Their need for closure can be destructive if it causes them to be fanatically rigid and overly punitive and punishing for minor offenses.

Example: "An unintegrated 'SJ' [i.e., insufficient 'N' and 'P'] came to visit and got upset when I threw away leftovers that my youngest child hadn't finished eating. She said that I should force him to finish so that he would learn not to waste food. I told her it was more important for me not to destroy his spirit. I assured her that I am not a wasteful person, but that I just can't force food on a child. She said 'A rule is a rule and must be followed.' I asked her to put a dollars and cents value on the food I had to throw out. It came to just a few pennies. I asked her if those few pennies were worth making the child miserable. But she repeated, 'A rule is a rule.' So then, in her presence, I called my Rav's wife and asked her if throwing scraps of food away was a major sin. She laughed and told me that when Ya'akov came to Egypt, Yosef provided for his father and all his relatives 'According to the little ones.' She said that the commentator, Mizrachi, interpreted this last statement to mean that Yosef gave to his father in abundance because it is in the nature of little ones to waste food. *(Bereshith 47:12)* That reduced my temper on this matter. However, my relative was still upset. Obviously, we were on completely different wave lengths."

PROBLEMS IN RELATIONSHIPS: Ideally, the "P" and the "J" should balance each other: the uninhibited spontaneity of the "P" is held in check by the good judgment of the "J", and the conservatism and hesitations of the "J" are overcome by the enthusiasm of the "P"; the I'll-manage-your-life tendency of the "J" is held in check by the drive for independence of the "P".

In reality, however, the differences between them can be the cause for a great deal of antagonism and irritation, especially if either is extreme, such as the "J" who wants the house to look like a museum, or the "P" who doesn't even care if the house looks like a tornado just hit. Serious problems will also arise if one of the partners is a very domineering person who wants to manage and control others' lives. Dominance implies lack of trust in the other person and the unspoken message, "You are a failure." No one likes to feel this way. "P"s, in particular, must feel autonomous and independent and relate from a position of equality.

INTEGRATION: Both "P"s and "J"s must be capable of using the skills from each other's mode when necessary. As with all the pairs, there are advantages and disadvantages to both preferences. Sometimes it is essential to make quick judgments

about people and situations at other times it is imortant to
be flexible and open-minded. In other circumstances, this would
be harmful. Sometimes one needs to be spontaneous and tolerant.
In other circumstances, such a position might be very damaging.
Sometimes it is important to step in and help people take control
of people; at other times this is disastrous. Each mode be used in
the proper way, at the proper time, or it becomes negative. A "P"
without "J" is capricious, irresponsible and wishy-washy. A "J"
without "P" is intolerant, prejudiced and overly rigid.

REVIEW:
WHEN YOU THINK "P" (PERCEIVING), THINK:
spontaneous - to wholeheartedly experience the moment even if
some intended things go undone
impulsive
open-minded - willingness to admit to new ideas even if
they conflict with one's own
understanding of other points of view
tolerance for a variety of legitimate standards
curious and adventurous
zest for experience
adaptability arising from a willingness to let go of the old, and a
freedom to improvise to meet altered conditions.

WHEN YOU THINK "J" (JUDGING), THINK:
seeks closure
manages, organizes, directs, plans, sets limits
restrained, self-regimented, purposeful and exacting
integrity, reliability, dependability, trustworthiness
aims to be right
  systematic and orderly, follows proper procedures
sustained effort through will power
decisiveness
the exercise of authority and willingness to advise people along
with managing, executive and organizing skills
settled opinions
acceptance of routine

CHAPTER VI:
THE INTUITIVE-THINKING
TYPE (NT)

The eight modes discussed in Chapters 1-5 combine in such a way to provide a four-initial description of each personality type which is discussed more thoroughly in a later chapter. However, in order to avoid overwhelming the reader, we will start with a two-initial combination. Each of the following four descriptions provides a basic unifying principle within the sixteen possible types: NT (Intuitive-Thinking), NF (Intuitive-Feeling), SP (Sensing-Perceiving) or SJ (Sensing-Judging).

Dominant NTs and NFs, with their "inspired," intuitive, vivid imaginations, are in sharp contrast to the sense-oriented, down-to-earth approach of the "S"s: ST, SF, SP and SJ.

Note that these descriptions focus mainly on the talented, highly intelligent, developed personalities. Obviously, many people will not reach a high level of development. At the end of each section, a brief description of the underdeveloped and unintegrated personalities of each will be given.

INTUITIVE-THINKING is dominant in about 12% of the American population.

Dominant NTs are profound and scholarly. They are usually quite intelligent, often brilliant, and have a strong thirst for knowledge. Whereas the ordinary person requires time to consider, understand and fully digest an idea, the NT goes through the same process much more quickly, often with a speed-of-lightening grasp of the underlying ideas and relationships. They can often pierce to the heart of difficult problems in an instant, seeing solutions no one else would have thought of with simple reason.

NTs' quick comprehension of theoretical abstractions, such as in *gemorah*, math, law, physics or philosophy, is in contrast to the ordinary step-by-step process which most people have to go through in order to reach their conclusions. Therefore, they are referred to as "N"s, Intuitives, for only someone with intuitive perceptiveness could so easily follow very complex, intricate ideas to their conclusion. Their intuitive ("N") ability enables them to grasp seemingly contradictory ideas, and visualize connections and conclusions where others only see a tangle of confusing or irrelevant data.

NTs love to spend their time exploring new ideas, developing theoretical models, or rearranging things in new and interesting patterns. Because of their rich inner world, NTs dislike having to focus for long on repetitive, mundane physical chores. NTs enjoy contemplating metaphysical abstractions, paradoxes and theoretical puzzles.

The NT is a "gemorah kohp," able to concentrate for hours. Sometimes, NTs are so involved in their world of abstract ideas and theories that they are oblivious to the world, to what they are wearing, to whether or not they have eaten, or to the time of day. They are driven by "knowledge lust" - the need to understand, to know the internal laws which make things work, for the sheer pleasure of gaining knowledge. This is in contrast to the "S" who may also have a hunger for information, but is more concerned about its practical application.

The history of the Jewish people is replete with giants in Torah wisdom, many of whom had mastered difficult tractates of Talmud at the age of five or six and were already coming up with *chidushim* at an early age. This is NT brilliance.

The developed NTs of great intelligence have a visionary, inspired quality. The richness and complexity of their thinking is beyond anything which ordinary people could ever grasp. A *shiur* with an inspired *talmid chacham* leaves one feeling uplifted, transformed out of ordinary, daily reality.

A beautiful description of the NT world in Eastern Europe, at the turn of the century, is given in David Zaritsky's *Beyond the Sun*. In one of the chapters, he describes the struggles of Aaron, who, because his mother was so against his learning full time, was forced to leave his beloved *yeshiva* when he was only 15 years of age. For the next three years, he earned a living as a mason. Then, one winter day, when his masonry equipment had frozen, he walked back into his *yeshiva* to get some hot water. Drawn to his beloved books as though by a powerful magnet, he sat down in his dirty clothes, looking longingly at the books he had loved so much. He simply could not go back to work.

"He would weary himself over an acute, keenly analytical discussion of...the theme he was studying in the Talmud. At times he would strike the *shtender* with his fists and cry out, 'All right: Come, let us look again, you stuffed-up blockhead of a brain. Let us look again at what it says here....' And suddenly he would leap from his seat in an explosion of joyous enthusiasm: a spark of understanding had kindled in his mind, making everything clear. The right explanation had been found at last, the difficulty was resolved. Then his entire being glowed in a happy radiance.

"'If you knew, Mother, what great pleasure a person has when he produces a new thought, a new point of view, in his Talmud study. ...it is literally like experiencing Paradise; simply beyond human comprehension... when you succeed in arriving by yourself at the very thought of a *rishon* [an early authority]..., when you arrive by the force of your own mind and you get to the answer, to the resolutions that he gave...I simply cannot describe it to you at all; I cannot convey it or explain it. I can tell you only this: I am happy! Now I know what I am. I feel alive and creative every minute, every hour; I feel my life is filled with content and meaning....'"

"His hunger for Torah study did not abate. It seemed to him that the more he went on to learn, the stronger his hunger grew. He craved to know more and more.... There he still stood - as on the first day he had entered the yeshiva - bent over the *shtender*, open-mouthed, with a yearning, craving spirit - like a thirst-stricken man bending down to a spring of cool water." (pp. 280-286)

In the end, his mother understood how important it was for her child to learn, and she gave him her full-hearted approval.

COMBINATIONS: NTs can combine either with "P" or "J".

NTPs are independent theorists and innovative pioneers in the field of philosophy and science. The enjoy finding ingenious solutions to challenging problems.

NTJs, while just as analytical and logical, are more concerned with the particulars of laws, and with management, analysis, goals, policies, and organization. They are often excellent grammarians, being attentive to every meticulous detail.

Either type can be extraverted or introverted. Extraverted NTs (ENT) are witty conversationalists and inspired teachers. They enjoy exchanging ideas, facts, and theories with others. Introverted NTs (INT) prefer more solitary pursuits. (These combinations are discussed more fully in the chapter entitled "16 Types.")

THE SCIENTIST: The NT is essentially a scientist. He is at his best when dealing with things that need to be done impersonally: giving precise explanations, figuring out instructions, and analyzing data. He wants to understand, predict and explain, in an impersonal, logical manner. He often feels like a "fish out of water" when he has to deal with people's emotions or talk about his personal feelings.

Thinking is essentially impersonal. Its goal is objective truth. The NT's judgments are based on whether something is true or false, and that conclusion is the product of having thought about objective realities. Thus, when the NT comes to a conclusion, he believes that he has reached that truth objectively and that it is, therefore, The Truth.

CHILDHOOD: The NT child is usually a voracious reader and is always asking, "Why?" This is a manifestation of his hunger for knowledge. These children may delight - or exasperate - their parents with their exuberant desire to know everything there is to know. They do not have to be nagged to learn or read; they devour books and beg for more. They catch on quickly to new material, often showing amazing aptitude for math at an early age. They are apt to be bored in school, which generally cannot supply enough stimulation for their fertile minds, and where teachers must explain abstract concepts in a step-by-step process for the sake of the majority of children.

The NT child may not want to be cuddled or held much by his parents once he is past the baby stage. NTs tend to be independent and somewhat non-conformist. They usually dislike repetitive, routine activities.

NTs can seem somewhat backward socially because they tend to be oblivious to the reactions of others. Introverted NTs tend to be loners. Extraverted NTs may be strong leaders.

Other children sometimes call the NT "the brain" or "odd ball." Unlike the NF, they usually do not mind the fact that they are different and don't fit in, because they do not have the strong NF need for emotional intimacy. They seem more self-contained than "F"s.

NTs are usually intelligent and high achievers academically. If they have a strong SP side, they also enjoy sports. They also like challenging intellectual games, such as Biblical quizzes or chess.

ASCETIC: Many NTs are "natural ascetics," i.e., unconcerned with physical necessities, such as food and clothing, and the material world except insofar as various machines, instruments or books may enhance their knowledge. They may be able to detach themselves so easily from sensual pleasures that they may not comprehend why others are attracted to them.

EMOTIONAL DISTANCE: Integrated NTs, i.e., those with with a healthy sense of self-esteem and a balancing measure of "F", are caring, insightful and communicative. However, NTs sometimes fail to communicate because they assume that others will not understand the intricacies of their ideas. In addition, NTs often fail to pick up the subtle physical and verbal cues which a more sensitive person would readily grasp. Most NTs are not as sensitive as NF s to the complexities of interpersonal relationships. In fact, they may actually be emotionally oblivious, not on purpose, but because their minds are wrapped up with other matters. They may make a tactless remark and, when told how devastating their words are, will respond with bewilderment that they could possibly have caused others pain. With time, healthy NTs learn to be more sensitive to the effect of their words.

"T"s do not "bond" like "F"s do, i.e., through self-disclosure. It is almost painful for "T"s to make self-revealing statements, and when and if they manage to do so, they may feel ashamed afterwards. This is more true for male than for female NTs.

RELATIONSHIPS: NTs who have a developed "F" side will be caring and sympathetic partners, taking great pains to listen to others and to help them come to their own insights, providing uplifting advice and ideas, and doing small things which show how much they really do care. Mentally healthy NTs are good conversationalists, are usually highly intelligent, insightful and deep, and are very devoted to their families. There are many wonderfully caring NT scholars, teachers, scientists, doctors, lawyers, home-makers, etc. However, they usually do not have the depth of empathy which the NFs have. [See following chapter]

NTs may not always remember to go into their Feeling mode and allow time for the expression of feelings when necessary. They really may not "see' emotional distress even when it seems so obvious to the "F". Since dominant NTs tend to suppress, undervalue and ignore their own feelings, it is not surprising that they tend to do the same with others' feelings. Since they see how quickly logic can overcome negative emotions, why is the mate or child still upset?

The NTs' ability to quickly "disengage" emotionally may give others the impression that they don't really care, when the truth is that they do, but are simply not as focused on the primacy of relationships as "F"s tend to be.

"F"'s need to accustom themselves to not always getting the degree of sympathy or appreciation that they might like. However, by focusing on the positive qualities of healthy NTs, by treasuring the moments of closeness which do occur, and by patiently developing the "F" side of the partner, the relationship can be a very rewarding one.

"F"'s married to NTs find that it is sometimes helpful to talk in "telegram language," i.e., to say what they want in the least number of words possible, and say it quickly, as the NT does not have patience for talk, unless it deals with their particular area of interest.

NTs usually view strong "F"'s as over-emotional, dense, "fuzzy headed," unstable, and irrational and are impatient when "F"'s talk about feelings.

NTs tend to discount conclusions which others have arrived at subjectively. Telling NTs "It just *feels right*," isn't enough to convince them that it is. Family members find that they need to come up with logical, convincing arguments if they want to win a debate with an NT.

FACTS: If the NT has to fire someone or make a critical remark, he has less of an internal struggle than the NF, for he is not concerned with the other person's feelings, but only with getting the facts across. A dominant NT doctor, for example, may not be able to provide much sympathy to patients.

PERFECTIONISM: Since NTs are so stringent and exacting with themselves, they may be very critical and overly exacting with others. They may not understand why others have to take so long to grasp what, to them, is so simple. To them, their critical remarks are a way of making others be more aware, competent and knowledgeable. But unless the relationship is very secure and loving, the criticism can destroys others' self-confidence.

THE UNINTEGRATED NT

As with all personality types, an abusive or neglectful childhood will push the NT to negative extremes, a cruel parody of all the brilliant talents of the NT. What can result in such a case is a person whose long-winded, complicated discourses make no sense; whose visions lack reality; whose piercing wit is used to humiliate and hurt others; and who is unwilling to make normal human contact. Instead, the strongly negative NT will compulsively attack people in private or take on the role of critic, dissenter, iconoclast, or nihilist in public.

Unintegrated NTs are usually the product of a cold home environment in which no one listened to or cared about their feelings. When they were in pain, they were told, "Don't be a sissy." "Be tough." "Stop whining." They never learned to see other people as sources of support or understanding. As a result, they never learned what it meant to have a relationship. To them, emotional closeness means having to experience the pain of being rejected and ridiculed.

Possessing only a primitive Feeling side, they are uninvolved and unconnected to the extreme, to the great anguish of those, especially family members, who want and need some show of emotional involvement and caring. As a matter of fact, such NTs may see any demand for involvement as a threat and may attack angrily. Any request to give — to tie a child's shoelace or pay for a new garment — is greeted with resentment. They refuse to give, unless the giving is at their own initiative. If the "T" is extremely unintegrated (i.e., very little "F"), the "F" spouse may go through the entire marriage grieving for a closeness which can never be had.

Negative, introverted NTPs, who lack the "J" sense of responsibility and duty, usually retreat from the world and will be unreachable and reclusive, often refusing to take care of any practical matters and oblivious to the plight of those who suffer as a result. Profoundly lacking in sensitivity and interpersonal skills, they rarely take the time to listen to people's feelings, and respond brusquely or not at all to any display of emotional pain in others. They feel threatened by any demand for emotional closeness and may respond to such demands with anger or hostile withdrawal. They spend little time with family members, and when they are present, they are critical, argumentative and oppositional in order to prevent any possibility of true closeness.

Feeling awkward with any show of emotion, NTs often respond even to close family members in a very detached, impersonal manner. They may talk to people, but not relate to them on a personal level. They are, reluctant to express affection. They assume that talk about feelings is unnecessary, silly, and childish. Family members of such NTs feel rejected and despised if all they get is either a curt reply to comments and questions or no reply at all.

In the presence of a negative NT who has little "F", a person may feel like a burden, a nothing. People will say, "Yes, my problem, (or "my question") exists for the NT, but I don't!" Such NTs will be cold to the point of ignoring people's suffering, especially that which they have inflicted by being so indifferent or critical.

To the unintegrated NT, people are superfluous and unnecessary. A wife may feel, "It's like I'm invisible. My needs don't count. He'd rather be with his books, hobbies, or stock reports."

OTHER DESTRUCTIVE SIGNS: Because the NT is so alert to his mental shortcomings, he can become immobilized by self-doubt, perfectionism, and the fear of failure. The more ashamed he feels about himself and his inability to reach the heights of knowledge he thinks he should have reached, the more he projects that shame on to those around him with devastating criticism for any minor fault or mistake. If he feels like a failure, he is going to make sure that everyone else feels the same way too.

He may also become indecisive because he can become overwhelmed by so much information that he misses the central unifying points and principles and so cannot act with confidence.

Unintegrated NTs often retreat into a closed world of abstractions, refusing to deal with practical, physical realities such as fixing the broken faucet, staying neat and clean, or remembering to pay the bills. Like disturbed types in any category, the NT can be cruelly sarcastic and cynical, arrogantly looking down on everyone else as incompetent idiots.

Such NTs are devastated by the most minor mistakes and hate to admit to them, for they think that they *must* always be competent and knowledgeable, in order not to be considered total failures.

HEALTH THROUGH INTEGRATION
Integration for the unintegrated NT mainly involves developing "F" sensitivities — "the duties of the heart" — such as sharing others' pain, allowing others to talk about feelings, and showing interest and concern. This is best done with a third party initially (Rav, family therapist, etc.). Because NTs are so unused to sharing their feelings, they become so anxious when feelings are discussed that they may quickly close up again unless there is a very safe environment.

If you are an unintegrated NT, realize that you lost trust in people at some point early in life. You have probably continued that pattern of mistrust by alienating others with criticism or indifference. Those habits have created much misery. But they can be changed. You can develop "F" sensitivities. Spend some time thinking how you could make your family members happier: little gifts, some word of appreciation each and every day to each and every person in your immediate environment, or mental appreciation for the good in others. Spend time thinking about others' needs. When you feel the need to "disengage" emotionally, learn to reassure the "F"s in your environment that you really do care. If someone says that something you have done is painful, don't get angry and defensive. Try to understand that person's point of view, and how you would feel if someone talked to you in the same manner. You don't have to be perfect. Most people will love you more if you're just human.

At first, all these acts of loving-kindness may be a kind of "intellectual caring" which comes from the mind rather than the heart. For example, you might call home if you are going to be late, not so much because you feel the anxiety that others feel when you do not arrive on time, but because you realize, intellectually, that calling is the right thing to do. You can give compliments and listen to someone's problem not so much because you want to, but because, intellectually, you realize that that is the only way to create closer relationships. Giving positive reinforcement to others will not feel "right" or "good" at first. You may feel phoney and uncomfortable. But little by little, such efforts will make these "forced" responses more natural.

Integration also involves getting out of the NT ivory tower and coming "down" to "S" realities: taking care of your appearance, clothing and appearance, earning a livelihood, if that is necessary, making sure that things which need to be fixed get fixed, and learning to enjoy life's pleasures without feeling guilty or silly.

NTPs need to follow those structures and regulations which will bring order and predictability into their lives. In contrast, overly stern NTJs who lack "P" flexibility can work on open-mindedness, tolerance for differences, and humor toward trivial mistakes and losses.

Those who live with NTs must be extremely patient and yet persistent about helping the NT develop trust. That takes many years. It requires that others not being overly demanding or critical, yet at the same time, making non-hostile requests for the fulfillment of the Torah law, which requires us to act with loving-kindness.

When communicating to NTs, it is important to let them take the initiative and not to overwhelm them with conversation or demands. Let them talk about their ideas. Don't expect them to express personal feelings. It is helpful to keep conversations brief. Introverted NTs are the most difficult to communicate with, and may be able to handle only one-sentence, eight-word conversations. Unintegrated STs (Sensing-Thinking) types are even more difficult, as they may not have even ideas to share. If they are also introverted, the problem is compounded.

To help overcome your anger when the NT responds angrily, or with indifference, realize that when NTs withdraw, it is probably not because they purposely want to hurt you, but because this is what makes them feel safe. Unintegrated NTs do not know what emotional intimacy is. That is why they don't miss it. They really do not *see* people's pain or needs. Whether or not an NT will even want to become more aware, communicative and emotionally intimate is the big question.

If you are an "F" (NF or SF), living with an unintegrated NT (or any other unintegrated type) is very painful. Later chapters will have some suggestions as to how to go on with your life despite this great loss.

Parents should make a special effort to talk to their children, ideally each and every day. This is especially true of their male children, and, in particular their "T"s. The creation of a warm and caring relationship early in childhood is the best way to ensure that, as adults, these children will want to make close connections with others and will be able to sustain healthy relationships based on mutual trust, consideration, and respect.

CHAPTER VII:
THE INTUITIVE FEELING TYPE (NF)

The NF is dominant in 12% of the American public, of which about 2% are introverted NFs: 1% INFP and 1% INFJ.

The dominating themes of the NF's life are a strong yearning for close, emotionally intimate relationships, for self-knowledge and for self-transcendence. NFs are extremely empathetic, have an intuitive depth of psychological insight and awareness, are mystically inclined, richly imaginative, and have a love of words and poetry [Rabbi Samson Rafael Hirsch is an excellent example]. They can often pick up new languages easily, and enjoy using stories, metaphors and similes to illustrate their points.

Being so multi-faceted, NFs, especially NFPs, have the most difficulty of all types understanding themselves and knowing how best to manifest their talents. They may look with envy at those who seem satisfied to lead a less complicated existence.

"N"s may sometimes crave a "simple life" with "simple" people and "simple, pat answers" as relief from their inner complexity. But eventually they get bored and disillusioned with these choices. If they honestly face their innermost needs, their inner richness eventually drives them onward in search of new inspiration and meaning. Even then, they find answers, and are happy for a time, until sooner or later, they start questioning and wondering again.

NFs are eternal seekers. Their "undiscovered continent" is their inner world. They want to be known and understood, and to understand themselves and others, not like an NT —i.e., impersonally and objectively — but in a profoundly intimate, personal way. NFs hunger for a direct, personal experience of the ineffable: particularly a kind of "merging," or oneness with G-d and man. Emotionally healthy NFs continuously strive for self-actualization, to become more of what they are capable of becoming. They engage in a lifelong search for meaning, harmony, unity, uniqueness and authenticity. "Know G-d," "Know thyself," are the NFs'goals — goals which can never be fully satisfied.

Naive NFs tend to be overly optimistic about the power of "communication" to bring harmony in all of their relationships. They assume, "We'll talk it out, and everything will be fine." They long for a "perfect" marriage with "perfect" children and no conflict. Because they are so deep, they take it for granted that others are as well. When they do not find this depth, they assume that it is hiding just under the surface. Thus, they put a lot of energy into making relationships "work," often to be sorely disappointed when after all that effort, the other person still doesn't understand or cooperate.

NFs — as opposed to Sensing Feelers (SFs) — get their information not so much from observation, as from "vibes," premonitions, and an intuitive awareness not possessed by the other types. NFs are impressionistic. They get a quick feel for people and situations. In so doing, they may gloss over the details which an "S" would notice, or jump to conclusions which a "T" would not accept so readily.

Dominant NFs have a "knowingness" about people. They often begin having psychic experiences very early in life: instances in which they "just knew" that something was going to happen, or were able to know someone's thoughts, or receive communications telepathically.

NFs have a strong inner drive to make their mark in the world. They are very idealistic. They just cannot accept that some people, who profess to be spiritual, are not. They cannot bear hypocrisy and sham. It is usually the NFs who spearhead movements to help the poor, the underprivileged, and the handicapped. Yet they are always wondering, "Why don't people care more and show concern about other people's misery? Why are people so apathetic and selfish, when they could be doing something to make the world a better place to live in?" NF children are the ones most likely to befriend the handicapped or "different" children in the classroom, even if it means that they, too, are ostracized. NFs wage a never-ending battle against mankind's indifference and cruelty, whether it is in their own living rooms or the world at large.

Emotionally healthy NFs love globally, not caring about external appearance or status or group affiliation. They exemplify the ideal of Aharon,

"Loving peace and pursuing peace, loving others, and bringing them close to Torah." (Avoth I:12)

An American patriot gave the SP battle cry when he said, "Give me liberty or give me death." For the NF, it is "Give me meaning, or I cannot go on with this relationship, with this work, or with this life."

Like the NTs, NFs live on a multi-dimensional plane of existence, seeing potentiality where "S"s see actuality, seeing complexity where others see simplicity. NFs tend to imbue every experience with significance, otherwise the event feels stale and empty. The falling of a leaf, the soaring of a bird, or the flickering light of a candle have overtones of deeper meaning to the NF. Likewise, a sigh, a pursing of the lips, a wrinkled brow will draw their attention and may arouse deep feelings.

NFs do not like to feel that they, or their lives, are ordinary or standard. To them, "ordinary" or "standard" means dry and lifeless.

COMBINATIONS: There are two major types of NFs, both of whom have the "N" qualities of creative imagination along with a strong capacity for empathy. Many are creative artists, singers, writers, and teachers.

INTUITIVE-FEELING-JUDGING (NFJ): Emotionally healthy NFJs have the "J" sense of stability, responsibility, trustworthiness, and decisiveness. They are excellent pedagogues, [experts in the art of teaching] able to manage and organize ideas, develop methodologies for learning, and plan a creative, inspiring curriculum.

INTUITIVE-FEELING-PERCEIVING (NFP): NFPs are also highly creative and empathetic, but are characterized by their "P" love of excitement and variety, their non-conformity, impulsivity, independence, spirit of adventure, and greater adaptability and flexibility. (All of these factors make it more difficult to control their emotionalism.) They retain their childlike curiosity, joie de vivre, and enthusiasm into old age. Unlike NFJs, NFPs may dislike formalities, rituals, rules, and regulations, and resist pressure to conform to social proprieties, and maintain strict structures and disciplines. NFPs may lack the self-assurance and self-confidence of the NFJs.

NFs can be either "I" (Introvert) or "E" (Extravert). Both are acutely aware of inner signals. However, the Introverts (INFP or INFJ) are even more intense, introspective and reflective.

FEELING V. INTUITIVE FEELING: Everybody feels. But to be "intuitively feeling" is to have a special talent. Although we cannot ever truly understand what another person is feeling unless we have undergone a similar situation, the ability to be intuitively feeling means that NFs grasp what others are experiencing without them having to go into a long explanation. It means that when NFs see someone in pain, they cannot help but feel that pain, almost as if it is their own. It means that when someone is happy or smiles warmly, the NF immediately feels that warmth and may instantly duplicate it back. (Unfortunately, they also experience people's negativity just as quickly.) Intuitive feelers are extremely empathetic. They are the types who cry when they see strangers tearfully greeting each other or saying good-bye at the airport and feel insulted when they hear a stranger insult someone else.

Thus, being naturally empathetic, NFs suffer along with others who suffer, whether they are relatives, friends or strangers. Even when they are happy, tears may be close to the surface.

A supreme model of NF loving-kindness and empathy was Rabbi Aryeh Levin (z.l.). He once went with his wife to the doctor when she complained of pains in her foot. "My wife's foot is hurting us...." he told the doctor. (*A Tzaddik In Our Times*, p. 150)

Reb Aryeh didn't just feel bad for his wife. Her pain *was* his pain. It was a part of him.

Example: "Every time I go into labor, my husband gets severe stomach aches. There is nothing either of us can do about it. He is simply an extremely empathetic person."

Example: "Two days after my youngest turned six, someone asked him how it felt to be such a big boy. He said, 'I'm happy and I'm sad. I'm happy to be big. But I'm sad because my mommy wanted another baby and now she doesn't have one any more."

This child was not just sympathizing with his mother's pain. Her pain was his own. This is the difference between sympathy — where the person is separate from the one in pain — and empathy, in which there is a merging of two, so that one feels the other's pain as his own. NFs also want this empathy from others, and may feel terribly frustrated and hurt if they don't get it. It helps somewhat to understand how rare this quality is, for then they do not have unrealistic expectations of others.

This tendency to unconsciously and automatically duplicate people's feelings means that NFs must constantly make a conscious effort to protect themselves from the hostility of people in their environment, with continuous thoughts of forgiveness and acceptance, if not physical separation or assertive demands for respect.

LONELINESS: NFs, especially introverted NFs, often suffer from profound existential loneliness. This is not only because they constitute such a small percentage of the population, but because few people have the same empathetic capacity which would make the NF feel really understood and cared about. Even as children, NFs often worry more about loneliness, even to the point of feeling guilty at leaving their parents alone.

NF children often feel that their classmates are rather shallow and superficial. They may not find the kind of depth-relationships they crave until they understand themselves and know how to make contact with like-minded NFs. Otherwise, they may spend a lifetime feeling defensive about what they see as their over-emotionalism and unreasonable needs for closeness. They may also waste much emotional energy trying to prove to themselves or the world that they really aren't different, though they know they don't really fit in.

It is ironic that the group which wants most to "connect" has the fewest people with whom to do so.

FAITH: At a very young age, NFs are already asking about the meaning of life and what our purpose is, especially in the face of evil and death. The Holocaust looms as an ever-present shadow in the lives of many NFs, as they struggle to understand how people could be so cruel, and life so seemingly unfair. Answers to the deeper questions about life are apt to come not so much from impersonal rationality and logic, but rather from an intuitive grasp of the ultimate meaning, wisdom, and fairness of all that happens.

Example: "It was only after one of my sons was killed in a car accident that I realized who he really was. I found journals full of poetry and Torah wisdom in his drawer. Friends from his *Yeshiva* came throughout the *shiva* period with stories about his incredible deeds of kindness. He was so modest that we never knew about most of them.

"Afterwards, my older son and my husband (both strong NTs) immersed themselves in Torah with renewed vigor and determination in dedication to his name, while my 'NF' son needed to talk about what happened over and over again. At first, I thought that my NT son and husband were suppressing their feelings, and I kept asking them if they wanted to talk. I thought maybe they didn't want to make me feel bad by talking about it. But they really didn't feel the need to talk. They weren't suppressing anything. We all loved this child deeply and sincerely, and I wondered how they could just go on with life. At first, I thought that perhaps their level of faith was greater than mine. But now I understand that it is simply because people with different natures react differently. I had to find my own personal meaning and *nisayon* in this event over and over again."

AUTHENTICITY: NFs will often remark that they like a particular person "Because he is so *real.*" They are most attracted to people who are honest, open and warm, and who really are what they appear to be. NFs find it difficult to be insincere, unless it is for the purpose of saving themselves or others from hurt feelings. They dislike pretense, ostentation, phoniness, "show," and bluff.

While others can engage in "small talk," NFs aren't satisfied unless their conversations are deep, bringing greater understanding and closeness or spiritual elevation.

On the other hand, NFs do sometimes exaggerate when they repeat stories or express feelings. What others may see as "fancy lying" is usually done unconsciously, in order to emphasize the importance of what they are saying, or, in the case of the NFP, because of the "P" innate desire to perform and dramatize. Their drama can also be the result of a highly creative imagination which does not always make a clear distinction between fantasy and reality.

CHILDHOOD: All children need positive feedback in the form of physical affection, communication, and reassurance. Non-nurturing parents can provoke depression and self-deprecation, chronic anxiety, approval-seeking behavior, or hostile aggression. This is especially true of NF children, who have extra needs for closeness and communication. NF children who ask for attention are not just being maniuplative. They really do need to talk things out more than other children.

NFPs may feel "lost" in a large family, especially introverted NFs. NFJ children do better in a large family, enjoying a parental role toward younger children. Extraversion provides more social confidence and the "J" (Judging) provides a sense of inner stability and organization.

All children are sensitive to their parents' moods, but NF children are super-sensitive, and will usually become physically and emotionally ill if there is no harmony in the home.

Many parents of NFs are awed by the depth of their children's thoughts and feelings, but also drained by their need for closeness and conversation. Such parents may envy those with SF (Sensing-Feeling) children who seem more organized and "together" and less complex and demanding. Parents must provide a great deal of praise and opportunities to become skilled in important life tasks to build their self-confidence. Criticizing them for being disorganized or demanding, only crushes their self-esteem.

NFs usually talk early — and may talk incessantly to their parents, wanting to share everything that happens to them. Their early verbal fluency may astound the parents. They quickly identify and verbalize when they are disappointed, jealous, afraid, or hurt.

Example: "Once, when my husband said something unkind, I went to my room in tears. My five year old came after me, patted me on the head and said, 'Daddy's not really angry at you. He was just upset because of what happened at work."

Example: "After I screamed at my four year old, he said, 'Mommy, when you scream at me it makes me feel that you hate me. Tell me in a soft voice that you will give me a potsch if I don't listen and then, if I don't listen, give me a little potsch on my hand." The mother asked if he would rather get yelled at or get a potsch. He said, "A potsch. When you scream at me I get afraid. So when you get nervous, remember this."

Many mothers of NFs are surprised to find that children as young as seven are already writing stories and poetry expressing profound feelings about nature, G-d and man. One NF child was lucky enough to have a mother who was sensitive to his abilities, and developed his NF qualities by writing down imaginative stories which he dictated to her.

Many NFs remember being rather lonely as children, perhaps
having only one or two best friends, and rarely being understood
by parents. Introverted NFs, in particular, may feel socially
awkward and terribly self-conscious. Because they don't really fit
in, they may conclude that their unpopularity is due to some
terrible defect in themselves. The feeling of not belonging
anywhere may continue throughout life.   A move away
from the NF's one best friend is often quite devastating.

Parents often find that their NF children have more separation
anxiety than other children, clinging to them more anxiously
when it is time to go to sleep, or on the first days of school when
other children are scampering off happily. It is often difficult for
parents to know when those fears are real, thus necessitating extra
reassurance and time for adjustment, or when such protectivness
would only feed their tendency toward excessive emotionalism,
increasing the child's fears, and delaying the development of self-
confidence and independence.

NFs function best in a small, harmonious classroom or work
atmosphere, as opposed to the competitive atmosphere which the
tougher SPs (Sensing-Perceiving) enjoy (see next chapter).

With their rich imaginations and ability to fantasize so
realistically, NFs can easily become frightened by their own
thoughts, which are as real to them as the sensory world is to
others. Their super-sensitivity to both the sensory and non-
sensory dimensions means that NFs are receiving more stimuli
than other people do, both from their inner world (thoughts,
feelings and sensations) and the external world as well. Parents
should help them develop "T"-type logic in order to check out
whether or not their psychic impressions and fantasies have any
basis in reality.

NEED TO BE NEEDED: NFs are extremely people-oriented.
They are often involved in service professions and in volunteer
work, going out of their way to help others and to fight against
man's inhumanity.

Rabbi Aryeh Levin (z.l.), was offered a week's vacation at a
resort hotel free of charge by the mayor of Ramat Gan. However,

after only one day, Rabbi Levin became quite downcast and decided to return to Jerusalem, saying "No one comes here to pour out his heart to me. I don't have the opportunity to do a single thing for anyone, to help a single human being. At this very moment, someone is quite likely coming to my home to talk out his troubles with me ...and the door is shut.... I cannot go on staying here." (*Ibid.*, p. 199) To Reb Aryeh, life's main purpose was to help others.

POSITIVE AND NEGATIVE IMAGINATION: "N"s do not always differentiate between reality and imagination. They may truly believe that what they are saying is true, when in reality, it is only a fantasy which, to them, seems as real as a factual event. Unfortunately, others may think that they are deliberately lying.

If they use their imagination in a positive way, then "N"s seek ways to improve themselves and the world. However, if the imagination is negative, then "N"s are constantly working themselves up with visions of possible future disasters.

To live with a strong sense of possibilities and premonitions means that the NTs and NFs are not always in the here and now, but off somewhere else, in another time-space reality. They tend to go into these "alterted states of consciousness" rather easily. This can be a very inspired, even ecstatic, G-dly state, or a dark tunnel of doom and gloom.

NFs often experience a lot of "anticipatory anxiety" (such as sleeplessness, stomach distress, and other nervous symptoms) even if the event is a happy one. Their anxiety results not only from their rich imaginations, but also because they are attempting to protect themselves from shock by preparing mentally for what might happen: "...when the baby comes... when the in-laws arrive...; when I get old...; when the money runs out...."

Being in an "N" altered state is why "NF"s can so easily become discombobulated when forced to deal with "S" facts or people for any length of time.

Example: "I'm an NF artist with a strong SP side. But I hate managing the business aspect. I can't even do basic arithmetic when I'm under pressure."

Example: "Some of my relatives are very dominant 'S's. If I have to spend a lot of time with them, I feel a little schizophrenic because I cannot be myself. I'm an INFP (Introverted-Intuitive-Feeling-Perceiving) and they are all ESTJs (Extraverted-Sensing-Thinking-Judging). At least, I understand why I used to feel so threatened in their presence. Now I just feel uncomfortable, but not irrationally endangered."

VOCATIONS: "N"s usually show little interest in or aptitude for business, and tend to bankrupt unless they have a well-developed "SJ" side. On the other hand, they love words and love to communicate, making them excellent writers, counselors, psychologists, teachers, and journalists.

SELF-QUESTIONING: NFs are self-questioning, always wondering, "Am I contributing enough to the world?" "Am I being creative enough or being attentive enough to other people's needs?" "Am I doing all I could be doing to manifest my potential?" They have a restless inner drive to do more and be more. They also have a tendency to blame themselves when relationships don't work out.

Many NFs, no matter how intelligent, feel inferior to other, less emotional types. They are ashamed that they become so flooded with strong feelings that they do not think or function effectively, becoming easily confused and overwhelmed. They often stand in awe of the aloof, cool-headed NTs and those dynamic "S"s who are so capable of handling the physical world.

Example: "I used to get all tied up in knots whenever I would have to deal with a very decisive, unemotional type. Often, when I'd try to explain something, I'd start stammering. I've caused myself a lot of pain by trying, my whole life, to be a very organized, coldly rational TJ (Thinking-Judging) person when, in reality I'm an NFP. Only now, after working with this typology, am I slowly learning to accept who I am."

LACK OF PSYCHIC ARMOR: NFs lack the protective "psychic armor" of the other types. They cannot *not* feel. They automatically and unconsciously pick up on what others are feeling. If they lack self-confidence and self-esteem, they are easily shattered by the merest hint of rejection. It is not helpful to blithely tell the NF, "Don't take it to heart," when they already have. However, advising them to adopt a Torah outlook on the situation is helpful, i.e., to give the benefit of the doubt, to work on one's own *middoth,* to give rebuke with love in one's heart, etc.

RELATIONSHIPS: Although SFs (Sensing-Feeling) are also extremely caring, emotionally healthy NFs are the most empathetic of all the personality types. NFs form close relationships rather quickly, and even after years apart, can pick up at that same level of intimacy in minutes. They are also natural harmonizers, and will go to great lengths to avoid conflict and make peace. NFs of all ages thrive on physical displays of affection and praise and need a lot of reassurance that they are loved.

If the people around them are critical, NFs often become physically ill with all kinds of psycho-somatic illnesses, especially with digestive disturbances. Their physical pain is exacerbated by their tendency to blame themselves for misunderstandings and for other people's bad moods or fits of anger.

NFs are very concerned about people fulfilling their potential and can be impatient with those who are more superficial and shallow. The danger is that they can feel excessively responsible for others, thinking that they must be a never-ceasing well of nurturance, strength, and inspiration to all those around them, and feeling unnecessarily guilty if they cannot be.

Like SFs, NFs are romantics: they need to love and be loved. They are sympathetic, tender and passionate in their physical and verbal expressions of love. They may want to give and receive on-going attention and affection. This will be very problematic if the NF's mate is someone who equates positive reinforcement with flattery and, therefore, refuses to give it.

The "F"s (NFs and SFs) are the types most likely to remember birthdays and anniversaries and may be dramatic in showing their constant affection. "F"s enjoy showing appreciation to others, and expressing it, often with small tokens of gratitude, and want some show of appreciation in return.

NF spouses are usually very warm and accommodating if their mates offer words of appreciation. Any attempt to intimidate the NF with criticism is disastrous, and will deaden the NF's feelings. On the other hand, their need for warmth makes it easy to manipulate them with nice words and a pleasant manner.

Being linguistically gifted, NFs are not afraid to express their love in words, poetry, and literature. Strong "T"s may find NFs' talk repetitive, "mushy" or long-winded. The NF is slow to recover from personal hurts. If the "T" has been critical in the morning, he may wonder why the "F" is still smarting from the pain and acting cold in the evening. The "T" must be made to realize that his critical remarks have made a shambles of their bond of trust, which is the foundation for any healthy relationship. Unless some repair work is done to re-establish trust, the "T" cannot expect closeness and warmth.

NFs need to be able to relate spiritually, as well as physically, to their mates, or the relationship feels empty, no matter how nice the partner may be. Emotional nourishment is as important to them as physical nourishment, and NFs experience great pain if the relationship is superficial, without a true feeling of communion and contact.

NFs are apt to make great personal sacrifices to help others, to comfort and guide them. *A Tzaddik In Our Times* is replete with stories of Reb Aryeh's love of his fellowman, such as his visits to Jerusalem's prisoners every Shabbath, over a fifty-year period. In freezing winter, with snow filling his shoes, and in the intense heat of summer, he trudged miles to visit his "sons," even when he was quite old and in poor health.

Once, in an attempt to save an underground fighter who had been condemned to death in pre-State Palestine, he stretched out full length on the road, in the path of the limousine in which the British high commissioner was riding, and demanded that the boy's life be spared. It was. (*Ibid.* p. 284)

When he was unable to save two condemned fighters, Moshe Barzani (z.l.) and Meir Feinstein (z.l.) from death at the hands of the British authorities, he observed the full seven days of mourning, as though they were his own children. (*Ibid.* p. 278)

Men and women who have been widowed or divorced and then remarry often discover that their new mates do not have this special quality of being able to "incorporate" their new mates' children into their hearts. This is a very special quality which many people do not have.

MOTHERHOOD: Emotionally healthy NFs are very concerned about and sensitive to their children's thoughts and feelings. They want to know each child individually and nourish strong emotional bonds with them, yet also need time away from the incessant demands, as well as time to pursue their own quest for creative fulfillment and inspiration. It is this very intensity which necessitates time away to recoup their energies and reawaken a desire for closeness.

NF mothers need not feel guilty about these conflicting priorities. Wanting time away from children is not a sign that they don't care. Time away to pursue contact with other NFs or creative interests helps NFs to be more loving in the long run, since time alone helps replenish their fund of affection.

Given the NF's hypersensitivity and state of hyper-arousal, *every one child may feel like four or five*. Thus many NF mothers find themselves easily overwhelmed by their children, despite their great love for them. One NT husband decided to try being an NF for a day, by responding emotionally to everything that came up. At the end of the day, he told his NF wife, "I'm exhausted! I can't believe this is what you go through every day!"

NF mothers should take into account that they:

1) May be over-emotional and high strung,

2) May not have the physical stamina and endurance of the "S"s. Their hyper-sensitive, hyper-alert nervous system takes its toll physically. The NF is open to more stimuli than the other types, whether from the outer environment (sounds, sights, etc.) or the stimuli emanating from their own imaginations, muscles and organs,

3) May feel that mundane household tasks have a "deadening" effect on their spirit if that is all they do all day, and

4) May feel guilt-ridden over her inability to have the very close, special, intense relationship with each child, and greatly saddened at the thought that the children are not getting the time and attention she feels they need.

These stresses are exaggerated if the mother a) is an Introvert, which means she needs more time for herself and has very intense emotions which she may have difficulty expressing, b) does not have an understanding or nurturing husband, c) has critical relatives, d) has very exuberant SP children [See next chapter.] It is no wonder that such a mother would feel extremely stressed, as well as very alone and inadequate.

THE UNINTEGRATED NF

Like the disturbed NT, the disturbed NF is an ugly parody of all that is so noble and wonderful in the healthy NF. The depth of feeling with which the NF was endowed, and which was meant to enable them to "bond" to others, is turned inward and becomes fixated on the self. Instead of using their strong emotions to help others, the NF is dragged down by his emotionalism as though stuck in quicksand.

NFs who never received proper nurturing, loving closeness or confidence-building experiences in childhood, or who are in relationships with non-nurturing spouses, will usually lack the self-confidence and feelings of worth which well-loved NFs have. An emotionally impoverished childhood leaves scars, which in the case of the NF, manifests as an insatiable need for reassurance and approval. Unfortunately, that craving for closeness can be highly irritating to mates and children, who may experience her neediness as a bottomless pit which can never be satisfied. NFs may make others feel like failures for failing to be sensitive enough to their needs. In response to the unintegrated NF's demands and emotionalism, others — even healthy NFs — often turn away in annoyance and frustration, bringing about the very abandonment that the NF always feared.

Unintegrated NFs are likely to have a number of other symptoms:
  *   People-pleasing arising from fear of rejection. Their

hypersensitivity to rejection makes them terribly anxious to please others. But since they cannot possibly satisfy everyone's demands or meet everyone's expectations, they worry obsessively about the possibility of being abandoned or rejected. Their compulsive "niceness" makes them dishonest about their true feelings to the point where they fail to protect themselves from those who would exploit and manipulate them.

* Dread. They use their fertile imaginations to think the worst about themselves, the people around them and the state of the world, thereby filling themselves with anxiety and despair.

* Self-preoccupation. The worst NF habit is to become overly preoccupied with their most minor physical sensations, insecure thoughts and upsetting emotions. This preoccupation can be paralyzing to the point where they do nothing positive with their talents and their intelligence, except to talk about what they should be doing or might have done. Immersed in self-doubt, and a sense of helplessness and fear, their ability to act is paralyzed, which further lowers self-esteem, convincing them that they really are helpless, weak, inferior, or even insane.

* Touchiness. Having experienced so much rejection, they become so overly sensitive to criticism that even a helpful suggestion may seem like a rejection, unless it is presented very tactfully. The slightest criticism or most minor hint of rejection (whether real *or* imagined) can be devastating. They can be very critical of those who lack their sensitivity.

* Idealization of others. Unintegrated NFs minimize their strengths and exaggerate other people's ability to cope. Being so super-aware of their own weaknesses, they exacerbate their inadequacy and helplessness. In addition, such dependency alienates imagining that they have no human frailties (especially the more stable SJs and cool-headed NTs).

* Excessive dependency. Because the unintegrated NF often sees himself as a weak and vulnerable child, he often chooses a down-to-earth, practical "S" to "take care of me." Such a match can be successful, *if* the "S" mate can provide stability as well as "F" warmth and sympathy, and encourages the NF to develop

independence, self-confidence, and stability. Unfortunately, the poorly nurtured NF often unwittingly chooses a mate who repeats childhood patterns by being emotionally oblivious or even physically cruel.

* Discouragement. The great danger to NFs is that they may be so frustrated with and disappointed in people, and so wary of getting hurt again, that they withdraw from relationships altogether.

They may run to therapists, expecting that their mates will change and suddenly become more understanding, sensitive and aware. But communication cannot work magic with an unintegrated person of a different dominance who has no real interest in emotional intimacy, or in an unintegrated NF whose needs are so great that no one could ever fill them.

* Fear of insanity. NFs, particularly NFPs, live in a multi-dimensional, ever-changing reality. Many NFs fear losing contact with reality, being alone, lost, out of touch. This, plus their degree of emotional pain, combined with a rich inner jumble of various inner voices and dimensions, makes such NFs think that they must be crazy and in need of therapy. Unfortunately, few therapists know how to treat NFs in a way which increases their feeling of self-confidence and stability.

* Identity crises arising from excessive suggestibility. When you empathize with someone you do, in a sense, lose your own boundaries temporarily. However, this ability to "merge" can cause the NF to feel that he has no stable identity. He constantly wonders, "Who am I, really?" The insecure NF who adopts others' opinions as if they are his own, loses sight of who he is and what he really wants. "P"s, in particular, may find that their personalities and opinions about religion and life change drastically depending on who they are with. In addition, when people are critical of them, they may accept those negative opinions as if they are absolutely correct. (NOTE TO NF READERS: Do not be suggestible to the negative tendencies mentioned here! You may never experience them. However, by

being aware of these possible pitfalls, you will find it easier to overcome them.)

* Utopian romanticism. NFs can spend their lives longing for romantic ideals which cannot be: "happily-ever-after" relationships, harmony between all mankind, continuous inner peace and joy, etc. They are easy prey for therapists and religious charlatans who exploit their naivety, promising them a perfection here on earth which can never be achieved in reality.

HEALTH THROUGH INTEGRATION

In comparison to "S"s, who are more heavily defended against self-awareness, and "T"s, who are more impersonal and rational and can immerse themselves in their work or studies, insecure NFs have no external pretense of togetherness to hide behind. They are raw and easily hurt. However, while it is impossible to stop being an NF, it is possible to become more balanced by cultivating SP optimism and activism, SJ discipline and orderliness, and NT logic and objectivity. The following suggestions help to do this:

* Study Torah, pray and read *T'hillim*. Ultimately, only your connection with G-d will save you from loneliness. Only your understanding of Torah philosophy will save you from being bitter and angry over the suffering which you and those around you must endure.

* Don't apologize for who you are. Do not feel that you are bad for having strong emotional responses. You have a G-d-given nature which is like fire — it can be used for good or evil.

* Love is oxygen for you. You must find people to love and who love you. If your spouse is a non-nurturer, then you must find others to whom to give and who will appreciate you. Without love, your spirit withers. Force yourself to make contact with other NFs and work or volunteer with people who appreciate you.

* Don't condemn those who don't have your degree of sensitivity. Remember that people are generally doing the best they can with the tools they have. They usually do not mean to

hurt you deliberately. This thought is the key to good relationships. All people, yourself included, are sometimes selfish, lazy, and inconsiderate. Don't make a big deal out of such events, unless you or the other person are actually being deliberately destructive.

* Give up your "rescue fantasies" of being saved by an all-loving spouse or therapist. Even the most nurturing person could never satisfy the unfulfilled dependency needs of an adult who is looking for an external source of nurturance. Nor would this be beneficial, for dependency on others only feeds feelings of inadequacy and helplessness. In addition, such dependency alienates the very people the NF wants to be closest to, and hinders the development of self-reliance and self-sufficiency.

* Use your imagination positively. NFs can enter other states of consciousness more easily than other types. Instead of always imagining that things are going to get worse and that you are never going to achieve anything of value, use your imagination to see yourself acting in a confident, self-sufficient, self-disciplined manner, and becoming more loving, calm, and secure in the future. (See *EMETT* and *Raising Children To Care*, for suggestions on how to do so.)

* Don't "buy" opinions on impulse. If someone is critical, stop to consider whether or not you want to "buy" it and incorporate it into your mentality. You are the boss of your own mind. Practice "active indifference" toward negativity and negative people. If such "emotional separation" is impossible, as in the case of a truly abusive person, physical separation might be necessary.

* Be disciplined. An excess of "P" causes an NF to give in too readily to his impulses, so that he drifts through life without direction or purpose. NFPs are more prone to depression and instablity because they love to live spontaneously. The result is chaos. Mental health requires regularity and discipline: scheduled times for work, prayer and study of Torah; strictness about *mitzvoth* (such as *kashruth*) and keeping up your appearance and environment. Having predictable schedules helps build sense of self-worth and self-trust, thereby lessening anxiety.

* Choose a positive reality and live in it. This would sound strange to a non-NF, but NFs, especially NFPs, understand that they must make firm decisions about what kind of direction, goals, and principles they want to adopt in life and ignore the temptation to explore other ways of life. It is especially important to find a Rav whom you trust and respect and accept his guidance. This does not mean that one becomes rigid and intolerant, but rather than one accepts Torah as the one and only guide for one's life.

* Keep the external environment as calm as possible. With your vibrant inner world, you need outer calm and regularity.

Don't shirk the menial chores which keep the environment orderly. These activities are important "balancers" which keep you from losing touch with "S" reality. The home should be orderly and clean enough for peace of mind and self-esteem. However, neither should you spend all your time on uncreative activities. That would be just as depressing.

* "Wear the mask." It is a Torah principle that an insincere gesture of love and confidence will produce an inner conviction of love and confidence. Doing something positive, even if one does not feel like doing it, builds self-respect. Ironically, for the NFs, who pride themselves on being so emotionally honest and sincere, health comes by being a little phoney - pretending to be integrated, even if that is not the inner reality. Do this by using your non-dominant modes, such as "T" detachment or "J" self-discipline, even if those states do not feel comfortable or authentic. Soon, the external "act" will become an internal reality. Even a phoney pretense of calm (e. g, talking in a slow, low voice when upset) will arouse an inner calm. A regulated life and calming, confidence-building thoughts also lessen the roller-coaster syndrome (excessive highs and lows) suffered by many insecure NFs.

* Practice assertiveness. Don't be so self-sacrificing that you fail to assert your right to be treated with respect, to have "NF time" with friends, and to avoid having to be with those who exploit their good-heartedness or try to control them through

intimidation. Healthy relationships require finding the proper balance between self-respecting assertiveness and self-sacrifice. Avoid the tendency to "turn the other cheek" until you suddenly explode or go into a state of despair when you can't take it any more. Speak up before that happens.

* Practice "thinking average." NFs think of themselves, their problems, their thoughts and feelings as exceptional. Constantly strive to see yourself and your problems as "normal range" or "average." Sharing notes with other NFs will make you feel less exceptional, and thus less alone, weird, or crazy. You'll feel relief when you realize that most NFs are coping rather well with the same problems you are.

* Don't expect truly profound closeness with non-NFs. Non-NFs cannot understand NFs fully. You will only feel frustrated and pained when you see people's eyes glaze over in boredom or you are rejected as weird when you share your thoughts and feelings. Talk about concrete, sensory matters with "S"s (e.g., health, food, clothing, trips, plans for upcoming events, *halacha* and personal rules and regulations and methods of getting organized, recipes) and unemotional facts, ideas, and theories with "T"s.

* Practice strict indifference to all nervous symptoms. As much as NTs need to "engage" emotions, NFs need to learn to "disengage." NFs suffer from heightened awareness of bodily sensations and feelings. These must usually be ignored in order to function effectively. It is helpful, when the symptoms are strong, to say, "This is nothing but a *harmless* out-pouring of an over-excitable nervous system which will soon fade if I do not attach danger to it." This does not mean that you fight feelings or are ashamed of them, but rather that you detach from them, allowing the unpleasant feelings and bodily sensations (e.g., tightness, air hunger, stomach distress, teeth-clenching) to take up only a tiny portion of your mind, while going on with your life. While it is important to express appropriate pain over *major* losses and disappointments, indifference will help you to avoid "obsessing" about insignificant trials and tribulations.

* Take your grief and do something constructive with it! Pain can be an incentive for more action, not less — to do more chesed, to get busy and be involved in meaningful causes, and make meaningful contacts with others. When feelings become overwhelming, tell yourself, *"Stop emoting and start moving!"*

* Avoid long-term therapy with therapists who don't feel it is important to make a caring connection or who believe that mere talk is the answer to all problems. Short-term, goal-oriented therapy to overcome specific problems is often beneficial, providing you with an actual experience of being cared about and accepted, and practice in being emotionally honest. However, long-term therapy — especially therapy with a cold, detached therapist who focuses on insight alone — can actually exacerbate confusion and depression. This is especially true of NFs who think that to be "cured" means not being in pain any more, or means that they will turn into "T"s, or make some other dramatic change in their basic natures. Some therapists unwittingly strengthen their patients' feelings of inadequacy, anxiety, and helplessness, and actually increase their emotionalism and self-preoccupation.

Therapy should make people feel more effective, more in control of their lives, and more loving of themselves and others. If that is not happening, the therapy should be ended. On the other hand, it is not the role of the therapist to motivate his patients or make them happy. These are unrealistic demands which even the best therapist cannot satisfy. It is the job of each and every one of us to motivate ourselves and find fulfilling work and relationships.

* Avoid long-term medication for nervous symptoms. The side effects of medication for depression and nervous symptoms include insomnia, agitation, anxiety, nausea, feelings of unreality, reduced powers of concentration, fatigue, weight gain, allergic reactions, lack of co-ordination, blurred vision, loss of libido, fuzzy thinking (or no thinking), weight gain, urinary tract problems, permanent damage to the nervous system, as well as physical dependency. More pills are often required to counteract

the effects of such medications, all of which have more side effects.

Instead, try a natural diet and natural, non-addictive products to calm you down: vitamin B, calcium, L-tryptophane, and valerian. If you are a woman and suffer from mood swings, use Efamol (Evening Primrose Oil) and Spirulina every day. These products, along with *EMETT* tools, will also help you control your over-active imagination and your tendency to overreact. [An occasional prescription pill during major upsets is sometimes necessary. But do not make it a habit.]

* Be realistic, not romantic about people. Give up your romantic, utopian dreams of perfect relationships, with ever-lasting communication, appreciation, understanding and rapport. Realize that most people will not be able to handle your NF craving for closeness. Prepare yourself mentally ahead of time by visualizing yourself giving the benefit of the doubt to those who will misunderstand or criticize you. Accept others as they are instead of criticizing them. If necessary, go into a different mode to get along:

Example: "A family member refused to help me when I asked for his help. I began to get furious. Then, suddenly, I stopped myself. I know this person has great difficulty giving, unless it is at his own initiative. I know this person is afraid of relationships. Demanding that he be different is like demanding that an elephant be a horse. I calmed down by accepting the reality. When I no longer felt hateful, I asked him again, in a calm voice, adding a little humor. Then he was more amenable."

Example: "I saw a relative at a social event who had been very cold to me. I went into a 'T' modality, becoming the objective observer of my own emotions as well as of her responses. I remained analytical and aloof, like a disinterested scientist. I had such a sense of power! Inwardly, I 'celebrated' my ability not be sucked into her negative state."

* Find some creative outlet, even if the outcome isn't all you would like it to be. NFs need to create. Otherwise they feel that their lives are devoid of meaning, and often sink into despair and

depression. Unfortunately, NFs tend to bring that very state about by thinking, "If what I do is only mediocre, then I am a failure and there is no reason to continue." Health means being creative even if the product isn't spectacular and giving and loving even if others do not always appreciate what you do. It is the act of creating and the act of loving others which is important. Dance, teach, write, sing. These are all creative activities.

Example: "During a low period, a friend suggested that I take up weaving. I was sure that I would fail at this too, but I went to the classes anyway. I was surprised at how good it felt to use my hands, to be doing something creative in the world."

Example: "After my sixth child, I was really out of shape and embarrassed to give exercise classes as I had in previous years. But what got me going was the decision that it was just fine for me to have an average body. The funny thing is that I found that the other mothers I worked with loved me and my classes much more when they saw that I was struggling just like them."

Example: "I love teaching, but because I had learning disabilities I thought that I could never enter the profession. Then I decided that perhaps my own difficulties could be an advantage. I could identify more with the children because of what I went through. I went back to school and got a degree and love my work."

* Recognize trivialities, and refuse to "emotionalize" them. Only situations involving real and actual danger should be cause for anxiety or anger. In most cases, the feeling of being overwhelmed or endangered is simply the result of an over-active imagination producing a "doom-gloom-disaster" mentality. Don't condemn yourself for being emotional. That is your Divinely-determined initial response. But you can work it down.

The neutral "Oh...response" helps cut down the emotionalism over trivialities. This means looking at life's trivialities and people's annoying traits like a neutral newspaper reporter, without getting involved emotionally. You either ignore the person or the event, or find an assertive solution. For example:

"Oh...you're angry. Let's think of a solution."

"Oh...you don't like the food. That's fine. You can make something else for yourself." Or, "I'll make something else."

"Oh...the room is a mess. We'll just clean it up."

* Build "J" stability and discipline and maintain those priorities even in the face of your ups and downs and their varying moods. Self-control builds self-esteem: that means being disciplined, and focusing one's thoughts on *middoth* and *mitzvoth*. Have a regular schedule for Torah classes, physical exercise, cleaning, etc.

* Cultivate a sense of *simchah*. Humor quickly lifts you above the excessive drama, gloom, seriousness, and self-preoccupation which so frequently drags NFs down. If you are a "P", have you forgotten to do things which give you pleasure? Have you become overly duty-bound and serious? You can still maintain your responsibilities, but make them more pleasurable (e.g., see *Raising Children to Care* for fun-loving ways to get kids to co-operate), and can make time for outings, sports, and other pleasurable activities. Throughout the day, you can find much to smile about if you constantly endorse yourself and those around you and maintain a spirit of gratefulness for all that you do have.

* Keep a journal. Many people cannot handle NF's need for expression, especially the INF, who is so self-aware. Share your struggles and your spiritual progress with your journal.

* Join a goal oriented group devoted to spiritual elevation, self-improvement and community activities.

* Be active and cultivate friendships with active, positive people. Excessive introspection tends to paralyze the ability to act with determination and enthusiasm. As soon as you become self-conscious, the spontaneous quality of 'N' inspiration is lost. You start questioning and stop living. The more you introspect, the more painfully self-conscious you become, which creates even more confusion and self-doubt. Find positive activities which build confidence and a feeling of personal power.

If you are an integrated person of any dominance, dealing with an unintegrated NF is as difficult as dealing with any unintegrated type. Listen to the NF's pain, but then push the person gently onward, to think logically and rationally about solutions, to be more detached and impersonal, to be self-disciplined and actively involved in the world.

CHAPTER VIII: THE SENSING-PERCEIVING TYPE (SP)

Sensing types (SPs and SJs) relate to the world differently than "N"s. "S"s are both more down-to-earth, more practical, more observant of details which can be grasped with the five physical senses. "N"s (NTs and NFs) are both more oriented to the intangible, to inner meaning and symbols. This makes an enormous difference vis-a-vis their connection to material objects, to religion, to people, and to life in general.

Although "S"s may lack the brilliant erudition of the NTs or the intuitive sensitivity and psychological insight of the NFs, they certainly can become masters of *halacha, mussar* and *middoth*.

THE DOMINANT SENSING-PERCEIVING TYPE (SP)

This type is dominant in approximately 38% of the American public, and is equally divided between males and females.

Emotionally healthy SPs are adventurous, good-natured, resilient, and optimistic. Many SPs are also artistically or mechanically inclined. Craving independence and autonomy from an early age, they are very individualistic and often somewhat defiant and anti-authoritarian. They enjoy work which involves concrete skills, such as medicine, art, mechanics, electronics, cooking, gardening, music, dance. ("N"s may enjoy the same activities, but with different motivations and goals.) Their optimism and enthusiasm for Torah is infectious, making them good at fund-raising for Yeshivas. They are also good at business negotiations. They often have a Yissaschar-Zvulen relationship with the Torah world.

With their unbounded energy and optimism, SPs come to the fore in a crisis and may even create one in order to test their strength and courage. A strong SP would be attracted to activities such as "Hatzolah," which is a voluntary cadre of Jews who drop whatever they are doing to race to various emergencies to help those in trouble.

High level, integrated "S"s (Sensing Types) are often described as having unflagging energy and indomitable spirits. SPs experience a kind of restless sensation-hunger — enjoying activities simply for the physical stimulation which they provide, regardless of the goal. They seek jobs which provide variety and excitement. An SP doctor, for example, will prefer surgery to research.

Young SP children will be constantly touching, on the go, seeking a flow of sensory input. Their love of action and excitement, and disregard of danger challenges their parents' patience and creativity (as well as their nerves). For an SP to be deprived of such sensory experiences is as painful as being physically hungry.

SPs must have some exciting adventure to look forward to, some way of discharging their impulses (e.g., Spend! Eat! Move! Go!) Otherwise, life feels "dead." To plan, wait, save or prepare is difficult for the SP. If he has a "sudden urge" (a favorite SP expression) to do something, he wants to do it — Now!

Example: "I was a very popular SFP in high school and was involved in all of the school activities. Then I married, moved to a small apartment, and within three years had three children. All we could afford was a fourth-floor walk up that didn't have a phone. No one visited me because other women with little children didn't want to *schlep* up the stairs, and I didn't go out much for the same reason. We didn't even have money to go out for ice cream once a month. I got so depressed. My husband became much more serious when we moved here. We lost our 'SP' side: no fun, no variety, and no excitement — and no sense of a relationship. I felt like I was dying. Thanks to an understanding of the types, I was able to validate my needs and explain them to my husband. We moved to a ground-floor apartment in a less expensive neighborhood so that I could interact with people more often; I got a small part-time job teaching, and we go out for walks or ice cream with the children once a month. I feel much better now that I understand my needs and don't feel ashamed of them."

Example: "I always dreamed of marrying a brilliant NT who would study full time. At first, my SP husband thought that that was what he wanted, too. But the truth was that he really wasn't happy learning all day. After a couple of years, he told me he wanted to study in the evenings and work during the day. At first, I was very angry and ashamed. But once I read about the types, I understood his needs better. Ironically, my sister would like her NT husband to go out and work. But he just wants to learn!"

SPs are resilient and optimistic. Where others may see an insurmountable obstacle, SPs see an exciting challenge. If they get discouraged, it is usually only momentarily, after which they bounce back with new energy and determination as soon as there is a new challenge. Hardships seem to strengthen and vitalize them.

If SPs fail to discipline their strong impulses in a positive direction, their dynamic impulsivity gets them into trouble.

COMBINATIONS: SPs can be either extraverted or introverted. Introverted SPs are just as intense and dynamic, but an outsider might not realize it at first since their energy is directed inward. Introverts prefer solitary activities, especially with tools and crafts.

SENSING-THINKING-PERCEIVING (STP) The STP has the "T" quality of preferring to relate in an objective, impersonal manner. STPs are usually good in business or with tools and instruments.

SENSING-FEELING-PERCEIVING (SFP) The SFP is more warm-hearted and people-oriented.

A shining example of the SFP courage combined with NF devotion to people is Gary Moskowitz, a 30-year old, *kippa*-clad police officer and social worker in New York, who is founder of the National Association of the Jewish Poor. He devotes all his free time to helping Jews in whatever way he can - collecting food and clothing for the aged, counselling troubled children, and bringing the light of *Yiddishkeit* to anyone with whom he comes in contact.

SPs AS CHILDREN: With their restless nature and desire for hands-on experiences, SP children tend to be painfully bored in school. Sitting passively can be "torture," unless something exciting is going on. While the "N"s may be *energized* by a discussion, the SPs may be drained. They learn best when they are active participants, particularly when there is competition and excitement or they are allowed to perform or work with concrete objects, such as crafts, building materials, instruments, etc. Teachers may complain that SPs are restless and always fidgeting with something on their desks instead of paying attention.

Example: "Two of my children are precocious SPs. The eight year old can take a few wires and a couple of batteries, and some odds and ends and all of a sudden, he has produced a crane or a tow truck that moves and picks things up. I couldn't do that in a million years. My twelve year old daughter is already producing very beautiful, original pieces of embroidery using yarn and old jewelry which she picks up here and there. They are both very resourceful, individualistic and love action."

If their teachers are uncreative, boring or overly strict, SP children may act out aggressively: talking out of turn, making other noises, dropping things, etc. Even brilliant SPs are sometimes under-achievers academically because of their resistance to the passivity of most school systems and their dislike of abstract concepts. Parents of SPs may wonder dispairingly, "I know the child isn't stupid. After all, look how creative he is! So why can't he concentrate or catch on in school?"

The SP child is a staunch individualist, and will insist on doing things his way at an early age. An adult who tries to break this child's spirit and get him to be submissive and obedient with harsh punishments will find that the child only becomes more defiant and rebellious. Whereas the NF tends to break down under intense pressure, the SP child gets tougher.

Because of the SP sensation-hunger, the SP child may get very obnoxious when bored and feels compelled to get some action going, either positive or negative. SPs crave a lot of physical contact, especially SFPs. If they do not get it, they suffer from what is called "contact hunger," and may provoke a hit or slap to get that needed touch in a negative manner.

SPs tend to be mischievous. If they can't stir up some excitement with either positive or negative acts, they may lessen the "sensory deprivation" (i.e., boredom) by dreaming about some action-filled fantasy such as flying an airplane, driving, taking care of animals, making business deals with friends, performing in a play, going on an outing, or getting married — anything but what the teacher or parent is talking about.

Example: "My children are all NTs with a very strong SP part. They do very well in school, but are also very mischievous! We've already been to the emergency room four times within the last three years."

Few teachers know how to handle exuberant SP energy. They may say that the SPs are "lazy and stubborn," and punish them harshly. However, such tactics often make these children even more resistant to school. They learn best when they can use sensory objects (e.g., making letters out of clay, constructing an actual *sukkah*, sewing a replica of the High Priest's clothing, making a Temple out of blocks, performing a Biblical story in play form). It is a mistake to force a dominant SP into a life of exclusively cerebral activities, for such children usually end up feeling like dismal failures, and may take out their frustrations on others in hostile acts of aggression.

Although adults may be quick to label dynamic SPs as "difficult" or "hyperactive," they should be considered within the normal range for such children if they sleep well and are able to concentrate for long periods on the things which interest them, such as gardening, hobbies, collecting items, playing out some action-filled fantasy, or working with tools.

Many SPs are "late bloomers" academically, and do settle down to serious studies in their teens or twenties. Many who had been labeled as "failures" in school go on to do surprisingly well in business or fields which involve the use of tools and instruments, such as electronics, engineering or handicrafts.

Parents who find themselves in constant battle with their SPs should not despair. It is essential to set down firm rules and stick to them. If the SP has a role in formulating those rules, he is much more likely to abide by them. It is most helpful to praise the SP child often whenever he shows signs of self-control, and to share with the child one's own struggle to do the same. E.g., "Chaim, I see that you are controlling yourself. I'm proud of you." "Sara, it's hard for me to control myself right now, but I am not going to hit or scream. I can control myself and so can you."

Teachers who enjoy making the classroom exciting, who have the children participate actively in discussions and projects, who express physical affection, and who provide sensory stimulation, bring out the best in the SP child.

Parents of SPs must establish firm boundaries and regulations and keep them consistently. Otherwise, the child becomes confused and lacks trust in his parents. Parents should also expect that SP children will constantly test those limits, and be ready to stand firm. Expect that SPs will need to be told the same rule over and over again. They are not being purposely spiteful. Rather, they have an inborn tendency to be defiant, insubordinate, and crave excitement.

Yet discipline must be imposed. Whenever possible, it should be done firmly, not with hatred or anger. Instead of imposing decisions on SPs with coercion, it is best to allow them some freedom of choice or a hand in the decision-making process. They should be praised often whenever they manage to display self-control. It is also helpful to use their natural "polarity response."

As one mother said to her two SP teenagers before leaving, "When I come back, I want this kitchen to be just as messy as it is now. Make sure you don't clean up!" It was clean when she got back.

Note: If, in addition to being an SP, a child also has a form of PSI (Poor Sensory Integration) called ADD (Attention Deficit Disorder), then the situation calls for the intervention of experts. ADD is characterized by: hyper-activity, inability to tolerate frustration, inability to concentrate or sit still in the classroom; right-left confusion; poor spatial relationships resulting in sloppy handwriting; poor gross motor coordination resulting in clumsiness and disorganization; recklessness and seeming unawareness of danger; poor peer adjustment; impulsivity leading to violent outbursts and other acts of aggression, and sometimes hyper-sexuality at a later age. This problem can occur among any of the types and requires immediate professional guidance by an occupational therapist. However, SPs, with their tendency to poor impulse control are particularly in need of *organized* activities as outlets for their energies. This is not a problem which is ever completely overcome, though the symptoms may decrease as the child builds self-confidence and learns techniques for self-control.

SPONTANEITY: SPs love to act impulsively and spontaneously, to live in the moment. If not balanced with "J" discipline, they will squander their resources, both physical and financial. Yet, because of their optimism and self-confidence, they are sure that "Everything will work out. We'll manage somehow."

They like to pick up and go when the mood strikes. Natural performers, they are the ones most likely to perform for the bride or groom at a wedding, and to keep dancing throughout the evening. On an outing, the SP has great enthusiasm, and is ever ready to jump in the pool, roll down a hill, or discover some new aspect of nature.

Example: "I was always ashamed of my extraverted SP boys' enthusiastic natures. They seemed so wild in comparison to my next door neighbor's boys, who are very studious, obedient and introverted NTJs. Thankfully, my boys are very bright and do very well in school despite their exuberance. Now that I understand their basic natures, I no longer feel guilty for the way they are. Now, when I discipline them, I'm not so hostile like I used to be. I'm frustrated by the situation, but not hateful toward them. This new awareness has made a big difference in our relationship."

FREEDOM-LOVING: Because SPs have a "meta-need" to feel free, they may feel an inner resistance to commitments, schedules, restrictions and the need for order and routine. When an SP teenager is asked where he is going, he may simply say, "Out." They often feel - whether rightly or wrongly - that others are trying to control them or put constraints on their freedom to come and go as they please. It is helpful to remind SPs that you have no intention of restricting them unnecessarily, but that it is simply good manners to let loved ones know where you are and to be on time and fulfill promises. Without a strong "J" (Judging) component in the personality, others are likely to feel that the SP is unreliable, capricious, and untrustworthy.

Even as adults, SPs may have a strong "polarity response," i.e., "If someone tells me to do something, I have this overpowering urge to do the exact opposite."

Many SPs dislike routine 9-to-5 jobs. They prefer work which involves variety and freedom. Some SPs will work very hard for a few days or weeks, then want to do nothing for a while.

If nagged to be more reliable, stable, ambitious or helpful, they may be even more defiant against what they see as restrictive demands, rules and regulations. This response can be hard on them as well as their family members if the SP has no balancing "J" function to provide structure, reliability, and stability to their lives and relationships.

Example: "Once the children started to come along, I realized that I couldn't be as spontaneously 'P' as I want to be. I also have to do a lot of household chores which I dislike doing. I figured out a way to make it fun, which is to pay myself a small amount of money for doing major clean-ups. When my envelope is full, I treat myself to some reward, in keeping with our small budget."

ENDURANCE: "S"s in general have great physical endurance. SPs do not have the SJ work ethic. They have a play ethic. They will work long and hard hours, not so much because of "J" self-discipline, but because of an inner drive to be active.

Integrated (i.e., not lazy or violent) SPs will work hard on a process-oriented project which involves a lot of sensory stimulation: that includes the doctor who can perform a 17-hour operation, a politician or businessman who can sustain a gruelling schedule day after day, a soldier who can survive protracted combat situations, or a musician who can play in a band all night. SPs are best able to endure severe physical hardships partly because they do not worry about whether or not they can endure — they have the confidence that they can — and partly because they enjoy the excitement and challenge presented by difficulties.

"VERBAL DOODLING": The SP may talk about adventures and schemes which he may, or may not, have any real intention of putting into practice. Depending on your own personality and the circumstances, it will either be very exciting or very upsetting to be told by the SP: "Let's move to a different city." "Let's start a new business." "I'm going to Russia to visit the *Refuseniks* next week." "I'm quitting my job."

Often, it is difficult to know whether or not to take these expressions seriously. They might just be a form of "verbal doodling" - a product of their enthusiasm for life. Friends and relatives should get used to these expressions after a while and know that the SP has to be pinned down to see if he really intends to do what he says.

RELATIONSHIPS: Emotionally healthy SPs have a good sense of humor and are optimistic and sociable. SFPs, in particular, are charming mates, with "F" warmth and an adventursome, optimistic outlook. However, SPs (men, in particular) also like to be "free spirits," an attitude conflicting with the demands inherent in any marriage, especially when there are children. Some STPs (Sensing-Thinking-Perceiving), while capable of generosity, may have difficulty with sustained giving or intimacy because they do not want to be tied down or obligated. The act of giving often binds one to the recepient, thereby restricting their treasured freedom. They may make promises and plans impulsively, then forget them as they balk at the restrictions imposed by those decisions. STPs will usually have numerous excuses — all reasonable — as to why they do not have time for the relationship. But the truth is that many STPs simply do not feel the need for emotional closeness and, like the NTs, may prefer to relate to things more than people.

SPs may prefer a mate from a different culture or country, for such a person will seem more exciting, exotic, and challenging than someone from their own background. SPs like a lot of variety and action, and may be quickly bored with a mate who does not share their hunger for action, variety and adventure. They may also balk at the restrictions and demands of married life. STPs who have not developed their "F" side can be quite insensitive to and oblivious of their mates' feelings. It may take years of patient prodding to induce awareness and sensitivity.

OPTIMISM: The SP's action-oriented optimism can lift others out of their doldrums and pessimism. When others say, "It's impossible," the SP says, "We can do it! We'll win!" It is a wonderful quality which we all need in order to get things done. But as positive as optimism can be in some circumstances, it can be an exasperating one in others:

Example: "I'm an NF with a strong SP part, but not the 'P' optimism. When we moved to a new city, I was depressed and anxiety-ridden. My optimistic SP husband kept saying that everything would work out. It did. His optimism kept my spirits up. However, when I found out that one of our children was learning-disabled, he really resisted that diagnosis and kept saying that nothing was wrong. His unrealistic optimism kept me from taking action when I should have."

THE UNINTEGRATED SENSING-PERCEIVING (SP)

As we have seen, childhood negelct, abuse or over-indulgence hinders the proper development of each mode, causing the individual to become overly dominant in one or another. In the case of unintegrated SPs, they never learn "J" self-discipline and trustworthiness, "T" rationality, or "F" sensitivity to others' feelings.

The impulsive, unrestrained passions of the unintegrated SP often manifest in acts of cruelty and destruction or in self-centered hedonism. Such SPs enjoy fighting. Fighting makes them feel powerful, and makes up for the sense of powerlessness which they experienced as children. Being oppositional, saying "No" for no reason, being arbitrarily cruel or irrational is part of their "fun." They enjoy the excitement of a good fight, and may keep up lawsuits and battles with relatives for years. They tend to be pessimistic, gloomy, and hot-tempered.

The disturbed SP relieves anxiety by running away from problems, commitments and responsibilities, becoming more irresponsible, unreliable, and scattered. The SP may run away physically or emotionally, into workaholism or some pleasure-filled pursuit.

Unbalanced SPs live superficial existences which are mainly dedicated to satisfying their physical desires. Often, their only goal is to make an impression on the world, to keep others from discovering that beneath the charming external mask, there is no depth: no depth of feelings for anyone except themselves; no depth of insight, no authentic self. Everything they do is for show, to enhance their external shell and to hide their inner emptiness from themselves and others. Many were poor students as children, and they fear that others may find out that they are really not knowledgeable. They devote their lives to externals: possessions, status, appearance, food, house, vacations, etc., though they may, at the same time, work hard to insure that they do not appear superficial or self-centered.

Whatever choices they make, be it in furniture, books, cars, clothing or acquaintances, are made according to whether or not others will be impressed. They can be extremely ostentatious, greedily accumulating material possessions or "good deeds" to impress others. In religious matters, they may adopt the external habits, but without any real meaning or content, as they are concerned only with their own ego-enhancement. Their bookshelves may be stacked with books which are never read, but kept for show.

They are afraid of real intimacy because they are afraid that their outer "cover" will be blown if anyone knows what they are really like. They are threatened by, and often cruel to, people who are real, honest, truly warm and loving. Having little capacity for introspection or true empathy, they ignore the deeper needs of their spouses and children, though they can, at times, put on a show of concern - to convince on-lookers as well as themselves. They tend to be self-satisfied, not interested in changing themselves, but very demanding that others prove their love by doing what they want, not caring if that means that those "others" must deny their own needs completely. They will use guilt-manipulation ("If you really loved me....") to force others to carry out their will.

They usually will not "humble" themselves to be under the authority of a Rav or other person who might be helpful, such as a marriage counselor. If confronted about their short-comings, they will twist the circumstances, lie, go off on a tangent, or put blame on others instead of looking within. They make up their own rules, being strict or lenient where it serves their personal purposes. They may get violently angry if their mates want to go for counselling, as if the exposure of their faults is a far worse form of abuse than anything they have done.

Such negative SPs are likely to make fun of, deny, or minimize others' pain, especially if they have been the cause of it. If others react with hurt, the SP will typically blame the other person. They simply will not look within, will not see where they need to grow. They want their mates and children to enhance their egos. At best, they engage in only polite, superficial conversations.

In the unintegrated STP, the "T" has nothing to do with any scholarly or philosophical ambitions, but represents a perversion of all the positive "T" qualities: disinterest in other people, arrogant aloofness, cold, cruel silence, and emotional oblivion. Their cruelty is always justified with some image-enhancing excuse, such as, "I'm doing it to educate them." Like disturbed NTs, the disturbed STs never "bond" emotionally to anyone, and are oblivious to, or even proud of, their uninvolvement, which they think of as a sign of maturity and independence. While all types can be violent, STPs are the most prone to physical cruelty.

In the name of "freedom," they might engage in passive-aggressive acts, such as procrastinating, breaking promises, refusing to work, refusing to share (e.g., money, time, resources, etc.), and being generally irresponsible and self-preoccupied. They are petty tyrants, merciless in their criticism, and making others dependent on them so that they can feel superior. They may appear selfless and helpful to the outside world, but in their own homes, they show little or no real concern for others. They often convince themselves — and those in the community — that they are actually the long-suffering ones who are being victimized by the victims.

Ironically, many STPs, who are not "burdened" with "F" emotional sensitivity or "J" integrity, often accomplish a great deal as ruthless businessmen or deceitful politicians. Some are pathological liars who smile charmingly while planning to betray or otherwise harm their victim.

Less ambitious SPs are weak-willed, passive and wishy-washy, endlessly procrastinating about what "should" be done, but never doing it. They may excuse their laziness with head-in-the-sand optimism ("Don't worry. Everything will work out.") This is merely an excuse to avoid having to exert themselves. This unambitious, unmotivated, pleasure-seeking hedonist is happy doing nothing, or spending time eating, shopping, talking, or finding other escapes from responsibility and hard work.

The unintegrated SFP is persuasive and manipulative, using words to charm others into giving them what they want. Unbalanced SFPs tend to be gushy, over-talkative, hysterical, and theatrical. At best, they are well-meaning, but sometimes cloying busy-bodies with a kind of suffocating need to feel needed and close. They think of themselves as very self-sacrificing. What they do not realize is that when they give, they give with strings attached, trying to "buy" others' affections or to dominate them. They give in order to satisfy their own needs. Thus, they are out of tune with what others really want and need. For example, the "martyr-mother" may stand on her sore feet for hours cooking a gourmet meal when the children would rather have simpler food and a mother who is in a better mood. The "martyr-father" may tell himself that he is working so hard for his family members, and that that is why he is never home. But his family members might prefer a less fancy house, and a father who has time to relate.

Possessing the "F" hypersensitivity to rejection, but without NF insight into why, these SFs do not understand why their presence is not welcomed. They may complain bitterly and rail angrily about all the relatives and neighbors who ignore, exploit, or manipulate them, "After all I've done for them." They usually end up feeling that people are ungrateful, unkind and selfish - without at all realizing their role in alienating them.

HEALTH THROUGH INTEGRATION

As with the other unintegrated types, becoming well-balanced means acquiring the disciplines and sensitivities of the other modes. For example: adopting SJ disciplines and sticking to them, such as being very committed to a daily prayer schedule, not procrastinating, meeting deadlines and commitments, getting up at a set time each day and going to work, and keeping regular hours. SPs must be able to subordinate themselves to a respected Rav. A connection with an inspiring and understanding Rav can be very helpful in developing an awareness of the importance of focusing on *middoth* and *mussar*.

Group therapy is excellent for emotionally unaware SPs. Role playing and role reversal can awaken long-dormant emotions and help them become more sensitive to others' feelings. In a supportive atmosphere, they can learn to trust that they will not be rejected or ridiculed when they reveal their feelings and fears, particularly their fear of others' seeing their inner emptiness. They must sincerely want to do this. Otherwise, they can say all the right things, but not do anything about their stated desire to change.

What compels the unintegrated SP is fear — fear of being revealed and fear of being tied down. It is a relief when SPs learn that they don't have to spend their lives trying to enhance an external image, but can be "real" and human, and still be loved. By confining themselves to a healthy structure, they actually free themselves to become more stable and dependable, and to experience really loving relationships.

They can use their ego-enhancing drive to become proud of their impulse control, priding themselves whenever they are able to delay gratification or control their desire to indulge themselves or to hurt others. Adopting Torah values of human kindness, forgiveness, and compassion brings balance and healing.

Example: "I guess it was my SP part which enjoyed procrastinating until the last minute and then rushing around madly to meet deadlines, like lighting candles or getting to the airport on time. I guess I got a little addicted to the wild excitement and feeling of the adrenalin speeding through my system. But as a mother, I could no longer afford to function like this. I had to be more disciplined. I now try to prepare as much as I can ahead of time. At first, it was extremely hard to go against my old habit patterns. But I think of my priorities, which are peace in the home and my self-esteem and mental health. The pleasure of a calm environment substitutes for the negative 'pleasure' of rushing around crazily at the last minute."

Integration is never easy for someone who has led an unbalanced life. However, it can be done if one possesses a strong will and a strong desire for health.

CHAPTER IX: THE SENSING-JUDGING TYPE (SJ)

This type is dominant in aproximately 38% of the American public, and is equally divided between males and females.

In contrast to the uninhibited, impulsive passion, and individuality and independence of the SP, the "J" has an inner drive to be lawful, responsible, self-disciplined, steadfast, and accepting of external authority. Like the DOS in a computer, the SJ provides the necessary rules and regulations and overall structure so that people can function effectively in the physical realm. The SJ is the master of practical *halacha*. Emotionally healthy, highly developed "J"'s have a wisdom born of common sense, and are highly principled, with a firm sense of right and wrong, a strong sense of morality, and great determination to affect others with their principles. SJs can be strong, positive leaders with tremendous determination and stamina. They are known and looked up to for their strict interpretation of and adherence to Torah law.

To understand the "J", one must understand their craving for closure. Having things limited, defined and decided is what gives them a feeling of security.

The SJ is self-regimented and exacting, a real Rock of Gibraltar. The SJs are the ones to turn to in an emergency. They will survive and provide. They are the stabilizers and organizers.

Highly developed SJs put their energy into organizing, planning, managing, events, objects and people.

As much as the SP feels compelled to be free, the SJ feels just as compelled to be good, to do the right thing, to be obedient, dutiful, structured, to serve and conserve (by saving energy, money, resources, traditions, etc.).

COMBINATIONS: The unifying factor among emotionally healthy SJs is their love of law, order, tradition, and structure in order to satisfy their craving for closure.

SENSING-THINKING-JUDGING (STJ). The STJ is devoted to preserving institutions and things (e.g., antiques, old books, etc.) STJs are more stern and blunt and more emotionally detached.

SENSING-FEELING-JUDGING (SFJ). SFJs are also very dutiful and responsible, but because of their sympathy for people ("F") rather than because it is the right thing to do ("T"). They are very warm-hearted and sociable. Extraverted SFJs are often on many committees, clubs and in volunteer community organizations.

The SJ wants to "mother" or "father" others, especially by giving advice or providing for their physical needs. A female SFJ is likely to always make extra food, just in case people in need show up. And when they do, they are greeted with genuine warmth.

SJs are often found in business, catering, accounting, health services, managerial and supervisory positions, the health profession, school systems, and in all levels of bureaucracies.

SJs often serve as school principals. The difference between the STJ principal and SFJ principal is often striking. Even though they both have the unifying SJ qualities of orderliness and love of legalities, the "F" will tend to be friendlier and more flexible.

The SJ can be an "E" (Extravert) or an "I" (Introvert).

A personal example of an outstanding SFJ was the late father-in-law of a close friend whose name was Itzchak Stanislawski, z.l. During the *shiva* period, his son and daughter-in-law spoke about his many qualities, which typify this personality. To quote just a few of their memories:

"He was a steady rock all his life, the one who took care of others. He never complained. He talked little, but he did so much. He had tremendous devotion to Judaism. At the risk of his life, he kept the Sabbath in the concentration camps. He risked his life to sneak whatever food he could find to other starving prisoners. After World War II, he set up a make-shift synagogue in the D.P. camp and made sure that all the men were there for prayers. Out of his group of 200 refugees who were sent to Atlanta, Georgia, in 1950, he was the only one who remained Orthodox at a time when it was deemed economically disastrous to keep Sabbath and old-fashioned to keep the rest of *halacha*. Because he was forced to quit school at a young age to help support his family after his father died, he never had much of an education. Though not learned, he had true *emunah pshutah* (simple, but strong, abiding faith in G-d). He lost his first wife and daughter in the Holocaust, remarried in the D.P. camp, and had a son. Wherever he went, he was devoted to the synagogue, taking on the role of unofficial *gabbai*, leading the local *chevra kadisha*, and donating generously to the *shul*. He lived simply, working as an upholsterer, yet saved enough money to come to Israel in his 60's. Although he was a strict, and often uncompromising father, he was very devoted to his family. He was respected by all who knew him for his great integrity."

THE NEED TO BELONG: The SJ is a belonger. He will join or create a club or social group wherever he goes. He enjoys being part of a committee, engaging in planning sessions, having a position in a hierarchy with its particular rank and status. "J"s enjoy wearing the uniform of their particular group. They feel comfortable in an authoritarian atmosphere.

LAW-LUST: A "J" has a different relationship to laws than a "P" does. The SJ is driven by "law-lust," for laws provide a sense of closure. He hungers to know what the rules are and to follow them. Flexibility is far more difficult for a "J" than for a "P", because flexibility implies that there is more than one way to do something and more than one point of view, which threatens the "J"'s' desire for closure. To the "J", laws are holy - even the ones he makes up himself. For many "J"s, doing something even one time makes doing that very thing again obligatory. For example,

"We went to my mother's home last year for the holidays, so we will go again this year."

How different from the "P" (Perceiving) who wants to keep his options open, and who wants to do things differently than the way he did them before.

Whereas SPs feel happiest when they can give free rein to their exuberant impulses, SJs feel safe when they are in control, or controlled, restrained and restricted. What makes the SJ feel safe and secure, makes the SP feel stifled.

SJs have a sense of self-assurance born of their feeling that whatever they think or decide is right. Once they have made a decision, they are practically immovable.

Example: "My wife edits my work. We had a disagreement over one word which can be spelled in two different ways. She said that there was only one right spelling. I wanted the other spelling. The dictionary said both were equally correct, but my wife said that her way was really the only right way. The fact that I would even think to argue with her was, to her, a sign that I didn't trust her or respect her opinion. Only after I reassured her that this was not true did she calm down."

OBEDIENCE: The SJ is decisive rather than curious. He lives according to plans, standards, rules and "ought to" and "supposed to," what is efficient and right. When the SJ finds someone he believes in, admires, and looks up to, his attitude is, "Tell me what to do, and I'll do it, no questions asked." This is a necessary quality when that person is a *Gadol* in Torah. It is not a positive quality if the SJ is looking for an escape from adult responsibilities.

It is also a negative trait to think that one has the right to impose one's personal opinions and habits on others as if they were Holy Law.

A parent asked his SP child what he wanted to do when he grew up, and the SP child expressed all his hopes and dreams. His SJ child, on the other hand, said, "What would you like me to do?"

Differences between various types of "SJ"s are seen in the percentage of other modalities in the SJ, such as whether the person is an Extravert or Introvert, a Feeling or Thinking type.

Example: "I asked an STJ (Sensing-Thinking-Judging) nurse if I could stay an extra hour with my son, and she said absolutely not, that it was against hospital policy. But an SFJ (Sensing-Feeling-Judging) nurse the day before had been more understanding and told me she would get permission from her supervisor."

Example: "My son very much wanted me to buy him some fish and an aquarium. Since he is an SP, I wasn't sure that he would have the SJ stick-to-itivness to take care of them once the initial excitement had faded. But I decided to take the risk, and it turned out that he is very dedicated, trustworthy and loyal. I'm happy to see that he has this balanced SJ side."

Example: "My introverted 'J' daughter finds it much harder to get along with her classmates than my extraverted 'J'. She's much more bothered if people touch her things and much harder to reach. She also has to have things just so in her schoolbooks. She gets along very well with her 'J' teacher. However, my SP daughter, who is more of a free spirit and not so organized, has a terrible time with her 'J' teacher. At first, I tried to explain to this teacher that this child's artistic spirit and need for autonomy must be respected. But I saw that the teacher was hostile to that language, so I changed my tactics. I praised the teacher for her dedication and devotion and agreed with her that my daughter should be more organized. Then I asked her to look at her lack of organization as a slight handicap, and to realize that it is going to take her longer to develop certain skills. Since the teacher has an 'F' side, she said she would be more patient."

KEEPER OF TRADITIONS: SJs love ritual and routine. They are tradition-bound, feeling compelled to do things as they have always been done. This reverence for traditions - which are like "laws" in their minds - makes SJs (Sensing-Judging) staunch in their refusal to make any change in their time-honored way of doing things.

It is likely that the SJ will want a mate from the same background and with the same traditions and will want to settle down quickly to the duties and obligations of married life. SJs usually marry someone from their own immediate group, or with a very similar family background.

THE CONSERVER: SJs are conservative in relation to religion, politics, money, food, health, etc. While the SP is splurging as if there were no tomorrow, the SJ is a "practical pessimist," preparing for the inevitable hard times by being frugal now. He disdains the "buy-now-pay-later" or "play-now-work later" attitude. Since introverts are also worried about expending energy, the introverted SJ may be doubly concerned about the need to save. Extraversion would balance this tendency somewhat. When SJs marry SPs, they often have a big difference of opinion: what the SJ calls wise frugality, the SP might consider extreme miserliness.

RELATIONSHIPS: Emotionally healthy ESFJs are the most gregarious and caring of all the types. They are the kind of people who seem to be able to take care of the whole world. Their door is always open to those in need, and they dispense funds, advice, and food freely. They prefer to be the ones who tell others what to do, prefer to be the giver, and dislike being dependent on others or on the receiving end.

The positive SJ is not emotionally repressive. He simply witholds feelings in order to get a job done. In times of crisis, he will put his needs aside, become strong and stoic ("Stiff upper lip") and be a source of reassurance and support to others.

Example: "As an NFP, I have a tendency to complicate everything and become preoccupied with my own drama, pain and restless searching. Sometimes, the best thing is *not* to talk it all out, but to just cut through it all with a Torah thought. An SFJ friend has these little maxims which are often just what I need to calm me down. She'll hold my hand warmly and tell me, 'G-d is your best Friend. He doesn't give you more than you can handle.

Everything He does is good. Maybe you just can't see it right now. But you will.' Here is a woman who was widowed when most of her ten children were still small. She has been through so much. Yet all she thinks of is how to give to others. Her small apartment is always full of children and grandchildren. She always has a smile on her face, always has a phrase from *T'hilim* or   Mishlai. From her, I'm not going to get complicated analyses or profound insights into myself. But I get a pure Truth which is so spiritually uplifting. I need her, and I also need NF contact. Both are important to me."

Example: "When it was discovered that I had a lump, I had a desperate need to talk, especially before surgery. When I tried to talk to an SJ about 'What if...' he kept saying 'Don't even think like that. Everything is going to be just fine!' But I needed to share my fears with someone who could understand the 'N' realm of possibilities and not just be in the 'S' world of actualities. There were very few people with whom I could be really real. I kept my deepest feelings for those who could handle my pain without giving me pat-answers and shutting me off."

PLEASURE: Another possibly problematic area is the fact that strict SJs who have very little 'P' are not sensualists, and may in fact be somewhat repressive and repressed in this area. Relaxation and play are difficult for them, especially STJs. Duty and work are their priorities. The repression of sensuality can be a major source of conflict if the SJ marries anyone with a high percentage of SP or NF, both of whom need a lot of physical closeness.

DOMINATION IN THE GUISE OF HELPFULNESS: SJs are reformers. The SJ wants to make sure that others keep the laws and do what is right. The "J" (Judging — or judicious) desire to be good and organized combined with the "S" (Sensing) desire to excel in the physical environment makes SJs feel that they have the right — if not the duty — to advise others on how to manage their lives properly, or take control of the person or situation. They want everyone to be as duty-bound and responsible as they are and to conform to their standards as to what is right and proper.

SJs are acutely aware of the external environment and have such a strong sense of right and wrong. They are quick to "advise," whether it is telling people how to cook, clean, spend their money or manage their affairs. If SJs are not careful, their advice can be experienced as a form of domination - domination which the SJ is sure is helpful, but which others resent as an attempt to control. It is helpful to realize that such "domination in the 'guise' of service" can be very destructive to relationships.

CHILDHOOD: As children, SJs love the security of the same neighborhood, school system and friends. They like to please the teacher and their parents and to be good. When the SPs are being mischievous and naughty, it's likely to be an SJ who brings them back into line with a stern look or a word of warning. SJs do well in a large family and enjoy the responsibilities of taking care of others and being of service. They are usually obedient, self-assured, organized, efficient and decisive. They can organize a summer camp for younger children at an early age, plan a social event or organize their possessions with a natural talent for such activities. They are very devoted and loyal to their families and schools. They are self-sacrificing and anxious to serve and be right.

Example: "I came home from the hospital just before Pesach. A neighbor's seventeen year old came to help. I was amazed at how she cooked and cleaned as if she lived here! She just *knew* what to do and where everything went!"

Though lacking NT scholarly gifts, the SJ obedience and desire to do what is right makes them a teacher's delight. They enjoy step-by-step procedures, being class monitor, and obeying rules and regulations without argument (while the SPs care more about having fun).

THE UNINTEGRATED SJ

As with every mode, all the positive qualities of the SJ can become negative. Negative SJs were usually punished severely for

minor mistakes throughout childhood. The result is that they
explode over insignificant details which are not to their liking and
become compulsive about private rituals in order to avoid possible
future punishment. Whereas strict obedience to *halacha* is essential,
blind obedience to unnecessary rules and regulations results in a
restrictive, totalitarian mentality.

Whereas the positive SJ is noble, principled, reliable and
dedicated to goodness, the negative SJ is stiff, intolerant, mean,
obsessed with petty materialism, pompous, shallow, superstitious,
extremely bigoted and closed minded, and an inflexible stickler for
petty details. Instead of firm principles and integrity, there is
obedience to petty rules and details. Instead of inner integrity,
there is a phoney image of propriety and holiness which is
presented to the world to keep themselves and others from seeing
the severity of their inner disturbance. It does not matter how bad
things are in the home, as long as the public image is correct.
Instead of a kindly, "parental" approach, there is suffocating
domination and over-protectiveness and incessant criticism over
other people's incompetence in keeping standards of order and
cleanliness.

The negative temptation of SPs is to be so self-centered and
impulsive that they are totally heedless of others needs. The
equally oppressive, destructive tendency of SJs is to allow their
identities to become so submerged in the group, that they give up
all sense of selfhood, individuality or autonomy. However, in
their desire to control and "manage" other people's lives, they
become just as tyrannical and cruel — the only difference being
that they do this in the name of holy principles and high ideals.

Fearful of group disapproval, SJs can easily become like
mechanical robots, allowing authorities to dictate all their
thoughts and feelings. They may worship an authority figure,
fearful of making even the most minor decisions on their own or
taking any independent action.

In an attempt to appear perfect, such SJs adopt a stern mein,
arrogantly looking down their noses at "lesser beings," and
imposing their perfectionist standards on others. They often have

a phoney, arrogant bearing. Other unintegrated SJs live in a world of agonizing anxiety, torturing themselves throughout the day over every little detail, or pre-occupied with obsessive-compulsive rituals centered around cleanliness and order. They feel ashamed and dirty, never "good enough," never able to live up to their own or others' standards of perfection.

Because they need to see themselves as superior, they are often verbally abusive and tyrannical, yet excusing themselves with a "holier-than-thou" attitude and insisting, "I'm only giving this advice to make you a better person." They often do manage the physical world quite well, and go around trying to force others to do the same. They delude themselves into thinking that their incessant advice-giving and criticism are a form of caring. Often possessing "F" hypersensitivity to rejection, but lacking in "NF" awareness, they then wonder why others are so resentful of their "helpful interference."

Disturbed SJs displace their anxiety about being inwardly bad and dirty onto other people and things in the form of fear of contamination from outside sources, such as the "wrong" people, germs which lurk on door knobs and other places, or various sights and sounds. This fear can eventually cause them to isolate themselves from most of humanity, except perhaps for their own narrow "in-group," and to engage in obsessive behavior, such as excessive hand-washing or other compulsive cleaning habits. They can be very cruel to those they consider part of the "out group."

Example: "I had to deal with a very nasty clerk. The only way I could get through to her was to keep apologizing and telling her that she's right, a hundred percent right. Then she softened up a bit."

The obsession with the possibility of "contamination" can actually produce a kind of anxious, watchful look on their faces as they scan the environment to check: checking to see if everything is scrubbed, polished, and in order; checking to make sure that others are meeting their standards of religiosity and cleanliness; checking that the doors are locked; checking and rechecking that no mistakes have been made; and checking to see that others' actions are correct and proper, and not hesitating to glare disapprovingly or express criticism when their standards are not met.

Because they see themselves as self-appointed "reformers of the wayward," SJs feel justified in using threats and punishments for very minor mistakes or failure to follow their particular rules and regulations. The merest hint of disobedience is considered a major crime.

While one may want a bit of compulsivity in a dentist or some other field where exactitude is necessary, it is disastrous in the home, where tolerance for messes and mistakes are essential for a calm atmosphere.

Lacking "N" intuitive depth, the unintegrated "S" remains basically shallow, concerned only with pettiness. Philosophical or psychological concerns are of no interest to them. Instead, they are wrapped up in externals. Religion deteriorates to mechanical acts of no real meaning. Family members may be ruled by the authoritarian SJ in the name of religion, but without the loving idealism which is the foundation of Torah. Anything pleasurable is forbidden. Children may be denied toys, or the toys broken as punishment. Their "pleasures" consist mainly in saving, scheduling, and scrubbing, and feeling superior to those who don't.

Negative SJs are anxiety-ridden about doing the "right" thing at every moment of the day, never really feeling that they are right enough, and, as a result, being very joyless and excessively stern with themselves and everyone around them.

The positive "reforming spirit" of the healthy SJ deteriorates into "witch hunting," i.e., seeking out and persecuting those whom they judge to be beneath them morally, and seeking to have such people severely punished. Their stern and forbidding manner frightens others. While they can be charming towards those of their own "in group," they can be quite nasty, and even cruel, towards all others, and justify their behavior with pious words. Once they have judged someone as part of the "out group," it is as if that person no longer has any value nor even exists.

Negative SJs tend to exalt suffering. They pride themselves on their grim, dutiful approach to life and people. They pride themselves on their ability to withstand pain, and welcome suffering as an opportunity to prove their devotion. They look down on humor or playfulness and deny its importance, even to the extent of denying toys to children. They minimize all forms of pleasure in their own lives, except perhaps as related to food.

They make up their minds too quickly and then rigidly cling to their decisions, ignoring facts which might confuse them or weaken their stand. They dominate and manipulate others with their endless recitals of rights and wrongs. They insist on being right and will not admit to mistakes or learn anything new. If they could, they would impose their rules and regulations on everyone around them.

In the presence of a disturbed SJ, people may feel that their needs, feelings and opinions are quickly dispensed with and swept away in the name of the group or some "higher" ideal, such as an orderly desk or a spotless kitchen. To the disturbed SJ, "higher" has nothing to do with true human values. Things are far more important than people. That is why the kitchen floor or the committee meeting take precedence over relationships. Family members cannot help but feel intimidated and unloved. After all, if the SJ is willing to hurt a person's feelings so easily over a bit of dust on the shelves or a half-eaten tomato which has been left on the plate, that person is not going to feel that he has much value in the eyes of the SJ.

In addition, the SJ feels it is good to suffer and to go without. So, if people complain about their actions, the SJ is likely to say, "Don't complain. Pain will make you tough." Or, "You're just spoiled." Their stinginess causes tremendous emotional pain, and sometimes physical damage as well in homes where SJ "pride" is taken to the extreme, and family members are made to go without proper food, clothing or medical care.

Unintegrated SJs are so obsessed with doing what is "right" that they become almost paralyzed with fear and shame, since they can never meet their own highest standards. That shame is projected onto everyone around them.

Example: "Growing up with a very strict STJ mother was like living in a military dictatorship. I wasn't allowed to choose my clothes. I always had to finish everything on my plate, even if I was nauseous or sick. I was still going to sleep at 7:30 at the age of thirteen. I never expressed any personal opinion or preference. There was only one way to do things - her way. All decisions were made for me by her. My poor father, whom she berated for all kinds of minor infractions of her laws, just couldn't stand it. He left the house early in the morning and came back late at night."

HEALTH THROUGH INTEGRATION

As with all unintegrated, unbalanced types, health for the SJ comes only with integration of the other modes. SJs need to use "T"-type logic when they find themselves panicking over a triviality. For example, calming themselves down by seeing the "trivialities" in everyday situations, such as the child who does not finish everything on his plate, someone walking in and seeing that the dishes are not all washed and put away, noticing that the newspaper is not in the "right" place, or that everything is not spotless and perfect. There is no need to "criminialize" or "catastrophize" such events.

Whereas SPs have to become more regulated and tighten up on discipline, health for the SJ comes only if they can develop their "P" mode, becoming more easy-going and relaxed about minor mistakes, and less compulsive about getting everything right and proper. This is a long-range process, not one accomplished quickly.

The "F" function can be strengthened as well. The SJs can become more sensitive to their own needs for warmth and understanding. Whereas the NF has to be less needy and compulsive about seeking closeness, the SJ must learn to ask for and show warmth. The SJ has to ask himself, "What catastrophe will occur if I allow myself to love, to trust, to be kind and warm?"

The SJ has to learn to stop torturing himself with demands for perfection in the external environment. He must allow himself to be imperfect, to make mistakes, to be human. Instead of projecting his own secret negative impulses onto "out groups," he can practice tolerance, focusing on the good in people, and working to create closeness instead of distance.

Example: "My daughter-in-law just had a baby and asked me to help her prepare for the holidays. Well, I don't like the way she stacks the dishes in her dishwasher, and I saw her whip an egg with a spoon instead of a fork. And I very much disapprove of her giving her two year old a pacifier. I wanted to mention a number of other areas in which I think she could improve, but since my son told me that she was afraid of me, I'm trying to control myself more, even though I don't see why she could possibly be upset, when I'm just trying to help. I feel like my teeth are going to break from not saying what I want to say, but I'll go along for the sake of family peace."

Example: "My husband and I used to enjoy ourselves much more during the first year or two of marriage. He is basically a 'J' and I'm more 'P'. Under his influence and the pressures of marriage and a growing family, we lost all connection with our fun-loving side. Everything was grim and serious. That wasn't so hard on him, because that is natural to him and anyway he was very happy in his studies. But I got very depressed to the point where I woke up crying and cried pretty much throughout the day. However, once I got in touch with our need to be more balanced, I began insisting on doing pleasurable activities together as a family, like going on hikes and having an inexpensive meal out once a month."

Example: "I know that my tendency is to be up-tight and severe. My own children were actually frightened of me. In order to help me overcome my perfectionism, I began telling them when I made a mistake. Like, the other day, I gave my six year old a hard smack, which he didn't really deserve. I ran to my room to calm down. When I came out, I told him that I was sorry and that I had made a mistake. He gave me a very hostile look. Then I told him that it is O.K. to make a mistake, that I still love him. Then I told him that he makes mistakes, and I still love him. I showed him how everybody makes mistakes, and it's all right, that Hashem still loves us. Little by little, he warmed up and hugged me. Later on, he put a *milchig* spoon in the *fleishig* sink. When I pointed it out to him, he trembled in fear at first. Then I smiled and said, 'That's O.K., it's just a mistake.' I've been using every opportunity to show him that it's all right not to be perfect. This morning, he spilled some juice and said, 'It's just a mistake. I'll clean it up.' I was very proud of him. I hope I can undo the damage I've done by being so up-tight about silly trivialities."

If you are living with an unintegrated SJ in a kind of KGB atmosphere, where everything you do is scrutinized and family members are severely punished for minor mistakes or the slightest disobedience, you will have to be very patient in helping the person develop a less rigid mentality. Remember, however, that people are not motivated to change unless they feel that something is missing in their lives. The SJ must realize that something is wrong, or they will have no desire to change.

When the SJ starts to explode or humiliate you over some petty mistake, you might say, "Please put away your sledge-hammer. It's not necessary now." Or, "There was no major crime committed here."

Try to get the SJ involved in some kind of pleasurable activities away from the house. Praise him for being exacting when perfection is necessary, such as checking lettuce for bugs or Pesach cleaning. But in non-*halachic* matters, use the word "trivialities" often in your own everyday language, to help the SJ distinguish between events which should be ignored and those which call for a response.

Talk about the need for compromises. For example, strict meal schedules can be followed on days when there are no emergencies, but should not be expected on other days.

The most difficult aspect of the unintegrated SJ is their need for emotional distance. This is why they tend to be serious, formal and hyper-critical, and why they feel they must maintain an image of being always busy — cleaning, checking, and scrutinizing. Inwardly, they are terrified of being seen as "bad," wrong, or failures. Spouses and children of such compulsive SJs usually end up feeling like they are failures. After all, it is almost impossible to keep your sense of self-esteem up when someone is constantly pointing out all your faults and glaring disapprovingly and suspiciously at you even when you are trying to do things right!

The compulsive is afraid of emotional honesty or intimacy. He does not appreciate feedback. If you say, "You're hurting the relationship," the SJ will reply, "But everything I do is for you." Or, they will defensively ask, "Are you accusing me of doing something wrong?" If you say, "Yes," the response is to attack you. If you say, "No," the SJ wonders what you are so upset about.

As with all unintegrated types, be prepared for a difficult road. Try not to take the person's behavior personally. The unintegrated type is motivated by fear, especially the fear of being exposed as less than perfect. Their cruel demands for perfection and indifference to others' suffering is partly a way of getting back at all those who never allowed them to be imperfect. One reason they are so frantic about making sure that life and people follow predictable schedules and regulations is because this lessens their anxiety about what they fear are impending punishments or diasters.

Your goal is to help them realize the Torah ideal — that people are more important than things. Whether they ever *see* that priority is the big question.

CHAPTER X: ACHIEVING AWARENESS AND BALANCE

"The entire purpose of our existence is to overcome our negative habits." (Vilna Gaon, Commentary to *Mishlai* 4:13)

As you begin to become more aware of yourself and your own characteristics, you will notice that you are weak in some areas and strong in others. You new awareness will also provide you with the opportunity to change, to become more balanced by working on your weaknesses and more accepting of those things which cannot be changed. This is the "entire purpose" of our existence.

It is not so important that you "type" yourself. Many people will never come up with an exact formula as to what percentage they are of each mode, or even what their true dominance is. What is far more important is that you start to recognize when you are in each of the eight modes, so that you can plan your life in such a way that you have a balance between each of them.

DO NOT THINK IN TERMS OF EXCLUSIVITY

One of the frustrations of dealing with this typology is that classifying people is often difficult, since we are all mixtures of traits from all the categories. A healthy person must be able to use each and every mode at the appropriate time and place.

In addition, a weakness of this system is that you never know how extreme or how balanced a person is. A dominant "T" with a strong, but subordinate "F" side, (let's say a 60-40 ratio) is quite different from a "T" with a 90-10 ratio.

Remember, a mode refers to preferences and predispositions, not exclusive "prisons," though they may become that in an unbalanced personality. No one is all one thing or another. For example, a well-rounded person can be philosophical "N" (Intuitive) and still love "S" (Sensing) activities such as sports, gardening, gourmet cooking and making plans and schedules ("J"). Therefore, think of yourself and others in terms of percentages, not all-or-nothing terms.

Note your own ability to move in and out of different modes. For example, if you want to enjoy a wedding or an outing at the beach, you need to be able to move into a fun-loving "P" mode. However, if you're talking about a scientific matter, or talking to a financial advisor about your budget, you should go into your analytical, impersonal ("T") mode. To get the housework done, the SJ (Sensing-Judging) mode has to be empowered. When someone needs a sympathetic ear, it is important for you to "empower" your "F" mode. People who cannot move easily in and out of these modes have difficulty functioning and relating.

One of the reasons parents find their job so exhausting is because they have to be able to empower so many different sides of themselves so quickly. For example, you're having fun and being playful ("P"), when suddenly a fight starts and you need to be authoritarian ("J"); a child cries in pain and you need to be empathic ("F"), or maybe quite dispassionate ("T") if you think the child is being excessively dramatic. If you have many children with varied demands, you may have to flip quite quickly. Then, if there are adults in the environment, things get even more complicated if one is responsive to their demands as well. No wonder mothers are so tired at the end of the day! It is not just the physical labor which is tiring, but the emotional demands as well.

Remember that even if you refer to someone as dominant in a certain mode, it does not mean that he lacks the other half of the pair. The "I" (Introvert) is not without desire for human relationships, nor is the "N" (Intuitive) totally oblivious to physical realities. We all have some percentage of all eight factors in our personalities.

If you are equally balanced in certain pairs, you may often be ambivalent as to how to respond. For example, if you feel you are 50% "I" (Introversion) and 50% "E" (Extraversion), you may feel torn between whether to stay home or to go to a party: part of you says "Go," the other part says "Stay." A person with a higher percentage of either "I" or "E" may not experience such internal conflict. If you are more or less equal on the "J" (Judging) and "P" (Perceiving) scales, it will be more difficult for you to decide whether to be restrained or spontaneous, flexible or strict, whether to save your money or spend it. If your "T" and "F" sides conflict, you may feel torn, wondering whether you should get emotionally involved or remain detached.

With some people and situations, you may be more introverted; at other times, more extraverted. In some areas, you are more open-minded ("P"); in others, more traditional and not open to suggestion ("J"). With some people you are more "T" (Thinking); with others more "F" (Feeling).

People whose dominance is extremely obvious are easy to type, such as the scholarly NT (Intuitive-Thinking). Others are more difficult to categorize because they move so quickly from one mode to another and display so many aspects of their personalities depending on various events. Any highly developed person will, by definition, have many areas of expertise. Less well-developed people can be just as difficult to categorize because they have few skills in any area.

DIFFICULTIES YOU MAY ENCOUNTER

At first, you may find it difficult to remember what the eight initials stand for and to go through the laborious process of "translating" them into a meaningful reality each time you come across them. After all, a wealth of information is contained within each of these eight small initials. It takes time to grasp the enormous body of information contained within each one. It is even more difficult when you start combining the initials into patterns of two, three and four. Remember, you are learning a new language. After a few readings, you will become more comfortable with it. The more often you use the terms, the quicker they will become integrated into your consciousness. It is helpful to find a friend with whom to practice using the initials to gain understanding of the people in your environment. (Warning: avoid *lashon hara*!)

You are not alone if you read this information and think, "I just can't figure myself out." *Please Understand Me* contains a "Keirsey Temperament Sorter" which may help you figure out what percentage you are of each mode. Although some people feel that the resulting scores do not precisely reflect what they feel themselves to be, it is worthwhile to try it. It is also worthwhile to read *Gateway to Self-Knowledge*, by Rabbi Zelig Pliskin, to assess your strengths and weaknesses.

It might take several months of self-observation for you to gain a true perspective on yourself. Obseve yourself in many different situations, with many different people. When do you feel "like a fish out of water?" Which skills take more time and conscious effort. Which skills come more naturally? Think of the people and events which excite you and give you pleasure. Which people and activities make you come alive and *energize* you? These reflect your dominant areas.

WARNING: Do not be too quick to type yourself or anyone else. This may cause you to box yourself into a narrow prison of despair-producing self-condemnations or cause major rifts in your relationships.

DO NOT CONFUSE MODES WITH MIDDOTH

These categories are independent of *middoth*. Within any mode, people can range from the loftiest levels to the lowliest. People at the lower end in any category will be unreliable, selfish, self-centered, prone to negative thinking, and unable to bond positively with others. Those at the upper end of the scale will be multi-talented, tolerant, responsible, trustworthy, positive, and kind-hearted.

Any mode can be taken to a negative extreme, such as the "F" who becomes immersed in negative moods, the "J" who spends all her time compulsively cleaning and organizing, or the "N" who lives in a fantasy world, cut off from reality.

MISJUDGMENTS

Obviously, we can be confused and make mistakes about people. Our literature is full of such "surprises," such as the person whom everyone thought was a mean miser who, after his death, is found to have helped poor people by giving huge sums of money in secret. There were "hidden Tzaddikim" who seemed like simple shop-keepers or shoe-makers, yet were brilliant mystics and scholars.

We are not fortune-tellers, nor do we have X-ray vision into the entire nature of a person's personality. We do not know what people are capable of achieving. All we can do is describe general tendencies.

It takes time to get a realistic picture of yourself, even more of those around you. Confusion arises because some traits may be confused with others:

* Is his extraverted "P" enthusiasm a sign of true "F" caring, or only short-lived passion with no real commitment?

* Is his "J" strictness a reflection of true spirituality, or a manifestation of compulsivity arising from deep feelings of shame and excessive inhibition or strictness?

* Is his silence a sign of NT intellectual profundity, or is he silent because he has no grasp at all of what is being said?

* Is that friendly smile a sign of true "F" warmth, or a manipulative ploy to get me to do what he wants?

* Does he have a "P", relaxed approach to things, or is he lazy, wishy-washy, indecisive, and irresponsible?

Humility means realizing that our judgments are often incorrect.

"AHA!"

Despite the difficulties, you are probably having a number of "Aha!" responses by now. You now understand why you like some people and bristle with discomfort around others. With unintegrated types, you may experience feelings of distrust and antagonism for which there may be no comfortable solution - only patient forebearance or self-protective assertiveness. The possibilities are endless:

"Aha, so that's why I have so much trouble asking my clients for money. I just have so much 'F' that I feel sorry for people when they say they can't pay."

"Aha, so that's why my three children seem like fifteen. As a strong INFP [Introverted-Intuitive-Feeling-Perceiving], I have little managerial skills, dislike repetitive 'S' chores, am hypersensitive to noise and rejection and need time for quiet reflection - not the greatest combination for a mother! For us NFs, every one child is like five. The extraverted SJ [Sensing-Judging] mothers seem to manage better with a large brood. My forte is developing imagination and communication skills in children — preferably one or two of them at a time."

"Aha! It's not that she dislikes me; she's not starting a conversation because she is a very private, inhibited Introvert. That's also probably why, when I said I was recovering from an operation, she just nodded her head and didn't ask me what kind of operation or anything else about my life."

"Aha, so that's why that relative stopped relating to me ever since she found out that we disagree on certain issues. As a rigid SJ, her sense of security is based on the certainty that her views are right. In her mind, there cannot be two equally valid, yet opposing, points of view. One is either right or wrong. Since we differ in outlook, she can no longer see me or my views as valid. I'm sorry about this, but I understand her strong need for security."

"Aha, so that's why my 'T' husband can get the kids to bed so quickly. He doesn't have this heavy emotional relationship that I have with them. With me, they have so much to relate, and I'm so

involved with everything they say that the whole procedure
schleps on for hours. Also, as an 'F', I'm a harmonizer, not a
fighter, and not authoritarian. He just puts them to bed. No
nonsense."

"Aha, now I understand why my 'N' neighbor has a sign on her
kitchen saying, 'A spotless house is a sign of a misspent life.' She
doesn't have patience for routine chores and details."

"Aha, now I understand why my 'J' 'little mother' twelve year
old loves to take care of her younger siblings, while I have to
chase after my 'P' 'little rebel' fourteen year old, who wants to run
off and play and not be burdened with all these chores."

"Aha, now I understand why it's like pulling teeth to get a
certain in-law to talk. He's an ITJ with far less need for emotional
communication and companionship."

"Aha, so that's why that person hated this book, scoffed at it
and said that it was totally incomprehensible and useless. He's a
strong 'S' who dislikes dealing with psychological theories."

"Aha, so now I can stop trying to be what I am not! What a
relief!"

Awareness is the first step. The next step is having the courage
to change what can be changed, and accepting what cannot.

STATISTICAL PROOFS

An awareness of different types helps you understand what
traits can be changed, in contrast to what must be accepted as a
kind of basic, determining force in our Divinely-determined
natures.

There is an enormous body of statistical proof, based on
hundreds of thousands of subjects, confirming the existence of
these innate predispositions. Although no research has been done
on Jews in particular, it seems reasonable to assume that they
have a higher percentage of "N"s (both NTs and NFs) than the
general population. Nevertheless, the basic general trends in both
populations are probably similar.

A long-term research project was conducted at the University
of Minnesota beginning in 1979 and ending in 1986. This study

measured a number of personality traits, including aggressivity, ambitiousness, the need for personal intimacy, and vulnerability to stress (i.e., highly sensitive to stimuli, easily irritated, and generaly dissatisfied with themselves). The researchers studied more than 350 pairs of twins, many of whom were separated at birth and raised in different families. Comparing twins raised separately with those raised in the same home allowed researchers to determine the relative importance of heredity as opposed to environment.

The study found that many aspects of the personality have a high degree of heritability, i.e., are genetically determined, as opposed to the influence of parents and environment. The trait most influenced by heredity was called "social potency." A person high in this trait is masterful, a forceful leader who likes to be the center of attention. Such people can be found among any of the dominances. Among other traits strongly determined by heredity was traditionalism, strict discipline, managerial skills, and obedience to authority (SJ). Other traits which were more than 50% determined by heredity included risk-taking and zest for life (SP); richness of imagination and ability to surrender oneself and ones sense of reality, becoming enraptured by an esthetic experience ("N"); a sense of vulnerability (NF); cheerful disposition ("Has a positive outlook, feels confident and optimistic."); and "harm avoidance" ("Shuns the excitement of risk and danger.")

Other traits which were found to be more than 40% determined by heredity were: aggression ("Is physically aggressive and vindictive and has a taste for violence"); achievement ("Works hard, strives for mastery and puts work and accomplishment ahead of other activities); and control ("Is cautious and plodding, rational and sensible, likes carefully planned events.")

Another interesting finding was that the need for personal intimacy appeared to be the least determined by heredity among the traits tested (33%). It was found that the desire for emotionally intense relationships can be greatly strengthened by the quality of interactions in the family. The more physical and emotional intimacy, the more likely it is that these children will want close ties with others and will turn to others for comfort and help. Even though only 33% of the subjects displayed such a strong desire for intimacy, it does suggest that there is, nevertheless, a significant proportion of the population with less of a need for such.

A few of the major findings mentioned in *Gifts Differing*:

* In two studies done in 1965 and 1967 of 2,248 law students, only a very small percentage were "F"s. The overwhelming majority were "T"s, especially TJs.

* In a 1961 study of school administrators, 86% were "J"s.

* A study of 488 business students showed that the majority were STs, the majority of science students were NTs, and the majority of fine arts students were introverted NFs. The majority of occupational therapy seniors were extraverted NFs.

* In medicine, pathology drew a large number of ISTJs (considered to be the type least in need of contact with people), neurology drew the largest number of INTPs, and pediatrics drew the ESFJs. INTPs tended to go into neurology, research, and psychiatry. Anesthesiology made its strongest appeal to the ISTPs and ISFPs, due to their SP watchfulness and their introvert's capacity to concentrate for long periods of time.

As we see, people are attracted to vocations which satisfy certain innermost needs: for example, NFs seek to follow their inner creative urges; SJs like managerial and executive work; and SFPs with "S" awareness of detail, "F" desire to comply with expectations and "P" adaptability, are good at working with people.

Obviously, the more complex the profession, the more skills and integration required. An SP doctor would have to have much more highly developed skills than an SP factory worker. An SJ school principal must have a variety of executive skills which an SJ file clerk might not possess.

It is best to think of a dominance as a kind of "governing principle" within each of us. It must be recognized and respected in order to understand how best to fulfill our own unique purpose. Yet within that broad field, we are always capable of growth. G-d gave each of us certain predispositions for a reason. To try to be other than we are is to deny our Divine uniqueness.

HEALTHY FUNCTIONING: INTEGRATED V. UNINTEGRATED

"An awareness of your natural tendencies lets you know on what you need to put your emphasis. Self-knowledge is a prerequisite for a total fulfillment of our Torah obligations." (*Growth Through Torah*, p. 272)

A Torah way of life is meant to develop and balance all eight factors within us: outgoing sociability and *chessed* ("E" and "F") and introspective contemplation ("I" and "N"); down-to- earth practicality ("S") and inspired spirituality ("N"); objective logic ("T"), as well as warm compassion ("F"); decisive closure ("J"), and open-minded independence ("P").

The Rambam states that mental health is a function of maintaining balance by cultivating a middle course. His advice is similar to the cure for "lazy eye" in which the young child's good eye is patched so that the weak one is forced to function. If this is not done early in life, blindness can result in the weak eye. The same is true with own weak *middoth*. If we never practice using our non-dominant mode, it may wither altogether.

"To cultivate either extreme in any class of dispositions is not the right course.... The right way is the middle path in each group of dispositions.... He will not be tight-fisted nor a spendthrift..., neither frivolous and given to jesting, nor mournful and melancholic...." (*Hilchoth Deoth* 1:4).

"If one is arrogant, he should accustom himself to endure much insult...till arrogance is eradicated from his heart and he has gained the middle path, which is the right way. On similar lines, he should treat all his dispositions. If, in any of them, he is at one extreme, he should move to the opposite extreme like a tree which is bent in the completely opposite direction until it can be straight, and keep to it for a long time until he has regained the...normal mean in every class of dispositions" (*Ibid.* 1:2).

One of the aspects of our *Gedolim* which awes us all is their perfectly balanced natures: brilliant men of incredible wisdom and scholarship, vision and psychological insight; capable of heroic action and courageous self-sacrifice; possessing tremendous will and self-discipline, faithful to *halachic* strictness, yet with infinite love, patience, and understanding.

All around us, we find pious people who give of themselves to aid the sick and the poor, to bring people back to Judaism, to help others who are in need. These are our role models. Though few will achieve such brilliance or balance, we can all work toward the goal of becoming more integrated. This is an on-going struggle. To neglect that struggle is to neglect the purpose of our existence.

CHECKS AND BALANCES

The eight preferences provide a system of "checks and balances." For example, the reserve of the "I" (Introvert) can be balanced by the "F" (Feeling) function which would cause the person to reach out to others despite shyness and reserve. The impulsivity of the "P" can be balanced by the logic of the "T" and the limitations imposed by the "J" in the name of safety. The generosity of the "F" is balanced by the thrifty conservatism of the "J". The imaginative other-worldliness of the "N" (intuitive) is balanced by "S" practicality.

However, it is just as true that other combinations make it more difficult for a person to keep himself balanced. For example, the inner-orientation of the "I" is compounded if the person is also a highly imaginative "N". The combination of reserved "I", philosophical "N", aloof "T", as well as a restrained and stern "J", adds up to an INTJ, who is going to have a far more difficult time developing close emotional relationships than if any one of these four modes were different.

A very introverted person is not so attentive to details in the outer environment. If the person is also an "N", that tendency is compounded.

Or, take the case of a very responsive and voluble "F", who is also an exuberant and impulsive "P". That, in itself, is an exciting combination. If you add extraversion ("E") and a highly intuitive nature ("N"), then you get an even more emotionally expressive ENFP. If, in addition to this combination, the person also comes from a very chaotic, insecure background, then the result can be a person who is emotionally explosive and unstable, with the imagination used to arouse negative mental images and negative emotions in himself.

INNER CONFLICTS

We also have inner conflicts between various parts of ourselves. The meta-physical within us ("N") is often in conflict with the material ("S"). The part of us which wants to be spontaneous and impulsive ("P") is in conflict with the part which wants to be more cautious and deliberate ("J"), and our emotions ("F") are sometimes in conflict with logic ("T").

Example: "Logically ("T"), I know we shouldn't buy that house. But I fell in love with it ("F") and have this optimistic sense ("P") that we'll swing it somehow, although this other part of me ("J") tells me that I'm not being practical. Such ambivalence!"

Example: "I know that I have to start getting organized for Pesach already ("J"), but every time I think of starting to work, something in me rebels ("P") and I want to have a good time or talk to a friend ("F") or learn something interesting ("T")."

Example: "I would like to stand up for myself and be assertive and say 'No,' but my NF side says to be flexible, give in and just make peace."

Once you know your dominant preference, you can often resolve inner conflicts by doing the opposite of your past habit pattern in order to balance yourself. This might help in making choices on the basis of what is best for you, as opposed to what others think you should want.

Example: "My father and his brother, both SJ accountants, have been urging me for years to become an accountant too. They were putting a lot of pressure on me. As an 'F', my pattern is to give up my desires in order to please others. But my real love is teaching. I love children (NF) and want to work with learning disabled kids, even though it doesn't pay all that well. I am going to go against my pattern and have the courage to fight for what will help me manifest what I feel is my real mission in life."

The important thing is to use the right mode at the right time and stand up for your right to have your deepest needs respected.

LEARN TO ACCEPT YOURSELF

"This is the day which the Lord has made. We will be glad and rejoice in Him." (T'hillim 118:24)

No matter what the day brings, with its good times and its difficult moments, it is what G-d has made. And, therefore, we strive to be appreciative and "rejoice in Him." The same is true when it comes to our innate natures. We must learn to rejoice in what G-d has made in terms of the particular skills, talents and handicaps with which we have been endowed.

Example: "I wish I had a brilliant mind and could sit and learn all day. But the truth is that often I don't really grasp the depth of what is being said. I've spent a lifetime feeling like a failure because I don't have NT brilliance. Now I have to work to accept myself as Hashem has made me without feeling totally inadequate."

Example: I wish I were an extraverted ESFJ, a Rock-of-Gibraltar with great stamina, able to manage work and home along with numerous children and an endless stream of guests, with a smile on my face and an orderly home — kept orderly, of course, by children who do so naturally and do not even have to be told what to do. I wish I had just enough "F" to make me warm and sociable, but not so much that I would get bogged down in emotionalism over my own or others' pain. Now I have to avoid feeling like a failure for not being like this."

Many people cannot meet their ideals. There are men who are not brilliant NT *talmedai chachamim*, whose thought processes are slower, or whose restless SP energy makes it difficult for them to sit and learn all day. There are women who are so high-strung that taking care of even two or three children is so draining and nerve-shattering that they barely function. There are women with a great deal of exuberant creative energy who feel that being confined in a small apartment with young children with no outlet for her talents or social needs is like being imprisoned.

Many people feel guilty, ashamed and worthless because they do not live up to what are, in reality, impossible standards for them. Hopefully, by understanding the enormous differences between people, we will become more accepting of ourselves, instead of feeling like failures for being who we are.

DOMINANCE AND RESISTANCE

Just as few people are ambidextrous — i.e., equally adept with both right and left hands — so too are few people equally efficient and effective in both aspects of the four pairs. When using a non-dominant side, one may experience resistance, either slight or strong. Yet, despite the fact that one side is weaker, it must be developed in order to be able to function as an integrated, emotionally healthy person. When working with your non-dominant side, expect to feel less successful and more awkward.

Example: "As a strong 'I', when I have to make a phone call or meet someone new, I experience a kind of inner resistance which makes me think I shouldn't call, that it's better to withdraw. Now that I know I have to balance myself, I reach out more, but the first step is never comfortable."

Example: "When I'm in the presence of a strong 'T', I tend to feel very self-doubting and insecure. I try to be very rational and act like a 'T', but I know that inside, I'm bubbling with feelings. I used to think that that meant that I didn't deserve to be taken seriously. I've learned to be more assertive, but it is still a struggle to overcome my resistance to doing so."

Example: "When I first became Observant, I loved the classes on philosophy, since I'm a strong NFP. I loved *halacha* classes, too, but the 'P' in me put up more resistance to having to do things in a set, prescribed manner and follow an authority figure.

I do it because I know I need this strict framework to provide a sense of stability."

Example [NF]: "I'm an NFP and found a therapist who teaches techniques to lessen emotionalism by changing the negative perception of disappointing events. I hated it at first. All I wanted was to talk and talk about my pain. I thought that that would make it go away. And I thought that when he would stop me in the middle of a drawn-out recital of woe, it meant that he didn't really understand how much I was suffering. I really resisted developing 'T' logic and 'J' discipline. I thought life would be very boring and that I'd feel dead if I didn't have all this fearful and angry drama or destructive impulses. But little by little, I learned to focus on solutions instead of emotions. I became calmer and more confident. It was quite a struggle to give up my drama, but I feel much stronger now."

Others may see us as resistant because dominance alters our perception of events. Even though we believe we are trying hard to change, others may not think so. For example, five minutes of talk about personal matters may seem like an hour to a "T". An hour of talk about personal matters may seem like five minutes to an "F", who feels he has hardly begun to say all he has to say. An "I" might feel he is making an enormous effort to be more outgoing, but to a strong "E", the result may seem paltry and ineffective. The emotionally healthy "J" is just trying to make the environment safe by setting limits and getting things under control, but the "P" may feel that the "J" is being excessively controlling.

OVERCOMING THE INITIAL RESPONSE

Achieving balance is no easy task for someone who has never had the opportunity to develop his weaker modes. There may always be a strong initial response to do the opposite of what we know is good for us. When this happens, keep in mind an essential Torah principle: that doing something positive with the muscles (speech or deed) brings greater positivity to the brain, for "The mind is shaped by deeds" (*Sefer Hachinuch*, Precept 16). In other words, a forced, insincere, or phoney gesture of love, confidence, or enthusiasm will usually produce sincere feelings of love, confidence, and enthusiasm.

Example: "As a 'J', I have a strong desire to manage other people's lives and tell them what to do. Now I realize that if I use 'P' language, like 'Oh, we'll adapt as we go; I'm sure things will work out,' or 'I'll keep my options open,' the words help me overcome my initial response to tell everyone what to do."

Example: "As a 'P', my initial response is to fall apart just when I should be tightening up. Now I realize that if I just force my body to start getting things organized and use 'J' language, like saying 'These are the limits,' 'This is the schedule,' I actually start to feel more together and on top of things, even though I didn't believe the words when I first said them."

Example: "I'm a pretty insecure NF, with an imagination that always seem to be on fire with thoughts of impending doom and unbearable loneliness. Now, when I feel that feeling of dread descending on me, I force myself to overcome my initial response by talking in a calm, slow voice to them. I say over and over to myself, "Don't get upset. You'll find a solution. You have a lot of inner strengths. Things will work out.' Saying the words, even if I don't really believe them at the time, eventually calms me down."

Example: "Even though I'm a 'T', I often have a violent initial emotional response if I don't get my way. I can get totally cold and insensitive to my children, as if I don't care at all, when I really do care. Every remark, grimace, criticism, even someone just honking his horn at me when I'm driving or a child who won't cooperate, or a clerk who is moving too slowly — anything at all can make me feel like exploding. After understanding the eight modes, I realize that if I am going to improve I must resist the initial response to get worked up, and use my 'T' detachment and 'J' self-discipline to avoid getting so angry."

Example: "A very strong freedom-loving SP relative came for an extended visit from America. She's single and in her twenties. At first, I was happy to have her in our home, because she is so delightfully gregarious and funny. But then her habits began to get on my nerves. She likes to go to sleep in the early hours of the morning and get up whenever the mood strikes. She never held a job for long and had no idea what she wanted to do with her life. She didn't want to help with the kids on any regular basis. She wanted her freedom to come and go. Finally, I explained the system to her and pointed out that she really had to work on developing some STJ, or she would never have any structure or direction in her life. At first, she felt personally attacked, but I told her to go into her 'T' mode and use a little logic to see that I was really trying to help. I explained that I, too, don't always like to work so hard or be so disciplined. But that's what makes me feel stable and allows me to accomplish so much.

"Little by little, she began to accept more structure and responsibilities. She is even attending a Torah institute now. When she starts to fight the discipline, I remind her that she must often ignore her initial response in order to become balanced."

Example: "My husband usually says 'No' to most requests. I've learned that if I just find the right words, he'll usually soften up and be understanding and flexible. So, I avoid reacting to his initial response by telling myself, 'He's just in a bad mode [sic] right now.' With patience, he usually comes through."

Example: "I was trying to explain to my non-Observant SP relatives why I love Judaism, and how *halacha* gives me structure, direction and meaning in life. But all they could say was that religion made them feel stifled. They just didn't understand my spiritual needs. I controlled my initial response to condemn them and turn cold toward them. I focused on maintaining a relationship by talking about their SP interests. I encouraged them to visit Israel, give *tzdakah* for the pleasure it brings, and to do something special for each holiday. During each visit, I manage to spread a little of Torah philosophy. Perhaps by staying loving, I may have some influence some day."

Example: "I'm basically an emotionally detached person. My wife was always nagging me about the fact that I don't praise her or listen. Things got pretty bad in the marriage, and she finally made me sign a contract that I would make two nurturing statements to every family member each day. So, I've been overcoming my initial response of disinterest and 'wearing the mask,' which means pretending to be involved. I listen more and give more compliments. I'm developing my 'F' side for the first time in my life and beginning to enjoy it, especially when I see how much happier everyone is."

Example: "My very mechanically talented SP husband was trying to explain to me — a strong NF — how to work the computer. To him, it was so easy to understand. My initial response was to give up in frustration. But his SP enthusiasm was contagious. He kept telling me that I could do it. And sure enough, I did catch on eventually, though I certainly don't have the comprehension into mechanical things like he has."

IMAGINATION AND CHANGE

The best way to overcome your initial response is to first imagine yourself making this change. Take a minute, two or three times a day, to close your eyes and see yourself doing things differently:

* "Before I go to sleep, I imagine myself getting up in a good mood instead of being depressed and grouchy, which is my usual initial response."

* "I have a very strong 'P' twelve year old who hates to have her freedoms curtailed. But she was failing in school and I had to take the reins. She had a school project which was overdue and I knew I had to forbid her to go on a class trip. Before I told her about my decision, I prepared myself by imagining that I would be impervious to the anger I knew she would have towards me. I have to bear the discomfort of her tantrums whenever I have to restrict her. Lately, I've been having her do her own little imagination exercises [called P.E.P. in the *E.M.E.T.T.* book.] I have her imagine that she is disciplining herself and acting less impulsively. I tell her that 'J' means safety, means creating a safe environment and a rewarding future for her and all the family members."

* "Before the kids come home from school, I take a few minutes to imagine myself talking to them calmly and slowly, in a

low voice, instead of my usual response which is to feel overwhelmed by their excitement and demands and yell at them."

* "I imagine myself not eating that gooey dessert, which my impulsive, pleasure-seeking SP side would like to do."

* "After my husband and I had an argument, I went off by myself and imagined talking to him in a very cool, reasonable tone of voice. Then I went back and tried out what I had imagined on him. It worked much better than my bitter, hostile tone of voice."

Mothers find that they can use short "directed dreams" to help their children. When things are calm [hopefully, there are a few minutes of calm now and then], ask the child to close his eyes and imagine himself doing something positive:

* "My shy eight year old was being picked on by a bully at school. I got him to imagine turning away and finding someone to play with instead of standing there terrified, or doing something else which would make him feel less vulnerable."

* "I had my aggressive ten year old imagine himself not responding violently when his younger brother taunted him."

* "I told my children to close their eyes. Then I said that there was a special G-dly force in the room which we could all feel. I told them that when they opened their eyes, this force would actually make them *want* to help me clean up. It worked!"

CAN YOU CHANGE YOUR DOMINANCE?

An innate dominant trait or talent cannot be changed; it can only be suppressed by disuse or enhanced by practice. A strong dominance will somehow exert itself, no matter what, like a flower pushing through the cracks in a stone wall. We see that a Jew with strivings for spirituality will become Observant even in atheistic Russia, amid terrible oppression and hostility, or in the lap of luxurious materialism anywhere. A giver will give, even if he is in a concentration camp and has only an old crust of bread to share. A non-giver will be stingy even if he is a millionaire. Poetic souls will express themselves, in song, in poetry, to anyone who will listen, and to G-d if no one is around at the moment. An artist will draw in the sand if he must, and a musician will tap his fingers to some internal rhythm even if all he has in front of him is a table.

Likewise, EFs will be friendly even at a serious meeting; "I"s will withdraw, even in a crowd; "N"s will have their dreams no matter how many people tell them to, "Come down to earth;" "P"s will fight for their individuality in the most restrictive environment; and "J"s will make order and impose restrictions in the most permissive society. Dominance will find a way to express itself, unless conditions are such that the person's spirit is crushed.

Obviously, various situations can cause the suppression or lack of development of one's dominance. A child may have the potential to be a Torah scholar, but if he is in a totally secular environment and knows nothing of Judaism, that potential remains hidden until it is awakened. Poverty may deprive some children of the opportunity to develop certain talents which require expensive tutors, instruments or materials.

* As a child, a certain SP (Sensing-Perceiving) was very wild and uncontrollable. His mother just threw up her hands in despair. He ran away from school many times and bullied other children. When he married, his wife was sure that she could "heal" him with kindness and by giving in to his demands. But his demands were insatiable. At first, she was gregarious and sociable, and wanted very much to please him and find her place in the community. She invited people to visit, but her husband was critical of her friends and relatives, as well as her cooking and the way the house looked. He often sat in the midst of company in a withdrawn state. He bullied her and the children. She never knew when he would explode over some petty mistake or failure to get his way. Eventually, her self-esteem had fallen to zero. Though starved for closeness, she nevertheless cut herself off from people, as she was so ashamed of herself and her situation. Five years into the marriage, she was far more introverted than she had been at the beginning. Previously, she had been a very emotionally expressive person, but in time, she experienced the

depression and emotional numbness which often occurs in victims of abuse. Her path to recovery began when she found outside employment with people who validated her worth as a human being. She stopped feeling responsible for her husband's illness and began to take charge of her life wherever she was able to do so.

　　* A highly intelligent and out-going extraverted NT scholar was forced, due to financial circumstances, to take a factory job. The lack of intellectual stimulation and the crude atomsphere was extremely painful. Cut off from his studies, he felt that he was losing his spirit. In addition, having grown up in an affluent home, he had been quite "P" - easy-going and generous with money. However, feeling ashamed at the sudden lack of money and intellectual outlet, he withdrew from most social contacts and became more introverted. His usual optimism was gone, and was replaced by pessimism, hostility and depression. He was starving for Torah. His mood did not improve until he found a way to make a small study group of fellow Jews during the lunch hour. His role of teacher made him feel that he had given meaning and purpose to what had been such a great loss. Then he understood that he could bring the power of Torah into any situation.

　　Even if we have no ability to change our outer circumstances or inner nature, change of attitude is *always* possible.

　　Example: "As a strong NP who was quite pampered as a child, I never developed the SJ painstaking thoroughness for cleanliness and order. When I got married, I always had the feeling that someone else should be cleaning up the endless messes and cooking the meals. My initial response to work is to procrastinate, ignore it, or do it with a lot of resentment. But after learning about the types, I realized that I was being irresponsible. I have a family to take care of now. I'm not a child any more. Orderliness *is* important, even if I don't like to do the work involved. To help me get organized, I bought a copy of *Sidetracked Home Executives* (by Pam Young and Peggy Jones). As they suggested, I made out index cards detailing what jobs to do on which days. Now, when something needs to be done, I empower my SJ side by giving a stern command to my muscles to 'Get up and CLEAN!' I certainly can't compete with my SJ neighbor whose house always looks like a museum and who really enjoys cleaning, but as I develop my SJ side, my self-esteem improves and I feel more stable."

NON-PHYSICAL NOURISHMENT
Nourishment is not only in the form of food. We also need emotional nourishment in the form of closeness with people, intellectual nourishment which we get by learning new information, and spiritual nourishment through up-lifting experiences which bring us closer to G-d.

Just as different kinds of flowers require different kinds of soils in which to grow, so too, do each of us require our own particular circumstances in which to blossom. What energizes and enlivens one person may stifle and deaden another.

People who are unable to express their talents often become destructive or depressed. Their creative energy, finding no positive outlet, eats away at them internally and wreaks havoc in their lives. Like people starving for food, they feel desperate and not themselves. Many people, experiencing such feelings, seek the help of a therapist to make their pain go away. But no amount of therapy will change the fact that when a person is not fulfilling his potential, his spirit is languishing. If that is the source of the problem, then talking about it or trying to divert one's attention with unfulfilling tasks, or telling oneself that one "should not" feel this way, will not make the problem disappear. The person will not feel better until he finds the specific people and activities which will provide the emotional, intellectual, and spiritual nourishment which is now missing.

Example: "I was very depressed until I took a part-time teaching job. Suddenly, my whole mood changed. I felt I had an identity, something to look forward to each week to break up the monotony of being at home. I can be creative and be with people, which are my two loves. It's like oxygen for me."

Example: "I was very depressed until I quit my teaching job. It was really the wrong thing for me. I like routine work in a closed, quiet place and not to have to interact with people too much. I found an office job which is perfect."

NOURISHMENT FOR CHILDREN

If you are a parent, encourage your child to express his dominance in a positive way, and see to it that he also has the opportunity to develop his non-dominant side:

Example: "I have a gifted ten year old NT who was very bored in school. No matter how much his rabbi tried to challenge the class, the child was always ahead of everyone, and very frustrated. So I helped him start a little newspaper. He writes his own comments on the Biblical portion of the week and puts in stories and games. His whole attitude toward life has changed."

Example: "One of my children is a very exuberant SP with a cruel streak. She's just not at all sensitive to people's feelings. I tried hitting her, but that didn't work. I was really beginning to hate her because she creates so much tension in the house. I decided to spend extra time with her each night, talking about her feelings, doing role-reversal and role-playing with her to develop greater sensitivity to people. We also have 'Diary Time,' when I encourage her to write about what happened that day and her feelings about various events, as well as the *mitzvoth* she did that day. As a very impulsive 'P', I usually don't stick to projects, and I tend to react violently when frustrated. I start out with a lot of enthusiasm and then don't follow through, or I blow up in frustration. But this time I am determined to help my daughter, and, at the same time, work on my own weaknesses. I find that by keeping a list of her good deeds, I began to see her and myself in a more positive light."

Example: "One of my children is a strong introverted NF, quite moody, shy, easily hurt, and always complaining and whining about something. I'm trying to help him develop 'P' optimism and some 'S' sense of stability and persistence in the face of difficulties. I told his rebbe to encourage him to talk in class and to praise him when he did. This wonderful man has helped him a great deal. He also takes a self-defense class to build confidence.

And I give him lots of positive reinforcement when he tells me that he's ignoring some nasty remarks which other children have made and reinforce the notion that this will help him be less emotionally responsive to outer negativity for his whole life."

Example: "My husband and I do not believe in having toy guns. But my little SP son will make a gun out of a piece of cheese or a carrot. There's nothing we can do to stop him from seeing what he sees. When he looks at an object, what he sees is a weapon or a tool. We finally got him a little tool kit and he's in heaven!"

UNEVEN DEVELOPMENT

People's development is not even. At different times in our lives, we work on different aspects of ourselves. For example, while most young men are involved in developing a non-emotional, analytical, firm approach to life, most young women are developing sensitivity, adaptability, and nurturing behavior. Many men and women feel confident enough to develop their hidden side only when they reach their late twenties or thirties.

A "T" working woman who gets married and starts to raise a family will find that she must develop her "F" skills. Spontaneous, playful "P"s find that they have to suddenly think about devising and maintaining strict schedules and budgets when they become parents and have to deal with limited budgets.

Thus, it would be wrong to "type" a person too early. A child may be very rebellious for a while, and hate learning, then suddenly settle down and become more serious and devoted to studies. A strong NF teenage girl who is basically quite spiritual, deeply feeling and poetic may suddenly seem to be totally wrapped up in superficial, materialistic pursuits - clothing, make-up, nails, hair, and furniture because of peer pressure but revert to focusing less on the externals after marriage.

Like any talent, a dominance can be strengthened or weakened depending on the amount of energy one puts into developing it. Most people have many talents, but since we cannot work on all of them at the same time, development is uneven. A person who is well-developed in every trait is a rarity. Most of us have strong behavioral and attitudinal preferences and recognizable weaknesses. For example, there certainly are some very scholarly people who are also excellent craftsmen. But most scholars are not so proficient with tools or even interested in them.

Just because a person shows a weakness in some area, such as lack of compassion, organizational ability or academic aptitude, does not mean that these qualities cannot be worked on and developed. Rabbi Akiva and Rabbi Eliezer ben Hurkinos are examples of brilliant Torah scholars who were thought to be simpletons until they began to study. Most of us may never reach the same level of development as someone who has innate talents or developed those talents early in life, but we can and should work to develop balance.

Parents can also use this typology to help their children become more balanced. Rewards can help the child develop his weaker side. For example, a strong SP child may want to play a lot and balk at sitting and reading. He can receive coupons for each book he reads and be able to cash them in for a toy or extra play time. Or, a very introverted "T" child may be reluctant to show his feelings, but if you start early enough, you can make sure to spend time each evening sharing the day's events. Most of all, to have an emotionally healthy child, minimize the criticism and provide positive feedback, especially when the child displays positive behavior in the areas in which he is weakest.

CHILDHOOD ABUSE

People often ask about the effect of an abusive childhood. Parental criticism, indifference or physical abuse instill strong feelings of shame in children. Because they feel they are "bad," they are fearful of loving or being loved. Some children become frightened of succeeding, others become frightened of failing. They are often unaware of their innate strengths and talents. Such children usually grow up to be abusive of themselves and others, either passively or aggressively.

Another result of an abusive childhood is a feeling of inner disorganization and chaos. The effect will be either failure to be in control of onself combined with disorganization in the external environment, or the compulsion to be in control and have everything organized at the expense of relationships.

A dominance will assert itself no matter what, and will probably manifest itself in a negative way because the other modes will usually be suppressed:

* "E"s may become compulsive socializers, obsessive about externals such as their looks or possessions, and fearful of paying attention to their inner world,

* "I"s become more withdrawn and uncommunicative,

* "S"s become more petty-minded, shallow and superficial,

* "N"s become more out of touch with reality, less able to function or manage practical affairs,

* "T"s become more self-contained ("I don't need anyone, and no one should need me.") and fearful of emotional intimacy.

* "F"s become more hyper-sensitive, easily shattered by the slightest sign of indifference or disapproval, and insatiable in their need for reassurance,

* "P"s become more defiant, irresponsible, unreliable, unstable, disorganized, indecisive,

* "J"s become more rigid, inhibited, compulsively neat and obedient to the point where all sense of individuality and autonomy is lost.

For example, take the common example of an "SP" child who craves a great deal of physical activity, but is denied these outlets and told that he is bad for even wanting to do anything other than learn. He may assert his need for autonomy and sensory excitement by stealing, breaking household objects, vandalizing public property, and running off to play and then lying about his whereabouts.

A "P" may spend money recklessly. A "J" brought up in the same environment may be extremely miserly and not be able to spend money even when he does have it. Whatever the case, early abuse promotes adult extremism.

MENTAL ILLNESS: STUCKNESS

Mental illness can be seen in precisely the same terms described by the Rambam: an imbalance between various functions. Or, in our terms of reference, it is the failure to adequately develop all eight modalities so that the person becomes "stuck" in an extreme position. The result is a disturbed person who turns all the positive qualities in each mode into weapons of destruction.

Obviously, it is not easy to define mental illness. We all go up and down this continuum to some degree. Under stress, we all may get temporarily deranged. This is not a problem unless one gets stuck in a negative state for a prolonged period of time.

By thinking in terms of development and integration of these eight functions, a person can more clearly see where he needs to change. Thus, one might think to oneself, *"I'm not crazy; I'm just not integrated!"* That is a lot more constructive than thinking, "I'm hopelessly insane." Thinking in terms of balance makes one responsible for change. Though outside experts may be comforting and insightful, they cannot be depended on to provide the motivation, the perseverence, and the will power to make change a reality. That is something each person must do for himself.

For example, an extreme SJ has to "de-regulate," while an extreme SP has to become more regulated. Without "J, a person is like a ship without a rudder. He lacks direction and discipline, and is ruled by his moods and impulses. Lacking inner controls, he either avoids taking charge of his environment, or does so inconsistently and often explosively. He has to learn to be more regulated and disciplined, especially in matters of *middoth* and *halacha*. But an extreme "J" is compulsively addicted to plans, structures and rituals.

Example: "As an unintegrated 'J', I have to constantly remind myself that the terms 'right' and 'wrong' only apply to *halacha*. I tend to agonize over every little petty detail. But when I remember that in matters of personal opinion, there are no absolute rights and wrongs, I don't get so anxiety-ridden about getting everything perfectly right, or paralyze myself with my perfectionism. I can overcome my initial response by lowering my standards in *non-halachic* matters, like not getting angry if something is out of place. I'm learning that it's more important to be humane and tolerant of myself and my family members. But believe me, it's not easy. I have to overcome a lot of anger in order not to mention every little thing that bothers me."

Example: "I'm an unintegrated 'F'. I'm trying not to be so *porous* - not so prone to soaking up other people's feelings. I also have this tendency to always check people's feelings, taking their "emotional temperature" to see if there are any signs of rejection or disinterest. Now that I understand this syndrome, I'm less influenced by my fears. I'm slowly learning to be more independent and secure within myself, to believe in myself and my inner strengths."

THERAPY

People who are stuck in a negative habit pattern can often be helped with proper therapy. However, it is important to find the right therapist for one's particular problem, or the situation could worsen. For example, telling an "F" to get more in touch with feelings is not very helpful when the "F" is already too emotional. True, identifying the precise feeling may be helpful (e.g., anger, helplessness, jealousy, inadequacy). But, once identified and expressed, a good therapist will help the person move out of that state by encouraging logic and confidence-building attitudes and activities.

A particular problem concerns therapists dealing with NFs. NFs tend to have more difficulty accepting themselves than other types. Approximately 85% of the people in therapy are NFs. Approximately 85% of the therapists treating them are NTs. What an NT means by "cure" — becoming more like an NT — is not practical or realistic for the NF. True, it is essential for NFs to learn to use cognitive tools to get them out of their excessive emotionalism. But the NF will never be an NT. They have different internal "wiring." The NF cannot stop wanting closeness and cannot avoid being hurt by its loss. What they *can* do is not get stuck in that pain. Instead of allowing themselves to become pre-occupied with their own personal sadness and worries, they can use their depth of feelings to reach out and help others. "Cure" for the NF does not mean having no more pain in their lives. "Cure" means living with pain and using it as an incentive to understand more and to love more.

Assertiveness training is also excellent for NFs, who tend to be self-doubting and self-denigrating.

"T"s, especially the introverts, need to get more in touch with their feelings and learn to express them. "J"s may be best helped by behavior modification techniques to help them give up their obsessive-compulsive rituals.

Whatever therapist a person chooses should be an Observant Jew who is, him/herself, a model of Torah values.

CHAPTER XI: IMPROVING RELATIONSHIPS

STAY LOVING: GIVE THE BENEFIT OF THE DOUBT
"With fairness shall you judge your people." (*Vayikra* 19:15)
"...included in this commandment is that it is right for every man to judge his friend favorably and interpret his deeds and words only for the better." (*Sefer Hachinuch* 235)

One of the most important applications of this typology is in the area of communication. An awareness of differences will not completely eliminate the pain of dealing with different personality types or people with poor *middoth*. However, it can help you communicate with most people more effectively. More than anything, an understanding of these types will help you *dan l'chaf zchuth* (give the benefit of the doubt) instead of exploding (or imploding) with resentments and hostility.

Not only are we obligated to give people the benefit of the doubt concerning individual actions, it is just as important to refrain from condemning them in their entirety. Unless a person is a publically acknowledged evil-doer, we are obligated to leave judgments to G-d, not man. When you grasp how different people are in their talents, motivations and needs, you will more easily be able to avoid judgments, or judge favorably.

Your relationships will improve tremendously if you constantly tell yourself, "This person is doing the best he can with the tools he has, given the passions and pains of the present, his predispositions and intellectual abilities, and the conditioning of his past." Say the words over and over to yourself, even if you do not believe them at first. Say them because they calm you down and enable you to be silent or to rebuke in a Torah manner: i.e., in private, with a gentle voice, and having only the other person's good in mind. (*Hilchoth Deoth* 6:7)

The great master of loving-kindness, the Ba'al Shem Tov, said that the secret to loving relationships is to have an "intellectual awareness" of other people's flaws without allowing that objective noticing to become a negative emotional feeling (i.e., a condemnation). (*Kuntres Ahavas Yisrael*) At first, it may be an extraordinarily difficult thing to simply notice people's behavior, as would an objective newspaper reporter, without condemnations. But the more you practice this "Oh...response," the more natural it will become. Then, instead of your heart filling with rage and anger, you will be able to a) ignore the behavior, b) give rebuke with love, or c) simply talk things out with the person in a mutually respectful manner. You cannot do any of these if you are full of condemnations.

Example: "My wife did something which really disturbed me. I caught myself and just noticed her behavior objectively, in a neutral way, instead of condeming her. Finally, I just told her what was bothering me, without my usual hostile tone of voice, and she quickly apologized. End of what might have been a major blow-up."

Example: "I was always feeling either superior or inferior to everyone I met, which prevented all possibility of closeness. Now, I'm more accepting, both of myself and the people around me because I see that every person has his own struggle and his own purpose. It's not for me to judge. I may be frustrated at a situation, but I'm not so hateful of the people involved."

Example: "While I was trying to help my SP son with his homework, he kept fidgeting with anything he could get his hands on. I could feel myself getting enraged and about to scream furiously at him. Then I told myself, 'He's not doing this *davka* to drive me crazy. The material is difficult and he would rather be playing. He already has an aggressive streak, and if I beat him up, it'll get worse. He needs to firmly guidelines. As soon as my anger disappeared, I was immediately able to think of a more creative way to get him to cooperate and learn. My son needs a 'J' mother who can make firm guidelines and be consistent. As a 'P', that's my weakest point, but we'll work on it together. "

Example: "The other day, I begged my husband to please go talk to our upstairs neighbors about all the noise they were making, but he said that it didn't bother him one bit. I was furious, thinking that he just didn't care about me and was being mean and stubborn on purpose. Then I realized that I'm a hypersensitive NF and far more bothered by noise than he is. He's not being oblivious on purpose. He really doesn't hear what I hear. Realizing this, I was able to talk to him assertively, without hostility."

When you believe, "He/she's doing this *davka* to hurt me," you are immediately filled with anger and/or shame. Take away the *davka*, and you will calm down and be able to think more clearly, and feel more loving. Constant practice (i.e., hundreds of times a day!) of the "Oh...response" will make "taking away the *davka*" an automatic response.

GRIEF

Many people go through a period of grief as they gain understanding of these types. It is hard to accept that the people around you may never be all you would like them to be. It is normal to feel discouraged, angry and jealous. When this happens to you, don't fight your upsetting emotions. That only makes them last longer. Even if your mind accepts that this is the way things are, your heart cannot help but wish that things were different. There is no easy way to bear the pain of an unfulfilling relationship. All you can do to avoid dwelling on the pain is to practice on-going gratefulness and forgiveness, plus taking positive actions when possible. Two typical reactions:

Example: "Whenever I go to a lecture by certain Rabbis, I am transported into a world of such profundity and depth that I am busrting to share my insights with others. At the same time, part of me grieves that I cannot share any of this with my mate, who lives in a much more simple reality — cut-and-dried laws, shop talk about the children or what needs to be fixed in the house... When I think about this loss, I get a feeling of great sadness, knowing in my heart of hearts that no matter how much I rationalize and justify, that the relationship is essentially empty and unfulfilling. I rise above the pain by telling myself to be thankful for all I have, for health and children and a home and a Torah way of life...and for a mate who is really very good and caring. I really struggle to accept Hashem's will, for that is true love of Him...."

Example: "Whenever I see how a certain in-law deals with the children, I get a lump in my throat and my heart feels heavy. I see love and consideration for the children, whereas my mate is so critical, always shouting, calling names and hitting. I see how their children are bright-eyed and enthusiastic, and mine are often frightened and withdrawn. I try to keep the atmosphere in my home positive, giving the children as much love as I can, but I cannot completely overcome the effects of so much meanness and criticism. It's hard...knowing I will never have the warmth and love I want.., and even more, that my children will be damaged. I lift myself up by focusing on what I do have, with constant gratefulness."

The sorrow over a paralyzed relationship is no less than the sorrow over a paralyzed body. Yet the same tools are necessary to deal with both: a lot of prayer and taking whatever positive actions one is capable of making.

COMPULSIONS AND SAFETY

To help you give the benefit of the doubt when others do things which displease you, realize that the behavior makes the person feel safe. People are often under a compulsion to act in a certain way because that behavior lessens anxiety, providing some sense of psychic protection for an insecure ego.

Unfortunately, what makes a person feel better when he's under stress may not necessarily be what is best for him or his relationships. For example, when SPs feel anxious, they may do something impulsive, such as run away, shop, procrastinate, or ignore the problem.

"F"s may feel terribly insecure and threatened when they feel that there is no emotional contact with someone they want to get through to. They may become even more insistent about relating, and so wrapped up in their own needs, that they may not even notice that others do not have the time or the interest to talk to them. In addition, NFs, especially women, are the most self-doubting and self-questioning of all the types, even more so if they are introverts. Such NFs may feel that they *must* make contact with everyone, *must* get through, *must* have reassurance that they are loved, appreciated, and successfully fulfilling other people's expectations, in order to reassure themselves that they are worthwhile and are not going to be abandoned or rejected. They are the ones who most need to become self-validating, protectively assertive and self-reliant.

Unintegrated "T"s are at the opposite extreme. They *withdraw* compulsively. Safety to them means *not* revealing anything about themselves, *not* touching, and *not* relating at a personal level. They may get furious if demands are made on them to give of themselves.

This helps explain why previously cold and aloof "T"s suddenly become contrite and sympathetic when the "F" spouse can't take the "emotional Siberia" anymore and threatens divorce. As long as the "F" is angry and distant, there is no real relationship. Thus, the "T" feels it is safe to be nice and win the partner over. however, as soon as the couple reconciles and the "F" partner draws close to the "T" in trust and caring, the "T" usually withdraws again and becomes just as critical and aloof as before. Many couples play out this frustrating scenario throughout their marriage. The "F" knows the "T" can be caring, as evidenced by those "honeymoon" periods, and wonders why it cannot be sustained, not realizing that the unintegrated "T" is too fearful to allow a real relationship to exist.

Knowing that you are dealing with an extreme personality trait, may make it only slightly less painful to be with that person.

Remember, it is a mitzvah to give rebuke with love in your heart. (See commentaries on *Vayikra* 19:17-18). On the other hand, it is also a mitzvah to remain silent if you know that the person will not listen to you. (*Ibid.*)

"CAN'T YOU SEE!" "NO!"

We tend to fear what is foreign to us and what we do not understand. Therefore, when you find yourself feeling uncomfortable in someone's presence, become aware of what might be motivating that person. In addition, use this as an opportunity to get in touch with the possibility that it may be your own irrational fears or unrealistic demands which are creating your discomfort.

You might often think that others are being deliberately insensitive, stupid, selfish and incompetent. However, the Torah ideal is that you "excuse, not accuse." When you truly understand another person it is easy to forgive.

It won't be easy to overcome anger and impatience towards others. But remember that people really don't always value what we feel is important. How often we may say or think:

* "Don't you *see* that mess on the floor? Aren't you disgusted with yourself for being so lazy and irresponsible? How can you live in such mess? Don't you *see* how easy it would be if you just had schedules, if you just put everything back in its place after taking it out, if you would just follow the rules, etc."

* "Don't you *see* how much distress she is in?" "Can't you *hear* how upset I am?" "Don't you *see* how hurt he is by what you just said?" "How can you sit there while I'm running around like a chicken with her head cut off? Don't you see how desperate I am for help?" "Why do I have to explain every little detail?"

* "Don't you see how I'm trying to rest (or "study," "work," etc.)? Can't you just keep things peaceful and quiet?"

* "Don't you see how important it is not to hit the child for the

mistakes he makes when he is learning? Don't you see how much damage you are doing with your constant criticism?"

The person really may not see — at least not until you point it out. And even then, you may have to point it out over and over again. And if the person remains in his "emotional coma," he may never *see*.

Trying to get someone to see your point of view is a little like trying to wake up someone who is sleeping. If the person is in a light sleep, you will probably have quick success. But what if the person is in an "emotional coma?" In that case, you can rant and rave forever without having any effect.

The very realization that people are all handicapped in some areas is often enough to reduce the negative emotional charge and bring a more loving, solution-oriented approach to problems.

Therefore, if you see that a person does the same thing over and over again no matter how much you try to explain or rant and rave to get him or her to stop, you may be bumping up against that person's "blind spot" or a real handicap. Try lowering your standards and learn to give very concrete, specific requests which you know the person can handle.

It is impossible to force internal change unless the other person really wants to do so. You can sometimes arouse a desire for change by asking a person if he wants to become more balanced.

*"I know you want to become more organized and efficient. Is there anything I can do to help?" [The worst thing to do with disorganized people is keep calling their attention to the fact. This makes them even more confused, insecure and angry at you.]

* "We're down to about zero minutes a month on quality time together. Do you want to spend more time improving the relationship?"

* "The tension in the house is just too high. I'm sure you want to do something to improve the situation. So let's sit down and figure out what can be done."

* "I always feel guilty whenever I ask for anything for myself. I'd really like you to listen when I assert myself."

The next step is to praise even the most miniscule baby steps in growth in the desired area. Success breeds success. **People do not improve if you constantly imply in words, gestures, or facial expressions that they are failures.** They may be more open to change when they are encouraged, with positive feedback, to do so.

THE MIND UNDERSTANDS...BUT THE HEART DOES NOT ACCEPT

This typology gives you a means whereby to define and validate the pain you may have been experiencing in a relationship. It is like going to a doctor and getting a diagnosis. There is relief in knowing that those aches and pains were not just figments of your imagination but are symptoms of a real illness. Then you have to go home and wage that lonely battle of coming to terms with what you have.

Coming to a true, heart-felt acceptance of another person's emotional handicap may take years, especially if the handicap is severe. The level of a person's mental health is equal to his degree of loving-kindness in harmony with self-discipline. Unfortunatley, there are many disturbed people in the world, and most of them are *not* in institutions.

Don't take responsibility for people's abusive behavior. Even under provocation, a *mentsch* acts like a *mentsch*, or is at least sorry that he didn't. Truly abusive people are never really sorry for what they do. The tipoff is that they blame you, or other outside factors, for their violent tempers and irresponsibility instead of taking responsibility for it themselves.

Do not try to satisfy the demands of a verbally or physically abusive person. **The extremely unintegrated person in any of the categories can never be satisfied, no matter how much anyone tries.** There will always be new demands for more. A critical person with an explosive temper will explode over *anything* — the weather, the budget, the lights, *anything* you say, *anything* you do, the food, the noise, etc. You may never achieve your dream of a healthy relationship, i.e., one in which there is a strong foundation

of mutual trust, respect and appreciation. However, you can be
self-protective.
State firm rules and let others know your boundaries:
"I do not like being talked to like that. "You don't have to use
a sledge-hammer to get your point across. I'm sure you can find a
respectful way to say what you have to say."

Counselors always recommend that couples "talk things out,"
preferably each and every day. But many unintegrated "T"s are
not interested in communciation or relationships, and many
unintegrated "F"s feel even more overwhelmed, helpless,
hysterical and depressed if they talk about their pain as much as
they would like.

Do not expect to get along with everyone, especially
unintegrated types in any category. When dealing with such
people, it might be helpful to repeat the "Serenity Prayer" silently
to yourself: "G-d, grant me the serenity to accept the things I
cannot change, the courage to change those things I can, and the
wisdom to know the difference."

It is important to acknowledge the grief you may experience
over a disturbed relationship. The process of coming to a state of
acceptance is a difficult one. You will think you have come to
terms with reality, and then suddenly fall into grief again. You
will restrengthen yourself and renew your faith in G-d's wisdom,
then fall down again. One way to lessen the gap between what you
want and what you have is to constantly tell yourself to "Make
Hashem's will your will" (*Avoth* 2:4), to convince yourself that
things must be this way because it is Hashem's will and is
necessary for your growth.

There are no easy tricks for dealing with unintegrated people.
The less interaction, the better. If one has no choice but to work
or live in such an atmosphere, remember that the process of
learning to bear the pain is similar to the process of learning to
bear the pain of blindness, paralysis or loss of a part of the body.
It takes tremendous effort not to be dragged down by a sense of
having been unfaired against by man or G-d. That is why prayer,
and trust in G-d are essential.

People often ask, "How can I get 'X' to change?" You cannot make people change. It is impossible to motivate anyone to change unless the person desperately wants to. The more serious the disturbance, the greater the resistance to change — and the less likely the person is to seek help.

Signs of disturbance are: chronic anger, hyper-criticalness, jealousy, possessiveness, extreme impatience, control through intimidation, constant argumentativeness, Jekyll-Hyde personality, blaming others for their outbursts and moods, etc.

Don't be passive in the face of real abuse. There are agencies and experts who can help you deal with the situation.

COMMUNICATION

When forced to move into their non-dominant mode, people usually feel confused, overwhelmed, inadequate, threatened, and even angry, much like a person who has been forced against his will to write with his non-dominant hand. There may even be highly uncomfortable physical responses. If you have difficulty getting through to someone, it may be because you are talking in his or her non-dominant mode. What often happens is the following:

"Whenever I talk to ..... about ...... (Fill in the blanks) he/she gets this glazed, bored look in his eyes. I feel like I've lost him after the first sentence."

On the other hand, when a person is involved in his dominant side, the eyes light up, interest is sparked, and excitement is felt in the body.

You will get along better with people of a different dominance if you use their "language" when talking to them [See "Charts" at the end of this book]. Obviously, when speaking to highly intelligent, multi-faceted people with "integrated" personalities, it will be much easier to be understood, no matter what "language" you speak, because of their flexibility in understanding all modes. The more undeveloped and one-dimensional the person, the more rigidity and resistance you will experience.

NFs (Intuitive-Feeling), with their multi-faceted, fiery,

empathetic natures are the types who find it most easy to understand people's needs, to reproduce and reflect those feelings back, and move into different modes. However, most people are not able to do so, or to do so as quickly. If you are an NF, realize that the lower the percentage of NF in the people to whom you are speaking, the less awareness, sensitivity, and understanding you can expect.

Those who want to deal successfully with others must know how speak different languages, and also how to arouse understanding in those who seem oblivious to anothers' points of view. Two stories illustrate this point:

Story 1: A poor man knocked on the door of the village Rabbi in the middle of the night, in the middle of a harsh Polish winter. The poor man begged for some wood, as his wife had just given birth and there was nothing with which to heat their small hut. He was afraid that both mother and baby might die. The Rabbi, also being very poor, had nothing to give him. But he dressed quickly and, after telling the poor man to go back to his wife, he trudged through the heavy snow to the home of a rich man. It took some time before the rich man heard the knocking and came down to answer the door. Angry at having been awakened, he stood shivering in the doorway, and told the Rabbi to come inside and talk. The Rabbi said that he couldn't tell him the problem until he came outside. The rich man replied that it was too cold and would he please come in quickly or he would slam the door and go back to sleep. They argued like this for a few minutes until the rich man finally agreed to go outdoors. While the rich man shivered in the cold, the Rabbi told him what the problem was. Immediately, the rich man agreed to give him money and fuel. When they were comfortably indoors, the rich man asked the Rabbi why he couldn't have said the same thing inside. The Rabbi replied, "If you hadn't felt the cold yourself, you would not have been so sympathetic to the plight of this young couple."

Story 2: A young man suddenly went crazy. His insanity manifested itself in his belief that he was a rooster. He closed himself off in a cabin, stripped himself naked, and crowed night

and day. Everybody tried to get him to see the light and stop this
nonsense. The more they tried, the harder he crowed. Finally, a
Rabbi who was visiting in the village heard the story and asked
for an opportunity to reach this poor young man. Going into the
cabin, the Rabbi also stripped himself naked and started crowing
like a rooster. The young man stopped suddenly and said, "Hey,
you're not a rooster. Stop crowing." And the Rabbi replied,
"Well, you're not a rooster either." The young man laughed. That
was the breakthrough. The man saw that someone really cared,
and before long, he had recovered. (Attributed to Rabbi
Nachman of Bretslav)

These stories illustrate a number of points. For *Example*:

* We cannot force awareness on others; that awareness has to
come from within. However, people *can* often be sensitized. When
our purpose is holy, when we have deep faith in the others' ability
to change, and when we approach the person with a combination
of loving-kindness and firmness, we increase the possibility of
awakening awareness and cooperation.

* The best way to reach someone who seems totally oblivious is
to enter his world and talk his language.

* Don't put people down or nag them to change. That only
arouses resistance. Instead, manipulate the environment or in
other ways create the conditions which will make them want to
change.

* We all have our areas of denseness. To a great extent, we can
only really understand what we ourselves have experienced. Can a
healthy person really know what it is like to live with a chronic or
terminal illness? Can the young understand what it is like to be
old? We can never be completely sensitive to or understand
another's world in totality, but we can take off our outer habit
patterns and take on another's point of view temporarily in order
to demonstrate concern. The willingness to do so is a
manifestation of true concern for others.

* Love heals — if the other person will reach out and allow you
to make contact.

* Love gets better results than hostility. Even if you don't get

what you want, you have retained your dignity and your humanity. So, either way, you gain.

COMMUNICATION TIPS

We have a commandment to "Love thy fellow man as thyself." However, it is impossible to sincerely love everyone in your environment to the same degree. By recognizing and respecting the differences in needs and values of other types, you may be less annoyed, vengeful, or angry. This is the first step to fulfilling that *mitzvah*.

First, and most important, keep in mind the profound words of Rabbi Eliyahu Dessler:

"When demands begin, love departs." *(Strive for Truth!)*

It is not the realistic demands for respect and trust which cause relationships to go sour, but the excessive, unrealistic demands which make others feel oppressed or inadequate.

A relationship in which both parties accept the other as they are, is ideal. To help you move toward that ideal, try the following:

* If you are an "F", don't be so sympathetic that you become a doormat or a patsy.

* If a person hurts your feelings, and you know that telling him so will only provoke scoffing or defensive anger, try the following steps:

1. Ask, "Can you give me 30 seconds to improve our relationship?" (If the person says, "No," then you don't waste your time trying to get through to someone who doesn't care.)

2. Calmly ask, "Please take 30 seconds to think about how it would make you feel if someone said to you what you just told me."

3. WAIT! Give the person the chance to think and to feel. This is the best way to help others gain awareness of your position.

4. Say, "Now, please restate what you want in a way which does not put me down."

* Point out when people are invalidating your feelings. Few people realize what it means to invalidate another person's feelings. The more often you point it out, in a non-hostile, or even

humorous manner, the more others will realize what they are doing and will, hopefully, stop. For example:

"I just said that I feel that we don't ever really talk. You said we talk all the time. That is an invalidation of my feeling."

"I told you that I feel lonely, and you said that I can't possible be lonely when there is a house full of children. That is an invalidation of my feelings."

* When a "T" has undergone a painful experience, he will probably express his pain. Then he is done with it. It's over. He has gotten his feelings out and that's it. But when an "F" has been traumatized by some event, he wants to talk it out over and over again. The "T" may say, "But you told me last week how badly you felt about 'X,' as if, having talked about the feelings, they are no longer there. But for an "F", feelings don't go away just because they have been expressed! (Don't we wish it were so!) Oh, no. They come back again and again, craving a few more minutes of attention or expression.

* Recognize when you are dealing with an insatiable demand, and do not try to fill it completely. NTs will never feel that they know enough. NFs will never feel that they love or are loved as much as they would like. SPs can never have enough adventure, excitement or variety as they crave. SJs will never be able to get others to be as responsible and organized as they want them to be. You are not to blame for other people's unhappiness (unless you are doing something purposely to cause it).

NFs tend to feel responsibility for other people's unhappiness, and they can get taken advantage of because of their willingness to go out of their way to give of themselves. They tend to say, "You're right, I'm wrong." NFs in particular need to follow the self-protective, but balanced approach of Hillel: "If I am not for myself, who will be for me? But if I am only for myself, what am I?" (*Avoth* 2:14)

* If you are an "F", realize that you may be sending your "T" mate a double message. "F"s who feel weak and vulnerable often marry "T"s because of their aura of solid invincibility and strength. Then the "F" complains because the "T" is not

"feeling" enough. In most people's minds, "Be strong" is the opposite of "Feel things deeply." Emotionally healthy "T"s do have deep feelings for people. But they may not trust themselves to show those feelings. Be patient. Show your spouse that a person can be strong and still feel. You won't get that message across if your own deep feelings keep you a dither all day.

* Just because "T"s have more difficulty "bonding," or connecting emotionally, does not mean that they do not need positive feedback. They do. "F"s may feel like they are sowing seeds of love in vain, because there is no acknowledgment or appreciation from the "T" in return. Keep sowing anyway. This is especially true with those "difficult," hard to love people who you may have turned away from years ago because you seemed to be getting nowhere with them. One day, those "seeds" may sprout. In the meantime, try not to take their aloofness personally. It may be a compulsion which they do not know how to overcome. Endorse them when they do make even the smallest positive act. You may not be able to avoid feeling appropriately sad and lonely if you are married to a extreme "T", but you can avoid feeling hateful towards your spouse or guilt-ridden about your own inability to make him or her change, understand or communicate. By accepting that reality, you can all that much sooner find outside sources of nourishment. Even if those "outside sources" never feel the gap left by an unfulfilling marriage, they do give you something positive on which to focus.

Example "I went to a marital therapist because of the lack of communication with my husband. The therapist suggested that we spend fifteen minutes talking each evening. So, there I was, trying to tell my husband about my feelings. After a few minutes, he would glance surreptitiously at his watch, impatient for the time to end. It's not that he didn't care. He really tried very dutifully to stick out the whole fifteen minutes. But his heart wasn't in it. At first, I was going to give up completely. But after learning about the types, I see that I have to stop focusing on my feelings when we talk, and spend more time letting him take the initiative and talk about outside interests. When I do need to get through to him about something, I am much less emotionaly threatening and more patiently persistent."

* When arguing with anyone, first acknowledge that he does have a point and may be right. Show that you have heard what he is trying to get across. Hopefully, that will calm him down. When talking to an "F", first validate that the person has a right to feel the way he is feeling. When arguing with "J"s, acknowledge their need for safety and closure. Don't condemn feelings. Instead, focus on solutions.

* Try "telegram talk" with dominant "T"s. The more "T" in a person's make-up, the more he/she wants clear, concise instructions stating precisely what you want without any emotionalism. Strong "T"s often prefer to be talked to as though by telegram: short, quick, efficient, and condensed.

Example: "My INTJ husband often does not seem to respond to me when I talk to him. So I have to ask him, 'Are you thinking or are you off somewhere else?' It took me a long time to realize that he really was thinking about what I was saying, but that he just wasn't the type to give any indication that he had heard. I had to wait a while before he would respond. His talk is not spontaneous. It might take me five minutes to get an answer. I used to get so exasperated, which only made him more withdrawn. Now we can have a real discussion if I wait for him to warm up."

If "telegrams" don't work, try writing a note.

Example: "I am 24 and pregnant with my fourth. I felt like I was dying from social isolation and lack of inspiration. We didn't have enough money for a baby-sitter, and my husband studied every night. He felt that this was my task in life and I should stop complaining. Normally, I would say, 'He's right. I'll adjust. I have no right to think of myself so selfishly. But the depressions got worse. Finally, I wrote him a letter saying that I had to have intellectual stimulation and contact with other NFs. I avoided my usual drama and accusations, such as 'You don't care about me! You only think of yourself!' I was very decisive and logical. The next day, after considering the letter, he told me that he would have his study-partner come to our house two nights a week instead of him going there, and also for us to go out together once a month."

*If you are an "F", it is important for you to practice going into a "T" modality when appropriate. Try phrases such as: "I want clear, precise instructions." "Give me time to think about an answer." Or, "I can't talk now. Let's make time to talk later."

* You might start feeling a little schizophrenic if you have to go into a different dominance for too long. When dealing with someone of a different dominance, don't fight the uncomfortable feelings which arise or condemn yourself for not being able to get along with everyone. Accept that you may feel frustrated, misunderstood, insulted or annoyed. Make sure that you "come back to yourself" afterwards with people who can understand you.

* Use that person's own language when communicating to a person of a different dominance.

Example: "One of the supervisors I teach under is an extremely stern, unintegrated SJ. After she observes me in the classroom, she usually has nothing but criticism, despite the fact that both the children and their parents love me. I tremble when she just walks into the room. It got so bad that I was thinking of quitting my job just to avoid her. Then I learned about the types and understood her need to see herself as right and to have everything structured and done according to her rules and regulations.

"So I started using her language. I keep telling her that she is right, that her observations are correct, and how important it is to be orderly and structured and follow the rules. I don't talk about creativity or individuality. Now, when she walks in the room, I still get uncomfortable physical sensations, but I don't feel so helpless. Even though I haven't done anything differently, the last time she came, she said that I had improved greatly!"

* Do not expect men to relate as women do, particularly "T" men. For example, when women talk, especially "F"s, they provide on-going feedback in the form of "Hm...," "Oh...," and "Yeah...." Men do not do this to the same extent. It may seem

that they are not paying attention. That may or may not be true. Check it out. If you are female, you might even want to say to a man, "Please say 'Hm' if you hear me so I know if you're listening." Most men are less comfortable than women with self-disclosure, except during courtship. So don't pry. Even dominant "F" men may have difficulty acknowledging the strength of their feelings - especially feelings of tenderness, rejection, hurt, or inadequacy.

* Learn from opposite types how to "empower" the non-dominant parts of yourself by using the vocabulary of that dominance:

Example: "I'm an NFP — not at all a fighter. I usually give up my desires and give in to make peace. But with children, you have to take the authoritarian role at times or they step all over you. Most of the time, I can find some non-coercive way to get them to cooperate. But when I need to be tough, I use 'J' language to arouse a decisive, authoritative quality. I tell them things like, 'You must control yourself now. Don't give in to your impulses. These are the rules and regulations. You must accept my authority.' This language really helps get myself under control, and that's the first step to getting the kids in line."

* Expect an SJ to check up on externals: your work, your looks, the appearance of your home, etc. Also, when "J"s give instructions, they often check up to see if their orders were carried out prefectly and precisely. If this checking makes you feel nervous and untrusted, it might be necessary to assertively tell the "J" that you are trustworthy and competent, and to stop the constant checking as it implies that you are a total idiot. If there is no way to avoid it, learn to bear the discomfort of that checking with good grace. Don't "buy" the conclusion that you are totally incompetent. Don't take the "checking" personally, as it may be a compulsion which the "J" does not know how to control and which he needs to make himself feel superior and secure. On the other hand, "J"s may want *you* to check up on them and may feel that you don't care if you do not do so!

On the other hand, the compulsion of insecure "F"s, may be to constantly check to see, "Do you really love me?" Expect an "F" to constantly check up on the state of the relationship, continually re-verifying whether or not he or she is still loved. If this bothers you, work out some way of reassuring them that you care.

* Remember that between 20 to 30% of the population has some degree of PSI. Eighty percent of this group is male. That means that such people, no matter what type, are more prone to aggression, feeling overwhelmed, anxious and disorganized, more likely to see rejection where it does not exist, more easily shattered by criticism, less able to tolerate frustration, and more fearful of taking control or giving it up. If a person comes from a physically or verbally abusive background, the same phenomena may result. Such people really do need more reassurance. (See *Raising Children To Care*, Ch. 13, for more on PSI and *EMETT*, for calming techniques).

* "T"s tend to go immediately for solutions when the "F" complains about something. This frustrates the "F", who just wanted a little sympathy and often feels put down when given pat advice. Teach them the "REACH" technique mentioned in *Raising Children To Care*: i.e., 1. Reflect, 2. Encourage, 3. Acceptance, 4. Consider choices and changes, 5. Hug or honor for sharing.

* The "P" may present some plan of action (E.g., "Let's start a school/open a new business/buy a house/quit my job"), but not have the imaginative skills to think ahead and consider all the possible problems which may arise. On the other hand, the "N" may be so immersed in all the possible problems that he gets paralyzed and never puts anything into action. If the "N" is also an "I" (introvert), then the tendency to leave plans in the realm of imagination and never bring them to fruition is even stronger.

Each can get angry, thinking that the other is being insensitive. The "N" can try to get the SP to consider possible obstacles — but in a factual, non-dramatic manner. The SP should also validate the "N"s' fears of possible problems, and recognize that his tendency to be impulsive or even irresponsible can make other types very nervous. If you are an insecure "F" and someone makes a proposal, don't be so pessimistic about the possible disasters which might occur. One NF put up a big sign saying, *"Expect the best. Learn to minimize disappointments."*

* If you think no one respects you, check your own self-esteem level. Lack of self-respect leads you to think that no one else respects you.

* One of the most difficult disciplines of all in relationships is to avoid making assumptions and conclusions about people's behavior. Check it out: "Did you slam the door because you are angry at me or frustrated about something else?" "Did you say that to hurt me on purpose, or did you not realize it would hurt?"

* Don't ever think that anyone is totally unfeeling. Every person has his own areas in which he feels inadequate. Everyone can be hurt.

Example: "My husband had just come home from the hospital after major surgery. I was very anxious about him and kept asking him if there was anything I could do for him. Every move he made got me anxious. Suddenly he said, 'You're making me feel very anxious and very inadequate.' Since he is a rather uncommunicative 'T', I was surprised at the fact that he would express these feelings. So I told him to take the initiative in asking for whatever he wanted, and that it would be helpful if he would reassure me periodically that he felt all right."

* Realize that people will have different priorities according to their dominance. Expect that what is important to you will not necessarily have the same level of importance to another. You get your greatest emotional "charge" on the things you value most. But others may not share that same excitement or displeasure.

Example: "I feel that it is extremely important to spend money on visits to family members who are spread around the country. Contact with them is a priority for me. I'd rather go without new clothes or other extras in order to be able to see them. But my husband, an introverted TJ, thinks letters and brief phone calls are sufficient. Instead of moping or getting hysterically angry at him, I now firmly express my need and my right to these infrequent visits and we come to some acceptable compromise."

* What may seem like a perfectly normal emotional response to you may seem like extreme, irrational emotionalism to others. Just because other people don't respond so emotionally does not necessarily mean that they are uncaring or insincere.

Example: "A 'T' relative had done something which really hurt my feelings. She made a brief and what seemed to me, an insincere apology. After that, I refused all her efforts to make up, because I figured that she would repeat the same hurtful behavior and so I didn't want to ever get close to her again. Then, one day she stopped by my home, and said, 'Look do you think that because I don't talk with your dramatic emotionalism that I wasn't sincere about my apology? O.K., I'll make the apology in your language.' Then, with great drama, like she was putting on a theatrical performance, she began to wail, 'Oh, how could I hurt you! Oy, I feel so terrible. I'm such an awful person. How can you ever forgive me?' She went on and on, repeating herself.

"I had to laugh to hear this relative, who is always so restrained, talk like this. Then I realized that I had misjudged her. She had felt bad about what had happened and was sincerely remorseful. But she was more solution-oriented than I. I wrongly interpreted her calm exterior as signifying that she didn't care. I would have saved myself a lot of heartache if I had realized this sooner."

*Confront real abuse. Even highly abusive people have just enough "niceness" and charm to convince themselves — and most of the people they encounter — that they really are nice people. Don't fall for that pretense. If you feel scared in someone's presence, and if that person is constantly critical of you, you are dealing with an abusive person, no matter how "nice" other people think he or she is. Take appropriate steps to protect yourself.

IF YOU ARE A "T" WITH AN "F" MATE
Before responding to your mate, think:
* "Does my response convey confidence in his/her ability to

manage? Or, do my words imply that my innermost belief that he/she is incompetent, untrustworthy, or stupid?"

* "Have I said anything encouraging or caring in the last few hours?" (E.g., "It's so nice to be home." "I'm lucky to have such a caring spouse." "You're doing a great job.")

* "When I see that he/she is upset, do I automatically turn off, treating him/her like a childish nuisance which I wish would disappear? Or, do I take time to listen or offer to help?"

* "Is he/she exaggerating and irrationally oversensitive? Or has he/she appropriately upset?"

* "Does he/she want "F" empathy or "T" solutions?"

IF YOU ARE AN "F" MATE OF A "T":
Whenever possible, before talking to your mate, think:

* "Is my dramatic expression overwhelming him/her and turning him off? Should I tone myself down in order to foster better communication?"

* "Is he/she in the mood to hear me right now, or is he/she preoccupied with other matters and will resent the interruption?"

* "Am I forgetting the 'total view' - that he/she is a really good person who does care, but is simply not demonstrative?"

* "Am I demanding that he/she change and become more like me rather than being accepting of what he/she is?"

* "Am I being excessively demanding because of laziness or fear of rejection?"

* "Am I making him/her responsible for my happiness and for giving me self-esteem instead of taking responsibility for my own fulfillment?"

* "Am I being overly self-sacrificing and then blaming my mate for my unhappiness and resentment?"

CODES
During peaceful times, it is very helpful for couples to work out codes to defuse potentially explosive situations. You might try the following statements:

"When I start screaming at the kids, don't scream back at me and tell me what a crazy hysteric I am. Remind me to look at the total view, that I'm a caring mother and doing a pretty good job considering the overwhelming circumstances. Then ask what you can do to help."

"When I'm depressed, don't tell me that I should snap out of it. Remind me that I have a tendency to condemn myself and that I need to focus on solutions. Help me to talk out what's bothering me."

"Don't be afraid to hear what I have to say. I'm not going to go nuts, even if that's what it looks like at the time. I just get overwhelmed and confused sometimes because everything affects me so deeply. Don't turn off when I get emotional. Have faith in me. I'll sort it out if you'll just give me time to express myself. Reassure me that you love me."

"When I'm down, don't get hysterical. Leave me alone and let me work things out."

If you are an "F", avoid giving an on-going recital of your physical and emotional aches and pains. It might also be helpful to warn your mate that you may exaggerate and get over-emotional at times, and not to be upset if these occurrences are infrequent.

RAISING YOUR TOLERANCE LEVEL

We have a *mitzvah* of not wasting food. An equally precious commodity is time. Two of the biggest time-wasters are condemning yourself and agonizing over others' deficiencies. People will never be all we want them to be. Nor will we ever be all we want ourselves to be. However, people do not improve from constant criticism. Instead, of highlighting the negative, focus on the positive.

If you are a very self-critical person (a strong tendency of both "N"s) and critical of others, it is helpful to write down the positive things you and those around you do. This is the atmosphere in which improvement is most likely to take place.

Example: "One of my teenagers was going through a very difficult time. He would snap at me, which of course, made me want to snap right back. Instead, I started to keep a list of the positive things he did, and whatever happy memories I could think of. I showed it to him at the end of the week. He was really flabbergasted that I would do that for him. We became much closer after that."

If your body is flabby and very out of shape, it's going to take time to improve your health and muscle tone. But you can't make yourself shorter or taller. Likewise, we cannot change our inborn propensities and talents, but every human being can improve his *middoth* no matter what his dominance. Each of us has hidden potential and strengths which can be released — *if* we are willing to work on ourselves.

Example: "I always thought of myself as a very weak, untogether, dependent person with no special talents. I never had much confidence. Then, in my mid-forties, I was suddenly widowed. I was devastated at first, but I had to start taking action to survive. I got a teaching job which I thought I was really unqualified for. Much to my surprise, the students loved me. I was forced to budget and keep the house more organized in order to get to work on time. I found hidden strengths, talents and courage that I had no idea I possessed, especially my 'J' managerial skills and inner strengths."

Example: "My husband has always been the strong, silent type who always had to be dominant and right. We had very little in common and very little communication. Then he had a heart attack. Suddenly, he wanted to do things together, wanted to get to know me and the children. It was amazing. I never thought he could care so much."

On the other hand, some people become less flexible and more unintegrated as time goes on. Just as the body stiffens, so can the mind, unless one makes a concerted effort to stay open-minded, tolerant and self-aware.

One factor which can always provide hope for integration and balance is the realization that, beneath every dominance is some percentage of the opposite mode which may be capable of being developed. The extent to which that is possible depends on how much natural ability exists in the first place, and how determined the person is to change.

Example: "I thought a certain relative was an unintegrated TJ — cold and uncaring. But when I had surgery, she was the one who helped the most, and was very kind and sympathetic. I even had the courage to share my feelings and the information in this book with her. She was very surprised. She said that she thought I had been the one who rejected her! After she read about the types, she identified herself as an insecure introverted Feeling type who fears taking the initiative and withdraws because of the fear of rejection. We became much closer after that."

PERCENTAGE OF EACH MODE DETERMINES OUR UNIQUENESS

No two human beings will ever have the exact same percentage of personality factors in their make-up. Intelligence, opportunities for development of skills, and religious training all make an enormous difference in how a person manifests himself.

Example: "I'm a strong NFP, with a lot of 'J' reliability and structure. In looking for a job, I had to find a 'J' principal who had enough 'P' that he would allow me a measure of independence in the classroom and would value my creativity."

Example: "Both my husband and I are strong SJs. We're both very strict about family rules and traditions. Our oldest daughter has a strong defiant SP nature. My husband, who has very little 'F', had no patience for her. He just wanted a 'tow-the-line' policy. Since I have more 'FP' in my personality, I was able to understand her point of view. I explained to him that she would be more accepting of his rules if he would first re—establish his relationship with her and allow her to express herself so that she knew he really cared about her."

DROP YOUR JUDGMENTS

Just because we are not as successful when using our non-dominant modes does not mean that we should avoid using them.

On the contrary, we must develop all eight modes to the best of our ability, while remaining respectful of our limitations.

Example: "As a dominant 'F', I used to hate the fact that I would get so flooded with feelings almost all the time, and also that I give in so easily and don't stand up for myself. That always made me feel stupid and incompetent. But I accept this now and give myself more time to get my thoughts organized. That might mean that I now tell people, 'I'll think about it,' instead of giving an immediate answer. Or, I get my ideas down on paper, which helps me to get my ideas across logically and with less emotion."

Example: "When I dropped my condemnations of myself, I finally accepted that I needed a maid. This was after years of hating myself for not being able to match my incredibly competent extraverted SFJ neighbor who can cook up a storm for twenty people at a moment's notice, and have the house in perfect order even with eleven children. Plus, she gives so much to the community. Finally, I accepted that organization is her right hand, while it's my left. I used to think that the reason I didn't manage as well as she does is because I was fundamentally lazy, selfish and stupid. Having a maid seemed to be announcing that fact to the whole world! But I did it anyway. The first maid didn't work out because she had such a sad life. I felt so sorry for her that I didn't have the heart to make her do all the work that needed to be done. The second took advantage of me, like coming late and leaving early and not doing what I asked her to do, and then demanding more than we had agreed on. I didn't have the guts to say anything because she was so tough that I was afraid she would bite my head off if I complained. The third came and, when I showed her around, she kept grimacing and making remarks like, 'Boy, you sure do need a good cleaning here. When was the last time you cleaned?' My house isn't that bad! I didn't need someone who would intimidate me and make me feeling even more incompetent! On the fourth try, I found someone nice, but not talkative and who likes to work hard and doesn't criticize me!"

Example: "My SFP husband must often drive long distances at

night because of his job. I wanted him to get life insurance.
Typically, he kept insisting that nothing would happen. At first,
I put myself down for not being more secure, and resented him for
what I saw as a lack of responsibility, (but which he saw as lack of
emunah). But now that I understand myself, I accept that I have
insecurities and, as an insecure 'F', I get strong emotional
responses. Instead of feeling ashamed of my needs, I went with
him to a Rav and explained that I have difficulty handling all the
anxiety that these trips generate, and that anything which would
decrease my fears and give me a greater sense of reassurance was
important for my mental health. When the Rav heard this, he told
my husband to get the insurance. I felt so relieved. I do work
more on faith, but being an NF, I may never achieve my
husband's natural, indomitable SP optimism."

CHAPTER XII:
GETTING HEALTHY

One of the lessons of the year of *shmittah*, when one's land remains untouched, is that it is important to periodically shake ourselves loose from our habitual patterns of thought and behavior. In the case of *yovel*, we are to let go of both the corrupting influences of power (in the hands of the land owners) as well as of powerlessness (represented by the slaves) which are suddenly uprooted. Both groups get a "shaking up." The secure foundations and the stable support systems are suddenly broken, allowing for an expansion in consciousness and a change in their relationships with G-d and man.

After reading the previous chapters, you may have experienced a shaking up in your own psyche, and in the way you have been seeing yourself and other people. But what do you do with your new awareness? We know that change is necessary, for stagnation is death. But *shmittah* teaches us that it takes tremendous courage and self-discipline to let go of the familiar, even if loyalty to the known means slavery to negative attitudes and destructive behaviors.

For example, let's say that you now realize that you are a "P" with a tendency to get side-tracked and to fight keeping commitments. You now know that to balance yourself, you need to do what the Rambam said and go to the "opposite extreme," i.e., sticking to schedules and living up to your promises. Or, as an overly reserved and shy "I", that you have to start being more outgoing and less self-conscious. You now have the awareness. But the next step is more difficult: making real changes in your life.

OVERCOMING INERTIA

Every change involves a difficult initial transition period. There is always the impulse to do what is familiar. It requires a tremendous act of will to overcome the force of inertia which has been built up over the years. Furthermore, one must also overcome the mental programming which tells you, "You can't do it. It's too hard. It's just not you. You don't really need it." Thus, people say, "I'm hot tempered," or "I'm just an unhappy person." They lose sight of the fact that there are many traits which can and must be changed.

As time goes on, people tend to become "comfortable" with their defects and less prone to changing them. As a matter of fact, it seems almost "right" that things should be this way.

"To those who are sick in body, the bitter tastes as if it were sweet, and the sweet as if it were bitter. Among the sick, some yearn for things unfit for food, such as earth and charcoal, and others have an aversion to wholesome foods, like bread and meat, the perversity depending on the severity of the illness. Similarly, human beings whose souls are sick love evil dispositions, and hate the right way, and are too lazy to walk on the correct path, and find it extremely difficult to do the right thing because of their sickness. Of such people Yishayahu says, 'Oh, they that say of evil that it is good, and of good that it is evil, that turn darkness into light and light into darkness, who take bitter for sweet and sweet for bitter.'" (*Hilchoth Deoth*, 2:1, and *Yishayahu* 5:20)

An unintegrated "J", for example, not only feels comfortable being arrogantly self-righteous and miserly, but actually comes to feel that this is the only right, noble and even "holy" way to be, and so twists numerous passages in *Chazal* to support his stern and serious mein. The negative "T" not only wants to be emotionally detached, but actually prides himself on his coldness and indifference. He too twists various numerous passages in *Chazal* to support his lack of concern or involvement in human affairs, and ignores those which demand the opposite. The people-pleasing NFs may think it is right and holy to allow themselves to be exploited and manipulated and not speak up about it, but rather to suffer in silence."

In other words, not only is change difficult, it is difficult to even "see" that change is necessary or possible.

CHANGING

Anyone who has been through a radical life change involving great self-sacrifice and self-discipline, such as those who have become *ba'alai tshuvah*, know that the process of integrating new information into one's mind and making that information a reality is a long-term one, even though the outer trappings can be adopted in a few seconds. You learn a lot of lessons about human psychology each time you go against an old habit pattern. For example:

* Sometimes the only way G-d can get us to do what we need to do is to bring some pain into our lives. Back pain and heart problems force some people to exercise. High blood pressure forces others to diet or turn to Torah study for calm. The feeling of emptiness and meaninglessness brings many non-Observant Jews to Orthodoxy. Often, a marital crisis is the one factor which finally forces someone to work on controlling anger or getting involved in community activities to overcome a depression.

* We can use every painful situation to either raise ourselves up, or we can be dragged down. After all, the person with a bad back can just stay in bed, immersed in depressive self-pity, and allow the muscles to get progressively weaker, or he can start an exercise program. When you are in the presence of a difficult family member, you can be sucked into a whirlpool of hatred. At the same time, that very person can force you to work on yourself in order to rise above your negative response. It may impel you to

turn to G-d for solace. The choice is completely in our hands, and, to be more exact, our minds as well.

Example: "A neighbor was very rude to me in the elevator. I used this as an opportunity to avoid emotionalizing minor events, something which is very difficult for me, a strong 'F' who tends to emotionalize *everything*. I adopted the position of an objective newspaper reporter, noticing the situation, jotting down all the particulars in my mind, but not getting emotionally involved. He is a very elderly man who has suffered a great deal. So I worked on compassion for him instead of focusing on my feelings. Now, I almost welcome these uncomfortable situations as opportunities to overcome my tendency to be shattered by criticism and to sink into resentment, hostility and bitterness."

* Adopting the external positive habits, even if they feel insincere or uncomfortable, helps to eventually arouse internal positivity. Not every *ba'al tshuvah* feels immediately comfortable with more modest clothing. But wearing such dress arouses an awareness of and an appreciation for the concept of modesty. Likewise, most people do not enjoy the first few minutes of physical exercise. However, as you become more involved in healthy activities, your body wants to continue.

Example: "I was furious at my children for leaving the kitchen a mess. But I held my tongue and thought of the word 'SOLUTIONS.' I kept telling myself to think only of what would be useful, rather than just venting my anger. First, I gave them the benefit of the doubt. Then I told them how I felt and what I wanted them to do. I was frustrated about the situation, but not hateful toward them. That made a big difference in how I spoke to them."

It is often extremely difficult to be patient, loving, silent, or assertive. However, an insincere pretense or gesture of positivity will eventually awaken the sincere feelings if you persist. In the midst of those inevitable dark moments which we all must go through, any act of self-discipline (either restraining oneself from doing something harmful, or forcing oneself to do something difficult), will kindle some degree of light:

"If a man consecrates himself in a small measure down below, he is sanctified much more from above." (*Yoma* 39a)

* There will always be obstacles in the way of change. You will always have a number of good excuses not to change. Think how deprived you'll feel if you don't eat that piece of cake. Think of all the time it takes to get to an exercise class. Think of all the "pleasures" you give up if you become Observant. A little voice will make you question, "Maybe I don't really have to do this.... Maybe it's not really necessary... Maybe it's the wrong choice...."

Example: "When a certain person gave us bad advice which caused us to lose a lot of money, I was very bitter. The last thing I wanted to do was give the benefit of the doubt. It was like breaking through a wall of concrete in my own mind to overcome my condemnations of him. But I kept forcing myself to drop my judgments for the sake of my mental health."

* Be happy with baby steps and "endorse" for whatever you do manage to accomplish. It is important not to compare yourself to those who are already experts in whatever it is you want to accomplish. Otherwise, you'll get discouraged. Use the experts as role models, but don't compare yourselves to others if it produces a sense of despair.

* If you want to encourage change, make even the most minor act of self-discipline into a major victory. "Endorse" for every baby step you make toward balance.

Example: "My husband is an extremely introverted 'T'. I feel like a dentist when I talk to him — getting him to talk is like pulling teeth. My tendency is to give up in hostile silence. But I plug away, endorsing him whenever he opens up a bit, and praying that he will want more as time goes on."

Example: "As a very dominant SJ, I have many strict rules. For example, I have a firm principle that children must go to school unless they have a temperature. Well, last week, my ten year old daughter didn't feel well, but she also didn't have a temperature. Our relationship has been pretty bad lately since she's the oldest and I'm about to have my seventh child. She's been very angry at me, resenting all the extra work I've asked her to do.

"Because I am trying to balance myself, I did something totally out of character. I went against a rule and let her stay home from school that day. We baked and talked and felt good about each other again. I'm glad I realized that it was all right to balance myself by allowing the SP part of myself to be expressed: to have more pleasurable activities with my children, to have a smile on my face more often and to make relationships more important than my rules."

Example: "As an introvert, it is not easy for me to express myself. But I decided to *do the difficult* and ask my boss for a raise. He hasn't answered yet, but I'm proud of myself for going against my old habit pattern and doing something I feared to do."

* It is very exciting to engage in the process of overcoming a bad habit.

Example: "I was hit a lot as a child, so that's what came naturally to me. But as my children got older, I found that they were getting more and more violent with each other. The other day, my five year old very active SP did something which really annoyed me. I was going to give him a real hard smack. Instead, I used the same energy to give him a really hard hug. I told him I was squeezing the 'baddies' out, and he should tell me when to stop. I thought I was hurting him, and part of me wanted to, but he loved it. The more I hugged him, the calmer and more loving I felt toward him. I asked if all the 'baddies' were out and he said, 'No, squeeze some more.' That's when I realized that what he really needed was a lot of physical contact. It calms us both down. It's still sometimes very hard for me to overcome the impulse to hit, but I'm getting more control over myself all the time. I feel more self-respecting and we are better off for being more disciplined."

Example: "I have one grandchild, aged five, who has PSI (See *Raising Children To Care*). He is hypersensitive, hostile and wild, and cries hysterically if he doesn't get his way. A few days ago, he was visiting with his sweet and calm SJ sister, a year older. They were playing a game, and all of a sudden he started to get hysterical. When I tried to calm him down, he started hitting me.

As an 'NF', I immediately pick up on his feelings. Usually, I get so hurt and insulted myself that I cannot think of a creative solution. But this time, instead of getting sucked in to his negative state, I kept my center. I responded in a firm, but caring voice. I told him, 'I will not speak to you until you go into my bedroom and calm down.' I spoke softly yet sternly. I was surprised that he listened to me and came out a few minutes later and said, 'I'm calm now.' This was a major victory for us both."

Example: "I had surgery six weeks ago, and I still don't feel very good. I often wake up depressed and go into a panic during the day, fearing that maybe I won't ever get well. It takes everything in my power to put on a smile so that I don't upset my family members. It takes tremendous will power to push myself to function and not to fantasize negatively about the future. Now I get a pleasurable feeling of pride in my ability to carry on despite my pain."

Most of our most serious efforts to overcome our negative *middoth* will never be noticed by anyone, especially the disciplines of the mind, such as avoiding condemnations. Only we can "celebrate" these inner victories which take so much courage and love. And celebrate we must, for this is how we create new habit patterns and retain our sense of "O.K.ness" in the midst of pain:

"The smallest victory that you win [over the *yetzer hara*] regard as important so that it may be to you a step to a greater victory." (*Duties of the Heart*, vol. 2, p. 23)

Example: "All my life, I've been obsessed with what people think of me and overly concerned with making a good impression. The other day, wealthy relatives came to visit and I started to feel ashamed of our relative poverty. But I stopped the negativity by reminding myself that I have choices of what to think. I have made certain sacrifices in order for my husband, a very intelligent NT, to be able to learn full time. I kept focusing my mind on my priorities - i.e., doing G-d's will - until the uncomfortable feelings faded."

Example: "I've had problems with depression ever since my last child was born. Then, when I read this manuscript, I realized that maybe I'm suppressing some creative talent. I began to think back to when I was a teenager, and I realized that I had given up on all the things which used to make me feel alive. My spirit had diminished without those activities. As soon as I started actively making plans to do those things again, my mood lifted. I even enjoy my children more and don't mind doing all the household chores as much. No one but me will ever know what courage and determination it took to get myself out of that rut."

* A positive habit is as powerful as a negative one. If you have never prayed with a *minyon* each morning, you will find that it is not always easy to drag yourself out in freezing cold winter rains or bear the discomfort of stuffy crowds in the summer's heat. But if you do it regularly, then even when you wake up with the thought, "I just can't do it, I feel too awful today," some inner magnet will pull you, as if you are being led by a force greater than yourself. You will pray when it feels mechanical and when personal problems divert your attention from the words. A person with a regular schedule will find that even when he doesn't want to do that particular act, his body will push him to do it anyway. The same is true of the person who makes it a habit to judge others favorably. Even when the condemnations are filling his mind to the bursting point, he will be able to calm himself down by finding some merit for that irritating child or unpleasant adult.

* Positive habits must be engraved on the psyche over a period of time. You can get used to criticizing just as easily as you can get used to reaching for a cigarette after a meal. We all do our own engraving. It's our choice — sick thoughts and actions or healthy ones.

* Ignore the initial resistance when you start to change a habit pattern. People get excited about change, but many abandon their resolutions because their feelings drag them back to what is comfortable. Expect that you might feel nervous, angry, tense, inadequate, stupid, trapped, afraid, rebellious, or discouraged at first. Ignore those feelings. Do what you know to be healthy.

Example: "I'm a very unassertive, 'F' people-pleaser, always concerned about other people's needs and feelings. I tend to assume that it's all my fault when things go wrong, that I don't know how to explain myself and have no right to make demands. I thought I would just die the first time I said to someone in a very assertive voice, 'What you just said hurt me. I get tied up in knots when you talk to me.' Once I started being more assertive, it became easier and I felt much better about myself."

* It will require constant "acts of will" to go against deeply ingrained bad habits or a strong dominance. Do not expect that resistance can ever be completely overcome. The establishment of good habits requires constant, on-going discipline: doing that which is difficult; doing the very things which we fear to do. All change requires courage and involves taking risks; after all, you might get rejected or fail or make a fool out of yourself. But if you are not willing to take that risk, you won't grow.

Example: "I'm a very critical person. My tendency is to *pasul* [invalidate] someone the minute there is a difference of opinion or the person does not meet my standards. It is an act of will every time I avoid condeming and arouse compassion in my heart."

* Remember, "The mind is shaped by actions." (*Sefer Ha'chinuch*, Precept 16) In other words, by doing something positive, even if you do not feel like doing it, even if it feels phoney and insincere, you awaken a real desire for that which is good and healthy.

Example: "I'm a strong 'P'. I want to do things on whim, whenever I feel like it, according to my mood. It takes great effort for me to make up a schedule and stick to it. But I know that this is the only way to get things done."

THE MOST PERNICIOUS HABIT OF ALL

Change requires that the *will* be stimulated into action. But there is one thought pattern which, more than all others, paralyzes the will and floods you with a sense of discouragement. That thought is: "I'm a failure. I don't deserve any better." With those thoughts in your mind, you cannot really live or love fully.

This is a major problem for "N"s, who have a tendency toward self-criticism, especially if combined with "I" (introversion).

How do you get rid of a failure or "victim mentality"? First, realize that this thought is mental *traife*. Thinking it is just like eating *traife*, because thinking badly of yourself keeps you from being a self-respecting and loving human being.

You must deal with destructive thoughts the same way you deal with unkosher food which someone might offer you: i.e., you tell yourself, "This is bad for me. If I 'eat' this thought, I cut myself off from G-d. If I 'eat' this thought, I cannot do what I came into this world to do, which is to be a loving, humane being."

Unfortunately, if you were brought up in a critical household, then you have acquired this "language" of self-denigration as "naturally" as you acquired your mother tongue. Even if you want very much to learn the language of self-nurturance, you may find that it is difficult at first to remember the words and phrases, and that you must wage a battle to rid yourself of your strong "accent" (i.e., your tendency to put yourself down) just like any immigrant to a new country.

CHANGING YOUR PAIN LEVEL

If you had a physically or verbally abusive parent, then you are used to a lot of pain. Let's say that during your childhood, the chaos and contempt level in your home was about "8" on a scale of zero to ten. As you got older, you unconsciously tried to keep that pain level rather constant, because that is what is familiar. So, even if you're having a wonderful time and things are going well, you'll keep the pain level high by doing one of three things:

a) dredging up mistakes, pains and failures of the past,

b) fantasizing negatively about the future,

c) condemning yourself or those around you for not being more perfect.

Thus, you might be at a park or a party, washing dishes or making a meal, and you start thinking, "It's not going to last. I'm going to have to pay for this pleasure with some suffering." "I don't deserve this, because the truth is that I'm a terrible, bad person." Or, instead of enjoying the moment, you're thinking, "I feel good now, but things will probably be awful when I get older," or some such thought which keeps you from enjoying the moment.

To maintain a hostile or depressed state of mind, you must use your mental filter to screen out all the good that does exist in yourself and in the people around you. Instead of endorsing yourself for how well you're doing, you will constantly complain about all that you haven't accomplished. Instead of appreciating people for who they are, you will be full of condemnations and complaints against them for not doing better. In other words, you don't let yourself be really happy or loving. Understandably, you don't get close to anyone because, having been burnt so often by rejection in the past, you are sure that you are going to get hurt in the future.

But you are an adult now. G-d wants us to serve Him with joy in our hearts (*Devarim* 21:47). And the first place to begin having a closer, more loving connection with Him is by creating a nurturing environment in your mind, giving the benefit of the doubt, being a more understanding and caring person towards others, as well as towards yourself. What you choose to think about is what will most influence your emotional state.

The language of nurturance is:

"I made a mistake. I'll do better next time." (Not, "I'm a total failure." "I'm hopeless.")

"It's all right if I'm just muddling through instead of managing superbly. At least I'm putting forth my best effort in these trying circumstances."

"I said something stupid. That's pretty average. It happens to everyone." (Not, "No one else is so stupid. I'm a total idiot. I always say the wrong thing.")

"I have basic strengths which have always pulled me through difficulties and which will pull me through in the future." (Not, "I'm a psychological basket case. It's just a matter of time before I go completely bonkers.")

"I'm a basically good person with a lot to offer the world."

(Not, "Basically, I'm awful. I'm a burden on everyone. I have nothing to offer anyone.")

"I'm not trapped. I always have options." (Not, "There's no use in even trying. I can't do it. I don't have the self-control.")

"I chose to be depressed/angry this morning by thinking depressing/angry thoughts." (Not, "I got depressed/angry. The feelings just descended on me out of nowhere. I'm a helpless victim of these moods. I don't have any choice about how I feel.")

Just as you are stringent about not letting non-kosher food into your home, you can be just as strict about not letting non-kosher thoughts into your mind. It takes the same sense of discipline and purpose to do both.

Example: "Every year, a certain relative comes to visit for two weeks. And every year, I'm sick with diarrhea and insomnia from the time I get her letter until she leaves. Why? Because nothing I do is right in her eyes: The kids should have better manners; They should eat at the table instead of running around; I don't give them enough attention; I give them too much attention; I don't toilet train them early enough. I work too hard; I waste food; I don't budget properly.... The list is endless. Each and every thing is a veritable crime.

"As an NF, I'm so suggestible to everything she says. I take in all the negativity, and try to be so accommodating and try so hard to please and be sympathetic to her. I want harmony so badly that I don't speak up. As an 'I', I tend to withdraw instead of standing up for myself. But I had to do the difficult and do the thing I feared most, which was to protect myself and my children. So this year, when she started with all her advice and criticism, which she feels is only constructive and honest, I told her that I am working at creating a nurturing environment in the home, and that her comments and grimaces were paralyzing me. She was astonished and enraged. She had no idea what I was talking about. She is convinced that she is right. But each time she made a comment, I asked her to think about whether or not it was a nurturing statement. I didn't tell her that she was being critical. She would not have accepted that. I just asked questions, asked her to consider her words and their effect.

"At first, she became very hostile over the fact that she couldn't just say anything she wanted. She felt terribly rejected. As a 'J', she sees it as her mission to go around reforming people. Well, I've got a lot of 'J' too, and I'm using that part of myself to be protective and stick to my principle of creating a safe environment in my home — and in my head as well."

You must be just as tough about creating a positive atmosphere in your head. It is the foundation of mental health. Like any language, the more you talk it, the more comfortable and natural it will become. [A very helpful book for learning the language of confidence and nurturance is *Talk Sense To Yourself*, By Chick Moorman]

LIVING WITH THE PAIN OF RELATIONSHIPS AND LIFE

Some degree of pain is involved in most relationships, since we can never satisfy others' desires or demands completely. In addition, we all must cope with disturbed people in our homes, workplaces, or offices. Furthermore, if you are an NF, you will have a higher degree of existential pain in your life than other types. You feel everything more deeply. Man's inhumanity bothers you more. You cannot escape the deeper questions about the meaning of events and the purpose of life. Don't think the pain shouldn't be there or that there is something wrong with you that you feel things so deeply. That's the price you pay for being an NF.

However, you can lower your pain level tremendously by cultivating your ability to evaluate situations in a way which makes them meaningful in terms of growth. This will bring you in touch with the other side of the NF coin: i.e., your potential for experiencing great depth of joy and love.

An outstanding example of the power of attitude is given in the book *Israel Legends*, by Rabbi Dr. S. Z. Kahana and edited by Leo Gartenberg. The story called "The Sukkoth of Reb Ahrele" in particular, shows the power of attitude. To synopsize:

Rebbi Mendel Mezakritim and his friend, Reb Ahrele, were in a concentration camp the night before Sukkoth, 1943, when word spread that there would be a "selection" in two days. That is, those who were still healthy would be set aside for forced labor while the weak ones would go to the gas chambers. Reb Mendel was still strong, but Reb Ahrele resembled a skeleton. He refused to eat any of the camp food because it was cooked by non-Jews. Instead, he subsisted on potato peels. While Reb Mendel was sunk in sad contemplation of the next day, Reb Ahrele entered his room, also looking very perturbed. Reb Mendel thought it was because of the selection. With tears in his eyes, Reb Ahrele said that it was not the selection he was worried about, but rather how he could celebrate Sukkoth without erecting a Sukkah or obtaining the Four Species.

They parted and did not meet until the next evening, when Reb Mendel saw Reb Ahrele, whose face radiated with joy. Taking hold of Reb Mendel in ecstasy, Reb Ahrele exclaimed that he had figured everything out. He said:

"Reb Mendel, do you see the clouds of smoke ascending from the furnaces where our fellowmen are being burned? Aren't these 'clouds of glory' a Sukkah? G-d wishes us to fulfill the mitzvah of Sukkah with such clouds of glory. Formerly we were privileged to invite guests.... This year...all that is left to us is 'to rejoice before the L-rd our G-d.' And this we will do. I have even solved the problem of the Four Species. When a man holds the *Arba Minim*, he takes, as it were, G-d unto himself, for each of the species...symbolizes and reflects G-d. This year, we have turned the tables by bringing ourselves nearer to Him. For the spine of man is compared to a Lulav, the eye to the Myrtle, the mouth to the Willow and the heart to the Ethrog. Shall I not rejoice with such a celebration of Sukkoth?"

The next morning, they were lined up for the selection. Reb Mendel arranged to stand next to Reb Ahrele, hoping to shield him. Reb Ahrele's eyes still shone with joy, as they did the day before when he had told him how he was going to celebrate the festival. The only problem was the *ethrog*. He worried that his heart might be considered broken, and hence not a perfect *ethrog*. But he contented himself by repeating the words of Rabbi Aaron of Karlin, who said, "Nothing in the world is as perfect as a broken heart."

When the Nazi butchers thrust Reb Ahrele to the left, Reb Mendel's heart was rent with grief. The last words he heard of Reb Ahrele were, "'And ye shall rejoice before the L-rd your G-d.'"

The lesson: We all have unfulfilled desires. Some of us are broken hearted over various losses. But in the midst of pain, we can be grateful that G-d has given us hundreds of *mitzvoth* on which to concentrate. There is always something new to learn. There is always work on our *middoth*.

In other words, what we focus on determines our emotional state.

One of my "heroes" is a young woman of twenty-eight, named Sari. Sari is dying slowly of muscular dystrophy. Every few months, as her condition worsens, she comes to my husband, an engineer, for new adjustments on the car he built for her so that she could drive despite her extremely weakened condition.

While he works on the car, we sit and talk. I always ask her how she manages to go on, knowing what faces her in the future, knowing that she can never have the children she so desperately wants and, recently, having had to give up the job she loved as a teacher of learning disabled children because of the hospitalizations which have become more frequent.

The last time she visited, I wrote down Sari's response:

"First, I'm not afraid to feel whatever I feel. Sometimes I get depressed, really really depressed. I don't fight it. I know that sooner or later, it will be over. I allow myself to feel how sad it is - for me, for my parents and friends.... I go through dark times. Everything looks so bleak and black. I move through the day as though I'm in a thick fog. But I keep going, keep up my usual activities to the best of my ability. I don't let myself just lie in bed crying. Then one day, the darkness begins to lift and I'm O.K. again. It happens over and over again.

"Second, I force myself to find things to appreciate - the flowers, the sky, whatever.... Two years ago, the daughter of my parents' friends got cancer at the age of twelve. We became very close when we were both in the hospital together. I talked to her a lot. We encouraged each other. She died last month. But I still think about our conversations and how close we were, and it makes me happy to know that I helped her a little."

She looked at me and smiled, her thin face framed by her short blond hair, and I saw that that frail body contained great courage and strength.

Sari's lessons are the same for us all:

1) Be honest about your feelings.

2) Don't condemn the feelings which arise spontaneously, or judge yourself for having them. We all feel jealous, mean, hostile, discouraged, etc. at times. Let the feelings be. Don't fight them. But do work on your attitude, especially trust and gratefulness.

3) Trust: Trust that G-d is with you at all times, and that He has given you this test in order to force you to work on particular *middoth*, such as *emunah*, determined perseverence, self-discipline, or silence. Trust your inner strengths to pull you through the dark times.

4) Appreciate whatever is good and noble and beautiful in your life.

5) Feel the pain of your unfulfilling relationships. But don't get stuck in it. Don't forget to move on.

If you have a chronic, painful situation, do not let it take over all your thoughts. Think of your life as a piece of paper. Allow this painful situation or relationship to take up a small space in one corner. The minute it starts to spread out and threatens to take over your life, push it back again and go back to focusing on all the other important things you have to do with your thoughts and your actions. Joining a support group of other people with similar difficulties is strongly recommended.

MARITAL FRUSTRATION
Even the best of marriages have ups and downs. Even our

saintly Biblical couples did not see eye-to-eye. Nor were they always able to work out their problems by frank and honest communication. There are countless incidents which point out their differences in perception and feelings: e.g., Sarah forced Avraham to cast Hagar and Yishmael out (*Bereshith* 21:10-11)); Rivka had to resort to deceptive tactics because she felt Yitzachak did not "see" what was going on with Esav (*Bereshith* 27); Chana went on a hunger strike when she felt that Elkanah did not fully understand the depth of her grief at being barren (*Sh'muel I). And these were saintly men and women, with prophetic wisdom and insight. How much more so does the average couple suffer from differences in perception.*

Then there are the inevitable differences in middoth: the responsible, motivated, kind person married to one who is unambitious, lazy, and critical; the sensitive one married to someone who is mean and tyrannical; the orderly one married to someone who is unreliable and sloppy.

An inescapable fact of life is that there will never be enough "F" men for all the "F" women. Even "F" men may not want to relate to their "F" wives as the latter might want. Furthermore, many men simply never have the opportunity to develop "F" skills, since their work usually does not call for the development of emotional sensitivity. Indeed, such sensitivity may even be a handicap in many lines of work. This means that women will have to develop more "T" skills and to be sources of nurturance and encouragement for each other.

"N"s and "F"s find themselves in a kind of emotional or intellectual Siberia, unable to share with their spouses, because they know that the spouses will misconstrue their words and fail to pick up on the deeper meaning of what is being said.

"F"s are grieved if they cannot achieve the "best friend" ideal which they would like. Many describe their situations thus:

"I feel like I'm being buried alive in words, trying to get my spouse to understand, trying to explain what should be so simple to understand."

"I am so frustrated. It's easier to just act numb and not to talk about anything than to try to get through, knowing it will take so long and be so complicated and end up in misunderstanding anyway. Don't get me wrong — he/she's a good person. But it does feel so lonely sometimes."

"He/she says that as far as he/she is concerned, everything is just fine and if I want to go to a counselor, I should go. It makes me feel that something's wrong with me that I'm so unsatisfied."

Even worse is the person married to someone who is deliberately abusive.

There are no happily-ever-after solutions to these problems. Many times, all one can do, like Reb Ahrele and Sari, is focus on how these situations can be used as opportunities for the development of courage and determination. Every painful situation is an impetus to work on ourselves. One's mind and one's life need not be barren, even if one's significant relationships are unsatisfying.

If you have a partner with whom you have difficulty communicating or feeling close to, a part of you might always be in mourning. Part of Sari is always in mourning too. So are her parents. But they go on.

If we could have chosen otherwise, we would certainly have chosen that our relationships with family members and neighbors be characterized by warmth, consideration, mutual respect, appreciation and understanding of our deepest needs. We would certainly not have chosen to live with, or even come in contact with, people who are inconsiderate, insensitive, irresponsible, mean, cold or tyrannical.

Yet G-d, in His infinite wisdom, knows what we need, as opposed to what we want. And so He brings various difficult people into our midst in order for us to recognize what we must work on and force us to face it. Each person offers us the opportunity to balance ourselves, and to work on our kosher "M & Ms" - our mitzvoth and middoth: practicing giving rebuke with love, giving the benefit of the doubt, being less influenced by other people and their negativity, developing inner resources and strengths, and fighting for Torah values.

Eventually, after all the tears, you come to a realization that it doesn't help to brood about the fact that you didn't get all you wanted. If G-d wanted, He could have provided everyone with more compatible mates. He could have given us all financial security, just as He sustained us with manna. Obviously, having to struggle to confront our areas of weakness and overcome them is the inner jewel hidden within each loss and disappointment.

Rav Bachya Ibn Paquda discusses two reasons for Hashem denying us our wishes:

"First, Divine wisdom deems it necessary to test the disposition of an individual's soul, as to whether it will serve Him or rebel against Him. An individual's tendency to obedience or transgression will become manifest by his intent as well as by his choice of means, either those permitted or those forbidden....

"Secondly, if a human being had no need to work hard...he would become arrogant...and would pay no attention to the [gratitude] owed G-d." (*Chovoth Ha'l'vavoth* "Sha'ar Habitachon", Ch. 3)

In other words, every painful event offers us the choice: to sink into destructive thoughts and actions or to come closer to G-d. Those who work on their *middoth* know that when we struggle against obstacles, we see our greatness as well as our weaknesses. Every time you avoid the easy way out by ignoring a problem or giving in to your dominant mode when that mode is inappropriate, is a victory to be celebrated. Obviously, G-d wants us to be happy, for He gives us plenty of opportunities to celebrate!

CHAPTER XIII: THE SIXTEEN TYPES

Reb Zusha was once quoted as saying: "When I get to *olam habah* [the world to come] I will not be asked why I did not achieve the greatness of Moshe Rabenu. I will be asked why I did not achieve the greatness of Reb Zusha."

Each of us has some inner greatness, something special to give to the world. Sadly, we often do not see who we are or what we have to offer. The result is great unhappiness which is often manifest as depression or anger against others, particularly one's mate or parents, as if others are solely responsible for our dissatisfaction. Yet the fact is that the search for our unique way of manifesting ourselves is really our own task. No one can do it for us. Perhaps the following will help readers to accept who they are, and give them courage to be all they are capable of being.

The following descriptions are, for the most part, summarized from *Please Understand Me*. Note that they describe the most intelligent, talented and positive types of people in each category. Obviously, many people never develop their skills or fulfill their potential.

Also, the percentages are given for the American population. It can be assumed that the Jewish population has a larger percentage of "N"s and that Torah observance greatly enhances the "J" aspect of the personality.

It is understood that most women in the Observant community will be devoted mainly to home-making skills and that most men will be devoted mainly to Torah studies. However, for those who, for various financial or personal reasons, cannot do so, these descriptions will provide a direction in terms of possible vocations. In addition, those who are able to devote themselves to full-time home-making or study will be able to identify where their areas of expertise lie, providing them with a realistic self-appraisal and realistic expectations of themselves.

ENFJ: THE HARMONIZER & CARETAKER (5% of general population)

* "E" means that this type is out-going and sociable.

* "NF" means that they have a depth of psychological sensitivity, reading people's motivations and intentions with unusual accuracy.

* "F" means that they are very caring (and handle people with charm and concern). "E" means that they are usually well liked and popular.

* As "J"s, they are organized, like to plan ahead, and like to have things settled and decided. They assume that others will follow their advice, suggestions and rules.

* People turn to them for nurturance and support, which they usually get. But ENFJs may feel so excessively responsible for others that they may feel inappropriately guilty if they cannot be available at all times to all people. With their strong empathetic ability combined with an inability to disconnect emotionally, they tend to over-extend themselves.

* They place a high value on cooperation from others; they count on it and expect it, and themselves are willing to cooperate. Like all "F"s, they need positive feedback and reassurance.

* They are optimistic about people's potential, sometimes so much so that it hurts them deeply when people do not actualize that potential. People may feel so ashamed of their inability to

live up to the ENFJ's ideals that they prefer to stay away.

* Communication is their strong point. They have a remarkable fluency in speaking and writing, and, therefore, are influential and do not hesitate to speak out.

* They are deeply devoted to their children, yet are not domineering or critical.

* They can be victimized by mates or others who take advantage of their goodness and become more and more demanding of them. They have unrealistic expectations of their ability to please others and feel inappropriately guilty if they are not able to satisfy everyone's demands.

* As a "J", this type is parental and conservative, accepting of rules and regulations.

INFJ: THE INNOVATIVE VISIONARY (1% of general population)

* "I" means that they are more private, territorial, reserved, intense and focused on internal reactions.

* They come to decisions quite easily. ("J")

* They have great depth of personality and can understand and deal with complex issues and people. ("N")

* They are tremendously empathetic. (NF) They are sometimes aware of a person's emotions and intentions even before the person is aware of them himself.

* Psychic abilities may manifest in the form of visions, premonitions, auditory and visual images of things to come. ("N")

'* Like other "I"s, they are not ostentatious and have a rich inner life, but are reserved and tend not to share their reactions except with those few whom they trust.

* They have complex personalities which sometimes puzzle even them. ("N")

* Like other "F"s, they like to please, are good at human relations, value harmony, and cannot bear criticism. Chronic criticism from anyone close to them causes them to lose confidence, become immobilized and physically ill.

* Like the ENFJ, they are cooperative and willing to consult others and abide by group decisions. ("J")

* They make excellent counselors because of their personal warmth, enthusiasm, insight and depth of concentration.

ENFP: THE INDEPENDENT IDEALIST (5% of general population)

* As NFs, they are sympathetic and extremely perceptive about people, seeing life as pregnant with drama and meaning.

* Like the ENTP, they are original, independent and feel charged with a special mission to perform in the world. They feel desperately unhappy if their pursuit of that special mission is blocked. Both types want to be and do something extraordinary.

* They hate routine. ("N")

* They are charming and ingenious. ("E" and "N")

* They function on impulsive energy rather than will power. As "P"s, they are enthusiastic, adaptable, fiercely independent, and resentful of any kind of subordinate role in marriage or work relationships. They enjoy the process of creating, but are not as interested in the follow-through. They have difficulty working within traditional frameworks and following rules and regulations. As "N"s, they enjoy inventing new ways of doing things. They must personalize their projects or they lose interest.

* Being optimistic, enthusiastic, highly spirited ("P"), ingenious and imaginative ("N"), they have a wide choice of careers. However, like other NFs, they often have difficulty knowing what they want to do, for they have so many interests and are so versatile.

* Like other "P"s, they are highly unpredictable, have difficulty making commitments, and can shift from the role of parent to friend with their children, from being generous to being frugal, from being extravagant to being self-denying. They resist "future-oriented" plans like life-insurance, retirement funds, savings plans, etc.

* Being 'N's, they are very conscious of the gap between how things are (including themselves and their relationships) and how

they would like things to be, thus tending to be dissatisfied and sometimes highly critical of themselves for not being better.

* Like other "F"s, intense emotional experiences are vital in making them feel alive. However, in the midst of the excitement, they may feel split off from themselves, as though part of them is observing.

* They are excellent observers of people (NF), but often inaccurate in their negative interpretation of others' motives. Thus, they may be wrong in their judgments and conclusions due to their lack of "J".

* Hypersensitive and hyperalert ("NF"), they may live in anxious expectation of possible future emergencies.

INFP: THE MYSTICAL IDEALIST (1% of general population)

* They have the NF gift for language, poetry, simile, and metaphor. They excel in the field of literature, and any field that deals with possibilities for people, such as counselling, teaching, psychology, and sometimes even — surprisingly — science.

* Like other 'N's, they dislike small-talk, superficiality and shallowness, often feeling that they don't fit in because of their depth.

* As "P"s, they may resist or question external authority.

* As 'I's they are interested in internal reactions (sometimes overly so), and have great powers of concentration and depth of understanding. Though reticent and shy, they present a pleasant face to the world. Being introverted, they are reflective and introspective, and may prefer to communicate with written words, rather than making personal contact.

* They have a capacity for caring not found in other types. They care deeply, passionately, about a few people and causes, and are willing to sacrifice everything for that cause, which often involves helping others. To understand them, you have to understand their particular cause. ("N" and "F")

* They seek unity and harmony: of the physical and the spiritual; of emotions and intellect; of various factions within their group. Since the ultimate "merging" of disparate elements can never be achieved, a subtle tragic theme runs through their

lives, for reality never comes up to their visions of how things "should" be.

* They are very aware of people and their feelings and seek closeness, but also need time to withdraw, to reflect and create.

* Like other "I"s, they are not concerned with impressing others, and are quite self-contained and independent. ("P")

* They abhor showy displays of ostentation, although they have the "P" desire to perform.

* Like other "N"s, they are impatient with routine details.

* Like other "F"s, they are strongly devoted to their families, with an almost symbiotic bond with their family members.

* They don't mind if others make decisions, as long as it does not violate their value system. When it comes to values and ideals, the "fighter" emerges and they stubbornly fight for what they believe in. As "I"s, they can become so wrapped up in their internal processes (thoughts, feelings, sensations) that they fail to act.

ENTJ: THE COMMANDANT (5% of general population)

* They have a strong urge to give structure, to unify people in the pursuit of noble causes. ("J")

* They are like SJs in their tendency to establish plans for a task, but they are more concerned with policy and goals than with external regulations and procedures.

* They are impatient with errors and, as with other "T"s, not necessarily tactful in pointing them out to people.

* These are the ones who visualize where the institution is going and communciate that vision to others. ("E", "N" and "T")

* As "J"s and "T"s, they value efficiency and competency in others.

* Like all "T"s, they prefer to make decisions based on impersonal data.

* They enjoy executive positions ("J") and are tireless in their devotion to their jobs, often ignoring their personal lives.

* Their spouses should be self-sufficient and not make emotional demands which the TJ will not want to waste time

with. They are not concerned with romance. At home, they insist that meals be on time and the home attractive, well-ordered and maintained on schedule. They want their mates to be active in community matters, and to be socially sophisticated and well-educated.

* "T"s can be as devoted to their families as "F"s, but because it is the right, logical thing to do, rather than because of the kind of symbiotic relationship the NFs have.

INTJ: THE ARCHITECT OF THEORIES (1% of general population)

* They are supreme pragmatists - builders of systems and theoretical models.

* Their NT intelligence and "J" devotion to law makes them excellent *dayanim* and *poskim*.

* They are introspective, focusing on possibilities, and priding themselves on their logical conclusions ("N" and "J").

* Like other ITs, they can be away from home for long periods of time without suffering terribly from the lack of relationship.

* Like other "I"s, they have no need to impress others and are not impressed by authority based on position, rank, title or hierarchies. They conform to rules only if the rules make sense and are useful to them. If they don't, they won't go along, no matter who said it.

* They are like INTPs in their penchant for logic, but, as "J"s are more concerned with the future consequence of the application of new ideas. They are better at generalizing, classifying, summarizing, evaluating evidence, and proving and demonstrating their theories than the INTPs. The "J" always tests for usefulness.

* They have the "J" single-minded, ruthless drive to completion, always with an eye on long-term consequences.

* In relationships, they are very private ("I") and preserve a psychological distance, making them seem cold, unresponsive, and dispassionate ("T"). Like other "I"s, their emotions are hard to read, and they tend not to express their emotional reactions.

However, they are hypersensitive to signals of rejection.

* They drive others as hard as they drive themselves. Those around them may feel that they do not really exist and are incapable of satisfying the boss' demands.

* At work, people can come and go without fazing the INTJ, because their loyalty is directed to the institution above and beyond the individuals within it.

* Like other "J"s, they are firm and consistent disciplinarians with their children.

ENTP: THE DESIGNER OF SYSTEMS (5% of general population)

* They exercise their NT scientific curiosity and ingenuity in the world of people and things. ("E") They are good at analysis, especially functional analysis, and enjoy complexity of ideas. (NT)

* They are the most reluctant of all types to do things in the traditional manner just because that is how they have always been done. ("P") They have an idea of how it can be done better. ("N")

* If they don't like the way things are being done, they simply ignore standards, procedures, policies, traditions and authorities. ("P")

* With their extraverted "P" enthusiasm, they are a source of inspiration to others and easy to please.

* They don't want to "move mountains" like the INTJ, but rather act in the moment, improvising and adapting. ("P") They are like the ESTP in their risk-taking, but they focus more on competency and the sense of power which they derive from these experiences rather than the "SP" love of freedom of action.

* Like other "E"s, they are good conversationalists, with the "N" ability to follow and explain complex ideas. They enjoy debating, and are typically several steps ahead of their opponent. They are "masters of the art of one-upmanship."

* They make outstanding teachers, and enjoy making learning exciting. As mates, they are lively, adventuresome, gregarious and usually in a good mood ("P").

* Like other "P"s, they are so confident that they can adapt and improvise as a situation develops that they may neglect necessary preparations. Their excessive confidence about their ability to find a solution in a crisis can lead the family into economic problems because they do not consider the consequences of their actions and enjoy engaging in "brinkmanship," placing their careers and their financial resources in jeopardy.

* They tend to be non-critical and inconsistent in the attention they show to family members. As far as their attentions go, it is either "feast or famine," very attentive for a while, then suddenly not available at all. ("P")

* As "P"s, they are optimistic, fraternal, impulsive, recalcitrant to rules, shunning confining promises and duties.

INTP: THE ANALYST AND STRATEGIST (1% of general population)

* This is the most intellectually profound of all types, the logician, mathematician, philosopher and scientist all rolled into one. Their forte is detecting contradictions and inconsistencies in people's written or spoken statements. Thus, they are excellent in *Gemora*. ("N")

* This type exhibits the greatest precision in thought and language of all the types, with a quickness of understanding, ingenuity, and fertility of ideas in dealing with problems. Their weakness is to assume that an attractive possibility is as realizable in reality as it seems in theory. ("N")

* Principles are essential to them: they search for what is relevant and pertinent to the issue at hand. ("N" and "T")

* Like all "N"s, intuition makes routine difficult.

* They are more interested in analyzing a problem and discovering the solution than in carrying out their ideas. They are more interested in formulating principles and creating theories than sticking to dry facts. Like other "N"s, they see reality as something which is quite arbitrary. Thus, any possibility can be considered - or ignored.

* When giving an answer to a simple question that requires a simple explanation, they feel bound to state all the ramifications which their scholarly minds can bring to bear, sometimes coming up with an answer which is so complicated that few can follow it. But, to the INTP, anything less complicated would be too obvious and, therefore, not worth saying.

* They are able to concentrate better than any other type, and prefer to work quietly, without interruption, and often alone. If left to their own devices, they can retreat into a world of books, emerging only when physical needs become urgent ("I").

* Like other "P"s, they may resist external authority.

* They are open to new ideas and areas of intellectual conquest.

* Like other NTs, they abhor redundancy and incoherence, are not good at clerical tasks, and are impatient with routine details.

* Like other NTs, their driving force is a curiosity to understand the natural laws which govern the universe.

* They are sometimes intellectual snobs, impatient with those less endowed intellectually. This causes others to feel hostile and defensive in the presence of the INTP, whom they see as arrogant and aloof. The truth is that they are often brilliant, even geniuses, and it is difficult to be patient with more simple types.

* They make excellent teachers for advanced students, but are hard taskmasters, driving others as they drive themselves.

* Like other "T" mates, they are faithful and devoted to their spouses, but preoccupied. Introversion makes them dislike a great deal of social activity.

* They want order and organization in the home, but are usually compliant and easy to live with ("P"), though tend to be forgetful of appointments, anniversaries, bill-paying and other such routine chores of daily living unless reminded. ("N")

* Like other "I"s, they have difficulty expressing their emotions verbally. Their mates may feel taken for granted and unappreciated. The "I" does care, and does appreciate signs of loving gestures, only has difficulty expressing it in return.

* Because of their introversion, they are difficult to know and others may not realize their true level of competency. They are

shy except with a few close friends, and it is difficult for others to penetrate their outer reserve.

* They are adaptable ("P") until their princples are violated. Then they suddenly react very strongly.

* They have difficulty being understood by others because they are terse and blunt, expecting communication to be very precise, never redundant ("T").

* The home is usually well run and ordered, and they are serious about their children's upbringing.

* If the Feeling mode is quite undeveloped, they will be insensitive to others' needs or feelings and oblivious to others' distress.

ESTJ: THE ORGANIZED ADMINISTRATOR (13% of general populaton)

* They are very aware of the external environment, especially regarding neatness, cleanliness and order. ("J")

* Like other SJs, they are matter-of-fact, practical, and retentive of factual details. Like other "S"s, they are intolerant of complexity. They tend to dislike anything intangible, for their sense of security is based on judgments which they assume are absolutely correct. The world of intangibles, not being based on fact, undermines their sense of security, for they can no longer be so sure that their conclusions are absolutely true.

* Human relations are approached through traditions and rituals. There is a routine and a procedure for doing everything. ("S" and "J")

* Like other SJs, they are seen as pillars of strength.

* Excellent at organizing orderly procedures and detailing rules and regulations, they are good in business and industry.

* It is crucial for them to see that things are done correctly, and they become impatient with those who do not carry out procedures with sufficient attention to details. ("J")

* They are comfortable in evaluating others, writing reports on them and judging them on the basis of how well they are functioning in terms of the standard operating procedures.

* They are more interested in mechanics and processes than principles and theories ("S").
* They have "J" loyalty to their family members, institutions, work. They will do their duty even when it requires considerable sacrifice on their parts.
* They are punctual and expect others to be so as well.
* They enjoy holidays and functions where friends and family get together. Service to the community is very important, and they often belong to several community organizations. ("E" and "J")
* Though outgoing ("E"), they lack "F" responsiveness and may not always be willing to listen to others' points of view and emotions, especially if they are in a position of authority. It is often difficult for them to be open and responsive to those who are dependent on them - their children, spouses and employees.
* They are so comfortable with the established, traditional way of doing things that they don't understand why anyone would want to try anything new. ("J")
* They are dependable, consistent, and are what they appear to be. ("S" and "J")

ISTJ: THE MANAGING EXECUTIVE (6% of general population)
* They are decisive and practical. They make exhaustively thorough lawyers who catch the errors or loopholes in the fine print. They are very accurate and have great powers of concentration. ("I")
* They are the guardians of traditions and time-honored institutions. They work tirelessly for the institution of their choice, and are usually the ones who are most watchful that the institution's resources are conserved and not wasted. ("J")
* As "J"s, they worry about the future, and can be very anxious about the possibility of poverty or bankruptcy.
* As "I"s, they are quiet and serious, performing their work in an unostentatious manner, and are extraordinarily persevering and dependable.
* Their reliability, stability and exacting thoroughness with

details makes them suitable for work as examiners, auditors, accountants, officers, supervisors, etc. ("J")

* They tend to be patient with procedures, but not with people, as they tend not to understand needs which differ from their own.

* Like other SJs, they are pillars of strength.

* They are very dutiful, taking their obligations seriously. ("J")

* As parents, they have very consistent rules and definite ideas about "rights" and "wrongs." They scold and punish without hesitation. ("J")

* Interestingly, for such responsible types, they sometimes marry completely irresponsible people, with the idea of reforming them. The marriage develops into a parent-child relationship, with the ISTJ playing rescuer and reformer, as well as the one who must scold or punish the "wayward" one.

* They dislike ostentation in speech, dress or home. ("I") They like things to be neat, orderly and functional. Their clothing tends to be "no nonsense." ("J")

ESFJ: THE SOCIAL HARMONIZER (13% of general population)

* They are the most caring, self-sacrificing and sociable of all types. They are outstanding hosts and hostesses, remembering people's names, attending to others' needs, making sure that everyone is comfortable. Although they lack NF depth of insight, they care deeply.

* Their greatest desire is to be of service to others. They are often attracted to the health professions. They must work with people, in a friendly atmosphere, and feel very bad when isolated from others. ("F")

* ESFJ's are excellent supporters of established institutions, such as the home, school, and synagogue.

* Like all "F"s, they are very hurt by indifference. Initially, they give spontaneously, without any thought of reward, without strings attached. But eventually, they want to be shown appreciation for all they do.

* They are very concerned with their appearance, and take

others' opinions about what is "right" and "proper" very seriously.("S" and "J")

* They freely express their feelings and give advice about what people should and should not do. ("J")

* They respect rules and regulations, are loyal to their bosses, and do not mind living a routinized, scheduled life or doing routine, repetitive work. As children, they are responsive and obedient pupils. ("J")

* They are not interested in or excited by analysis of complex abstractions. What interests them are people and things, rather than ideas, ideals or principles. ("S")

* Like other EFs, they enjoy socializing and entertaining, freely showing their emotional reactions. They are soft-hearted, sentimental, and like to observe birthdays and anniversaries with some very special gift or party.

* However, they also have "J" pessimism, and may make others anxious with their gloomy predictions about what might possibly happen in the future if they do not follow the carefully prescribed rules and regulations.

* Like the ISTJ, they may marry irresponsible types (e.g., alcoholics). With their natural tendency to anticipate disasters, the result is usually that their worst fears are fulfilled.

ISFJ: THE MANAGER OF FACTS AND DETAILS (6% of the general population)

* They are the most self-sacrificing and least hedonistic of all the types. They believe in the work ethic, and usually work long hours. They will do everything humanly possible to complete a task, even if it means great self-sacrifice. ("J")

* Like other "J"s, they are very concerned with traditions and the conservation of resources.

* Like other SJs, they are greatly interested in commerce and business.

* Their lives are ruled by procedures dictated by law.("J")

*Their need to be of service leads them to seek work in medicine, teaching, bureaucracies, secretarial and administrative positions. They are especially helpful to those in need, as they like the parental position. As a matter of fact, if the recipient no longer is in a state of need, they may become indifferent.

* Like other "J"s, they have an extraordinary sense of responsibility and are particularly talented in carrying out routines which call for repeated, sequential procedures, such as in nursing, secretarial work, laboratory work, etc.

* They feel personally responsible for making sure that everybody else follows the rules and routines. ("J")

* Status is important to them, and they are usually interested in and impressed with people's titles, positions, and family background. ("J")

* They tend to be bored by speculation and theories, preferring to simply know and do what is useful and practical. ("S")

* It is very important for them to feel financially secure, to have a "nest egg" or a savings account. ("J")

* They may be uncomfortable if placed in a position of authority, and may become overworked because they will try to do everything themselves instead of delegating jobs to others. ("J")

* Their homes are likely to be meticulously maintained, both inside and outside as well. ("S" and "J")

* They like a few, quiet, modest friends, and are bothered by ostentation and boisterousness. ("I")

* It is very important for them to own and preserve their little "territory." Even as children, they must have their private space. ("I")

* They, too, may marry needy, irresponsible types and conduct a "rescue-rejection" game during the marriage.

ESTP: THE DIPLOMATIC REALIST (13% of general population)

* These are people of action. ("E") They are outstanding entrepreneurs, diplomats, and negotiators. They are at their best in dealing with mechanical and other concrete problems, rather than abstract theories or ideas. ("S")

* Life is never dull around them. They are gregarious and friendly and have the theatrical flourish of other "P"s.

* They are socially sophisticated. Their expertise in observing minimal nonverbal cues makes them masters at manipulating people and "selling" the client. This is not the result of "NF" intuitive feeling ability, but rather their acute powers of observation and awareness of external signals.

* Extremely resourceful, they enjoy working on the edge of a crisis. ("P") While others may find this nerve-wracking, the ESTPs are exhilarated by danger and brinksmandship. They seem to have nerves of steel. ("T" and "S")

* They make good negotiators. They can sell an idea to people in a way other types cannot. However, because of their tendency not to persist or to follow through with the details, they may cause even the best of projects to fail unless there are strong "J"s around to focus on the details and persevere to the end.

* If their desire for excitement does not find constructive outlets, their energies may be channeled into destructive, antisocial activities. ("S" and "P")

* Like other extraverted "P"s, they are charming, popular and exciting. They are unpredictable and do not always want to make deep commitments. They have a low tolerance for frustration and are apt to avoid or leave situations which involve interpersonal conflict.

ESFP: THE GREGARIOUS PERFORMER (13% of general population)

* They are charming, warm, witty, optimistic, and enjoy life to the fullest, refusing to acknowledge that anything bad might possibly happen. ("E" and "P")

* They can be generous to a fault. However, when there is illness or trouble, they may suddenly absent themselves.

* Like other "P"s, they are impulsive and always ready to try something new and exciting.

* They have the lowest tolerance for frustration of all types. They avoid anxiety by ignoring or denying the dark side of situations for as long as possible, sure that "Everything will work out." ("S" and "P")

* They are inclined to be easy-going and self-indulgent. ("P")

* They may agree with someone just to avoid a fight ("F"), but then go off and do things the way they want. ("P")

* Like other "F"s, they are gregarious and love to talk. They know everything that is going on in the personal lives of those in their community.

* They are not terribly interested in academic pursuits. If they want to know something, it is in order to determine its usefulness. ("S")

* They love anything involving social skills, drama and excitement: teaching (elementary grades), nursing, the performing arts, etc.

ISTP: THE MASTER OF TOOLS (15% of general population)

* They are masters of the tool: drill, needle, scalpel, car, paintbrush, hairbrush, hoe, tractor, etc. Whereas the INF is involved in the internal workings of human beings, these types are interested in the internal workings of things, in applied science, marketing and the mechanics of how things work.

* Like other "P"s, they love action for its own sake, even if it has no purpose or aim.

* They are sometimes extremely insubordinate, having no regard for status, rank, hierarchy and authority. The ISTP feels, "I must do my own thing and be free to move on." ("P")

* They tend to be fearless daredevils, thriving on excitement, hungering for action and speed of movement. ("P")

* They are expert warriors and love weapons of any kind. Like other "I"s, they can be away from home for long periods of time without feeling the lack, as long as they know there is a home to come back to. They get very restless if cooped up for too long.

* Their realism, sense of timing, and fearlessness make them good leaders. However, unlike the INTJ strategist or INTP logician, they are not "architects" in the way they think.

* Though they tend to be loners, they enjoy the company of

others who share the same interests. ("I" and "T")

  * They are generally non-communicative and show little interest in developing verbal skills or doing school work. They communicate with their bodies, through action and tools. Educators often think they are "hyperactive" or "learning disabled," but this notion is quickly discarded the minute ISTPs get near a tool and surpass everybody else in the speed with which they learn how to use it and the excitement and precision with which they relate to instruments.

  * They are quite unlike the ISTJ: The "J" is parental, pessimistic, conservative, accepting of rules and regulations. The "P" is optimistic, fraternal, impulsive, recalcitrant to rules, shunning confining promises and duties.

ISFP: THE GENTLE ARTISAN (5% of general population)

  * The most modest of all types, they tend to underestimate and understate themselves, taking their accomplishments for granted, not thinking of themselves. ("I")

  * They are also the most misunderstood of all types because they express themselves through action, rather than directly. Like other "I"s, if they cannot find a medium through which to express themselves, they retreat from the world, becoming rather "invisible."

  * Highly aesthetic, they possess an exquisitely attuned sensitivity to color, line, texture, shading, touch, motion, and sound. They are devoted to the fine arts: music, painting, dance. They are often gifted musicians, composers and artists. ("S" and "P")

  * They are reflective and sympathetic. They love people, love humanity, have an instinctive bond with animals, love nature and the land. ("F")

  * They lack the verbal fluency of the INFPs, preferring to express themselves in their artistry. Reserved and private, they are not usually interested in developing verbal skills in speaking, writing or conversation. Speech is abstract. Ideas are abstract. ISFPs prefer some more concrete way of relating, particularly

through the touch or creative activities. What they produce is far more eloquent than anything they might say with words.

* Like other "P"s, they tend to be impulsive, not liking to plan or prepare. They do not like to wait, for they fear that if they wait long enough, their impulse will die, and they will no longer have the desire to do what was so exciting to them such a short time ago. For the "P", to be devoid of impulses is to be devoid of life.

* They do not share the NF search for meaning and significance nor the NT fascination with science. They live in the here and now, preferring not to plan or prepare.

* They do not mind long hours of practicing with their instrument or tool, for the important thing is to act. ("I" and "P")

* Like other SPs, they are optimistic, cheerful, fraternal, egalitarian and insubordinate, impulsive, shunning obligations, rules, duties and confinements, enjoying excitement and chance, and tending to be trusting and generous. ("F")

CHARTS

As you read these charts, keep in mind that we are all mixtures of many characteristics. A highly functioning, healthy person, must, by definition, be a mixture of all modes. Dominance is determined by the percentage of each amount in any given personality. Obviously, not everyone will reach the high levels of excellence described here.

CHART #1:
MAJOR TRAITS OF THE EIGHT PREFERENCES

MAJOR TRAITS OF THE INTROVERT "I" :
likes quiet
likes to concentrate without intrusions and interruptions
intensive rather than extensive
may have trouble remembering names and faces
works contentedly alone
enjoys solitary pursuits
may have problems communicating freely
is energized by being alone
is reflective
interested in internal happenings
may be slow to respond to external cues

MAJOR TRAITS OF THE EXTRAVERT "E" :
likes variety and action
plunges readily into new and untried experiences
good at interacting with a lot of people
communicates freely
often acts quickly, without thinking
interested in external happenings
responds more quickly to external cues

MAJOR TRAITS OF SENSING TYPES "S" :
likes a pre-established way of doing things
acutely aware of external environment
reaches conclusions in a step-by-step manner
patient with routine details and precision work
rejects conclusions unless there is concrete, visible proof
good at observing the actual
possesses stamina and endurance
patience for routines
concerned with the pragmatic, with present reality, the here and
now
faith in common sense
dislikes complexity of thought
concerned with tangible, concrete sense objects and physical
needs
seeks perfection in action in the physical universe

MAJOR TRAITS OF INTUITIVE TYPES "N":
craves inspiration as the breath of life
wants to constantly change or improve what is
faces life expectantly
imaginative at the expense of observation of details
inventive, innovative, ingenious, and original
works in bursts of energy powered by enthusiasm, with slack
periods in between
reaches conclusions quickly

dislikes taking time for precision work or routine, repetitive chores
patient with complicated situations
excited by inner meanings, symbols, ideas, concepts
intrigued by fantasies, hunches, speculations and theories
always one step ahead, thinking about possibilities
enjoys complexity and profundity of thought
seeks perfection in the world of ideas and ideals

MAJOR TRAITS OF THE THINKING TYPES "T" :
values logic above sentiment
responds to words such as: principles, policies, laws, criteria, logic, objectives, justice, categories, standards, analysis
impersonal, more interested in things than human relationships
more truthful than tactful
can get along in a non-harmonious environment and may not even be aware of others' distress or hostility
blocks facial expression in a crisis
may hurt people without realizing it
firm-minded
able to reprimand and criticize more easily than "F"
stronger in executive ability than social arts
likely to question conclusions
brief and businesslike
good at organizing facts and ideas into a logical sequence
tends to suppress, undervalue and ignore feeling
intellecutally critical
not easily influenced by outside pressures or views

MAJOR TRAITS OF THE FEELING TYPES "F" :
values harmony, togetherness, relationships
sensitive to emotional climate: aware of people and their feelings
responds to words such as: values, intimacy, sympathy, harmony, devotion, appreciation
enjoys pleasing others and living up to others' expectations

dislikes telling people unpleasant news
values sentiment above logic
more tactful than truthful
stronger in social arts than executive ability
naturally friendly; difficulty being brief and business-like
may ramble and repeat what has already been said
may have difficulty organizing thoughts
may suppress, undervalue and ignore logic

MAJOR TRAITS OF THE PERCEIVING TYPES "P":
independent, autonomous, and insubordinate
spontaneous: has the ability to wholeheartedly experience the
moment even if some intended things go undone
open-minded: is willing to admit to new ideas even if they
conflict with one's own
understanding of others and tolerant of other points of view
curious and adventurous
zest for experience
adaptability arising from willingness to let go of the old and
improvise to meet altered conditions.
democratic

MAJOR TRAITS OF THE JUDGING TYPES "J":
judicious: wise, trustworthy, sound judgments
wants to manage, direct, plan, set limits
feels safe within strict boundaries
restrained, self-regimented, purposeful and exacting
steadfast, reliable, dependable, responsible
aims to be right and good
systematic and orderly
sustains effort through will power
decisive
exercises authority and willing to advise people
has firm, settled opinions
accepts routine
duty above pleasure

CHART #2:
GIFTS OF THE FOUR MAJOR TYPES

To be considered "dominant" in any of the four types, one must have a high percentage of the first five traits in that category.

THE SENSING-PERCEIVING TYPE (SP-"AMO") (dominant in 38% of U.S. population)
artistic/mechanical, good with tools, objects, weapons
adventuresome
fraternal
anti-authoritarian, insubordinate and defiant if coerced
independent, autonomous
optimistic, cheerful
enjoys taking risks
competitive
dislikes strict boundaries and long-term obligations
aesthetically sensitive to color, texture, line, touch, shading
impulsively passionate (Go! Do! Move! Spend!)
a natural performer
likes to be served
playful ("Play before work," or "Make work play.")

THE SENSING-JUDGING TYPE (SJ-"DOS") (dominant in 38% of U.S. population)
conservative (Wait! Think! Be thrifty! Save!)
dutiful, dependable, stable, reliable, responsible, trustworthy
devoted to traditions and rituals
seeks to do things the right way
conventional, formal, proper
does things according to plans, schedules
tidy, neat, organized
painstakingly thorough, attentive to details in the physical environment
hard-working and goal oriented
self-regimented and routinized
likes strict rules, regulations, orders and structures

paternal/authoritarian
meets others' visible, physical needs
believes in work-ethic, will power
dutiful; seeks to serve
puts group before individual

BOTH SP AND SJ SHARE "S" QUALITIES MENTIONED ABOVE

INTUITIVE-THINKING (NT-"KIP") (Dominant in 12% of U.S. population)

scholarly, scientific mentality
takes a logical, analytical perspective
objective and impersonal in their approach to problems
critical and naturally skeptical
hungers to be knowledgeable
understands the ideas, processes, and theories behind the obvious
intellectually ambitious
blunt, curt
exacting
holds firm to policies in the face of opposition

INTUITIVE-FEELING (NF-"LT") (Dominant in 12% of U.S. population)

warmly empathetic and appreciative
psychologically insightful
imaginative, intuitive, mystical
seeks emotional intimacy
enjoys a cooperative, harmonious environment
works toward mutual agreements
loves language, poetry, and the use of words to teach and persuade
enjoys similes and metaphors
cannot function properly in a hostile environment
seeks self-actualization

puts individual before group
responsive to inner, unseen needs
hyper-sensitive and hyper-alert
takes things to heart; easily hurt
easily influenced

BOTH NT AND NF SHARE "N" QUALITIES MENTIONED ABOVE

You will notice that you have traits in all the above categories. Just because a person is hard-working, trustworthy, and structured does not automatically signify that he is an SJ. We would hope that all types would have these qualities. However, if in addition to being hard-working, reliable, and orderly, the person is also very attentive to details in the physical environment and easily adopts or creates rules and regulations, then this would indicate an SJ. If an NT or NF is also very dutiful, structured, and attentive to details in the physical environment, then the person would be an NTJ or an NFJ. Doctors and dentists can be NFJs, even though they are using instruments in their work, if they are also empathetic with their patients and idealistic. They are not 'S's since their main preoccupation is actually with the metaphysical, not the physical. Their work is an avenue to a higher goal. Likewise, any of the types can be objective and logical, which are "T" traits, but only a real scholarly type can be a true NT.

CHART #3:
CHART DIFFERENCES IN COMMUNICATION STYLES

You will find that your communication with other types will improve if you use their own language. Sometimes, it works like magic to get the person's attention and cooperation.

KEY WORDS OF INTROVERTS:
"Let's leave early and go some place to talk quietly."
"I'm worried that I won't have the strength to go through with it."
"I really need to be alone for a while."
"Before I call, I want to plan what I'm going to say."
"I let others open up first. Then I can talk."
"A few close friends are better than a lot of acquaintances."
"I don't want to go to the party because I don't know anyone who's going to be there."

KEY WORDS OF EXTRAVERTS:
"It's important to be sociable and accessible to others."
"I like talking to people, even strangers."
"The longer I stay at the party, the more 'up' I get."
"Let's just plunge in. It will work out."
"I'll initiate; I'm sure others will follow."
"This is going to really make an impression on everyone!"
"Oh dear, my calendar is so crowded with social events!"
"I don't care if I don't know who's going to be at the party. I'm excited about meeting new people."

KEY WORDS OF THINKING TYPES:
"You'll have to give me logical reasons."
"These are my principles; emotions have no place here."
"Let's analyze why you are feeling this way."
"Give me a logical reason why I should go along with your decision."
"The data you've presented is not convincing."
"Let's analyze the situation logically."

"Let's understand the reasoning behind this."

"I'm looking at this objectively. I have no personal interest in the matter."

"Let's discuss it thoroughly."

"Let's not get side-tracked by diversions."

"I don't understand why I have to tell you again that I love you when I already told you before."

"I don't feel comfortable giving compliments. It feels phoney and like flattery."

KEY WORDS OF FEELING TYPES:

"Let me tell you how I feel."

"Let's take the humane approach."

"I'm trying my best to meet your expectations of me."

"The important thing is that we all work in harmony."

"Do you *really* like me?"

"What's the best method to teach this material so that we can arouse interest and enthusiasm?"

"I can't throw it out because it has sentimental value."

"We have to take other people's feelings into consideration."

"It's really hard for me to tell you this; but...."

"Please take extenuating circumstances into account."

"I so much appreciate your devotion and warm-heartedness."

"I am sympathetic to your cause."

"Let's come to a mutually-acceptable agreement on this."

KEY WORDS OF SENSING TYPES:

"Let's be realistic and practical."

"Let's deal with what we have here rather than what might possibly come up."

"Common sense is the best guide."

"Just tell me if it's workable. That's all I need to know."   "Is it useful? That's what counts."

"Where's the concrete evidence?"

"I don't trust hunches. Give me facts."

KEY WORDS OF INTUITIVE TYPES:

"Let's brainstorm and speculate about the possibilities."

"You have such a fertile imagination."

"I have a metaphor which can get this message across."

"I don't care if it's impractical. It's so ingenious!"

"I get so high just contemplating the sublime wonder of it all. It's all so inspiring!"

"What do you think would happen if...."

"Can you imagine...."

"Let's consider the unconscious motivations involved here."

"You can't always trust common sense. It's better to go with your intuitions and hunches."

"It's the principles that are important, not the dry facts."

"Just follow your instincts. It's probably the right choice."

KEY WORDS OF PERCEIVING TYPES:

"There are two points of view, and they're equally valid."

"Let's wait and see. Something is bound to turn up."

"Let's play it by ear. We'll adapt as we go along."

"Where's the excitement?!" "Where's the action?!"

"I'm wide open to suggestions."

"I don't need anyone else to tell me what to do. I'll do it myself."

"The deadlines can wait; we'll work at our own pace."

"I love to be spontaneous and impulsive."

"Stop trying to pin me down. I want to keep my options open."

"I'm so curious. Let's see what there is to discover."

"Just leave it there as it is; you can finish when you come back."

"You don't have to get there right on time. Let things flow and see how your time's going."

"I'm best at adapting as I go along and making do with what I have."

"Let's see what turns up instead of planning it all in advance. We'll let things unfold spontaneously as we go along."

"If it doesn't work out, we'll try something new. But don't worry. Everything will work out."

KEY WORDS OF JUDGING TYPES
"I'd like to know the rules and regulations."

"I'd feel better if things were settled and decided."

"Be responsible. You can't just think of yourself. There are other people to take into consideration."

"You can count on me to keep my promise, to be there for you."

"Let's take the conservative approach."

"I just want to be good and do the right thing."

"Let's consult a higher authority."

"We have to go through the proper channels."

"Make a schedule; you'll see how much easier things will be."

"A place for everything and everything in its place."

"Here's where I draw the line. That's it and no more!"

"Focus on goals! Have a clear direction!"

"I want to do it the right way."

"It's best to save. You never know what might happen."

"Let's make a firm decision right now."

"You have to think of your future, your goals."

"It's decided, settled, completed, planned, wrapped up."

"There's a deadline to meet. So let's get going. Stiff upper lip. The show must go on, no matter what."

"Justice must prevail even if it hurts."

"Make sure things are arranged, ordered, planned, structured."

CHART #4:
POTENTIAL WEAKNESSES OF EACH TYPE

POTENTIAL NEGATIVE TENDENCIES OF THE "I":
* remote, reserved, withdrawn
* tendency toward self-absorption and impracticality
* difficulty in communicating — has to be brought out
* trouble remembering names and faces
* takes too long to think before acting
* tendency to be self-doubting, self-critical and self-deprecating
* non-responsive to outer environment
* feels guilty and selfish about asking for needed time and space
to be alone
  * holds back when faced with something or someone unfamiliar
  * slower in responsiveness to ideas or objects

POTENTIAL NEGATIVE TENDENCIES OF THE "E":
* short attention span
* too much breadth at the expense of depth
* acts quickly, sometimes without thinking
* impatient with long, complicated jobs
* "driven" by hunger for variety and action

POTENTIAL NEGATIVE TENDENCIES OF THE "S":
* over-concern with external image
* lack of depth and content
* overly simplistic interpretation of complex concepts
* intolerance for complexity
* overly precise about external details
* uninspired, superficial, shallow, one-dimensional
* deterioration of religion into "religious materialism," (i.e.,
keeping the letter of the law, but losing the spirit behind it by
putting all one's attention on the external, material aspects of the
religion such as dress, food, furnishings, etc.)

POTENTIAL NEGATIVE TENDENCIES OF THE "N":
* inattention to practical realities

* tendency to be unrealistic
* imprecision in routine details
* overly complex intellectualizing
* impatience with routine details
* changeability, lack of persistence
* failure to live in the present
* idealization: places people on impossible pedestals, not seeing them as possessing human frailties

POTENTIAL NEGATIVE TENDENCIES OF THE "T":
* tendency to suppress, undervalue and ignore feelings and invalidate anything which is incompatible with their logical conclusions
* excessively demanding of competency and knowledge
* devastatingly critical
* tactless exposure of others' mistakes and deficiencies
* assumption that their conclusions reflect truth
* little awareness of people; may hurt people's feelings without realizing it
* excessive self-criticism over inability to always know all the facts and be knowledgable enough

POTENTIAL NEGATIVE TENDENCIES OF THE "F":
* overly talkative and repetitive
* exaggeration of discomfort and feelings
* suppression and devaluation of logic
* seeks harmony at the expense of honesty
* inability to stand up for one's rights or state views
* inability to give necessary rebuke
* excessively trusting, receptive and generous
* excessive reliance on emotions without reality-testing
* excessively merciful, soft-hearted, too "nice"
* over-eagerness to agree with others
* over-responsiveness and hyper-sensitivity to others' opinions and moods
* unrealistic demands for understanding and sensitivity

* excessive faith in communication to resolve differences
* self-torture over inability to please people or be sensitive enough to others' needs; critical of others' inability to be sensitive to their needs

POTENTIAL NEGATIVE TENDENCIES OF THE "P":
* unrestrained passion
* has to be constantly reminded of rules and regulations
* lack of perseverence, stick-to-itiveness and follow-through
* self-centered hedonism
* indecision, or impulsive decisions
* rebelliousness - refusal to accept external authority (May balk at having a Rav or accepting a Rav's decisions. Wants to make his own rules and live by them.)
* too open-minded and tolerant; lacking clear standards, principles, structures, and disciplines
* refusal to accept or keep commitments, responsibilities, obligations, duties, and promises

POTENTIAL NEGATIVE TENDENCIES OF THE "J":
* stiffness and propriety at the expense of human warmth and concern
* over-interference in others' lives (telling them what to do);
* closed-mindedness and rigidity
* excessive inhibition and strictness
* smug self-satisfaction with the known, the status quo
* mindless devotion to unnecessary rules
* over exacting perfectionism
* anti-pleasure
* inability to adapt to new and unplanned situations
* authoritarian, anti-democratic
* too quick to decide, to get things settled and finished
* bigotry - quick to condemn others in their entirety and write

them off completely on the basis of one or two statements or
actions, or because of differences of opinion
    * self-torture over petty details
    * self-torture over inability to be always good and right

CHART #5:
SIXTEEN TYPES

The various "talents" or preferences are combined in such a way that people will be described according to a four-initial description. Your decision is based on a percentage:

FIRST PLACE: Is the person more "E" (Extraverted) or more "I" (Introverted)?

SECOND PLACE: Is the person more "S" (Sensing) or more "N" (Intuitive)?

THIRD PLACE: Is the person more prone to use dispassionate logic - "T" (Thinking) or personal "F" (Feeling)?

FOURTH PLACE: Is the person more option oriented and open to new ideas ("P") or more decision-oriented ("J")?

Eventually, we end up with sixteen types.

Note that, although each is a separate type in itself, there is unifying principle in each of the four clusters:

Four NTs: ENTP, ENTJ, INTP, INTJ

Four NFs: ENFP, ENFJ, INFP, INFJ

Four SPs: ESFP, ESTP, ISFP, ISTP

Four SJs: ESFJ, ESTJ, ISFJ, ISTJ

Two people with the same four-letter combination will probably relate more easily to each other, as long as they are integrated. Each individual within these categories will be unique. Unintegrated people are very difficult — if not impossible — to deal with, no matter what the type.

*Much of this information is taken from *Please Understand Me*, by David Keirsey and Marilyn Bates and *Gifts Differing*, by Isabel Briggs Myers. The first can be ordered from Prometheus Nemesis Books, P.O.B. 2082, Del Mar, Ca. 92014. The second from Consulting Psychologists Press, 577 College Ave., Palo Alto, Ca. 94306. A book on differences in learning styles, which would be helpful to educators, is *People Types and Tiger Stripes*, by Gordon Lawrence, Center for Applications of Psychological Type, P.O.B. 13807, Gainesville, Florida 32604.

ADDITIONAL REMARKS FOR THE THIRD EDITION

First, I want to thank Tamar Kagan for her proof-reading and comments to this edition. Her help was invaluable.

I want to thank the many people who have read this book and have excitedly told me, "Now I finally understand myself!" Or, "After all these years, I have finally forgiven my spouse for being the way he [or she] is!" "It's so much easier to give people the benefit of the doubt now!" A number of parents said that their relationships with their children improved greatly (or even opened up for the first time after many years of being closed down) after they explained the system to them, for they now had a language with which to describe their needs and express their differences.

People often ask me, "What type am I?" I tell them that this is a personal decision and is not for me to say. One reason I do this is because I may inadvertently embarrass them by stating my opinion. Furthermore, an outsider never has a full picture of all the many aspects of any human being. I may help them figure out their type by asking pertinent questions, but I basically believe that each person should decide for himself. I tell them that it may take three or four readings of this book to make that decision.

People have pointed out that there are also other pairs such as hot-tempered v. cold and restrained, and ambitious v. phlegmatic. Such opposites can exist within any of the modes.

However you see yourself, do not let it be a cause for hatred of yourself or others. By accepting and understanding who you are, you then can give yourself permission to change and you create the atmosphere in which others may want to do so as well. So do not hate yourself for being who you are. That will only hinder your progress and make you hate others for being who they are.

If you meet resistance in your attempts to interest others in this system, you might mention that many people who were originally against the idea of classifications eventually came to see the many benefits of understanding the types. However, if you see that someone is really annoyed, change the subject.

Finally, a few people have mentioned that the information in this book could possibly be used to hurt people. That is true of almost any principle in Torah or in psychology. Used properly, this system will promote growth, understanding, forgiveness and love. Used improperly, the opposite will occur.

We read in the Passover Haggadah that, "In every generation, a man must look at himself as if he personally had gone out of Egypt." In Hebrew, the word "Egypt" is *mitzraim*, which means "places of narrowness." The purpose of this book is to help us identify our areas of "narrowness" so that we can then be better able to overcome these weaknesses. Anyone who uses this awareness as an excuse to avoid responsibilities or to condemn others has completely misunderstood the purpose of this book.

Please make sure that you do not hinder your growth by thinking that you cannot escape your narrow category. Readers should feel that they are mixtures of many categories and aim for balance.

INTUITIVE-FEELING TYPES

Dominant NFs are, in essence, mystics. Most "nice," caring people are SFs, not NFs. Mysticism is an impossible term to define. That is one reason why it is often so difficult for the NF to know himself and validate his innermost needs, since most of humanity cannot relate to those needs.

True NFs feel an interconnectedness with an extra-sensory dimension in people and in the universe at large. They have sensitivites to vibrations and energies that others do not experience. This can be either a blessing or a curse, depending on the emotional health of the NF and whether he can handle that energy and use it for constructive purposes. If used positively, this special sensitivity is a force for creativity, for bringing about closer relationships, for humanitarian activities, and for helping others understand themselves and the nature of the spiritual. On the other hand, it makes them more prone to various nervous ailments, loneliness and despair if they cannot find a means of expression or make the kind of contact they crave.

Example: "I love teaching, but since I have a large family, I have to spend a lot of time in the kitchen preparing food instead of delving into the secrets of Torah. I find it very helpful to think of the fact that the spiritual world is in the actual physical world, and even more present in the physical since the highest sparks of holiness fall the lowest. That means that there are sparks of *kedusha* in the food, and that by being aware of this when I'm preparing it, I am nurturing their spirits. Sure, I'd rather be learning or teaching all day, but as long as I have to be in the kitchen and doing housework, it helps to relieve the boredom by reminding myself that the physical is alive with spirituality. We should never think of the two as separate."

Most of humanity does not relate to this mystical approach to life. Yet when NFs find each other, it is very special.

Example: "I finally found an NFJ dentist and an NFP pediatrician for my children. They are both the kind of people who will call up after an emergency and see if everything is all right. That is the kind of care I seek in a professional."

Example: "People think that because I am so punctual and reliable, that I must be a 'J'. But actually, I am a 'P' and my strong sense of responsibility comes from my 'F' side — my deep caring for people. People also think that because I love people so much, I must be an 'E', but I'm really an introvert who just likes to be with people. However, I do need 'recovery time.' I used to feel guilty for wanting to withdraw, but now that I understand my nature, I take time for myself without feeling bad about it."

Example: "Before I had children I really, truly believed that the job of a mother is to be with her children. But when I was home all day, day after day, I felt like I was going to go crazy. I still envy women who can be home all day with their children. I just can't do it and stay sane. As an 'N', I have a stronger drive for self-actualization than the 'S's do. Now I teach part time. Those few hours give me a great sense of fulfillment and an outlet for my NF need for contact and creativity."

NFs can teach themselves to "toughen up" and not be so shattered by criticism and loneliness. They can even enjoy the challenge of retaining their sense of self-worth and interconnectedness to the spiritual essence of the world in the midst of rejection and isolation.

Example: "My NF husband used to be shattered when his SJ parents would visit — stomach upsets, insomnia, etc. Part of the problem is that to them, success means being rich, and being that my husband is in education, we will never be wealthy. Our values are very different from theirs. Once he understood their type and stopped expecting their approval and understanding, he stopped getting so angry about their comments. It's painful, of course, not to have the relationship we want, but he now has a lot more humor and detachment about the situation."

Example: "When my wife and I were having marital difficulties, I tried very hard not to let the children know. But the two dominant NFs picked up right away and were most affected. They quickly became very nervous and suffered from all kinds of psycho-somatic illnesses such as severe headaches and stomach aches. They had difficulty concentrating and eating. I had to give them a lot of extra reassurance that I would be there for them."

Example: "When I was younger, I was always running around to various experts, hoping someone could explain me to myself, calm me down, lighten the burden of my inner longings and chaos, and give me answers that would satisfy my need to understand myself and life. Eventually I learned that I had to manage the inner symphony on my own. I had to stop trying to find someone to take over, to give me refuge or reassurance. There are moments of sharing, but ultimately, we are alone. Ultimately, only Torah can give me direction and stability. My relationship to G-d is my ultimate relationship. I learned to bear the pain of the loneliness and the lack of answers by developing *emunah* and *bitachon*."

Example: "As an NF, I was really resistant to the idea that the majority of mankind falls in the "S" category. I just didn't want to believe it at first, because it made me feel isolated. But the truth is that most people really can't handle my intensity or complexity."

Example: "It gave me such a sense of power to realize that I could actually choose not to emotionalize minor irritations and disappointments. For an NF, that is one of the most important choices in terms of maintaining mental health."

Example: "After my fifth child was born, I was so tired and overwhelmed that I started getting cold toward my children, especially my older ones. Something in me snapped. I just didn't care any more about anyone. I got through the day mechanically. I felt like the most horrible mother in the world. I was nervous and criticized the kids all the time. I thought I had lost the ability to love. But discovering that I am an NF made me realize that the love was there. I just had to uncover it. I've been working hard to change my critical habit. For example, I made Fridays 'Endorsement Day.' We only say things which would make each other feel better. I hope I can make it two days a week and then eventually all the time. Another thing, when a child is misbehaving, I shut my mouth. Whenever possible, I just look the child in the eyes without saying anything until I see that the child feels bad about what was done and until I feel the poison go out of my heart and I can think of constructive solutions. It sometimes takes five or ten minutes of staring until I'm able to cool off and make contact."

Example: "I'm an NF who is about to be engaged to an ST girl who tells me, "I don't want to hear that nonsense," whenever I express a strong emotion. And we're not even married yet! Before I understood the types, I would have been certain that she would soften up after marriage. But now I am not so sure. One part of me says that I have to be loyal to my commitment to her, that it is my lot in life to have this pain, and that I can learn to bear it. The other part of me says that that's the attitude to adopt only when the pain is unavoidable, and that I'd be a fool to inflict suffering on myself when I can prevent it."

Example: "I think that the 'curse' of the NF is to assume that everyone has depth of understanding, and then be angry or bitter when it is not. Yet we often marry 'S's because they seem more stable and able to deal with the world, and perhaps because we want relief from our own intensity and complexity."

Example: "I've longed all my life for simplicity, order, inner calm, and to fit in somewhere. As an ENFP, I see I've been barking up the wrong tree! I better learn to like myself as I am!"

NFPs must perhaps be the most disciplined of all types. Their tremendous creative passions, "P" openness to new experiences, and "P" tendency to be scattered, all mean that they must work very hard to keep themselves balanced and focused.

NFs are utopians. This is often manifest in dreams of a society where there is perfect harmony and no conflict. Throughout history, NFs have begun various organizations and movements to bring this about.

The NF can use his special talents for good or evil. Some NFs, feeling unloved, become self-destructive, even suicidal. Other NFs use their charismatic personalities, verbal adroitness, and psychological insights to manipulate and control others. They may seem "spiritual" on the surface, but may actually have many of the traits of the abusive personality syndrome, which can appear in any of the types: a strong urge to hurt, humiliate, and punish others, and enjoyment from doing so; extreme jealousy and possessiveness; chronic criticalness; an explosive temper which is purposely used to terrify others into submission; stingyness and paranoia; no feeling or guilt, remorse, or anxiety about the pain they cause others; a split personality, in which niceness and rage alternate unpredictably so that others are confused as to whether the person is abusive or not; and the tendency to blame others for their own abusive behavior.

INTROVERTS

Example: "If I succeed in dragging my introverted husband to a social event, he enjoys himself once he gets there, and often does not even want to leave. I've learned that I must usually avoid taking his initial resistance seriously. But he's so introverted that he even feels uncomfortable if he has to eat in the presence of strangers."

Example: "My husband wanted me to hire a maid once a week. But I always felt so uncomfortable having someone in my home, moving around in my space, taking control of my things. It was a relief to discover that this territoriality is an aspect of my introversion. Now that I understand the source of my discomfort, I am better able to bear the thought of a maid in my home."

Example: "I've always harbored a secret fear that I would someday withdraw from the world and from people and not be able to make contact. I thought that this fear was very weird and a sign that I had some severe emotional problem. However, since I've begun talking to other introverts, most said that they had the same fear. Now that I understand the source of the fear, it no longer frightens me. To avoid letting the tendency to withdraw become extreme, I have resolved to work harder to maintain my contacts with friends, even if it means forcing myself to do so at times."

Example: "Now I know why I like to wear subdued colors and avoid anything flashy or ostentatious in my outer environment. As an introverted NF, my inner world is so dynamic and exciting that I need to be calmed by the external environment. I don't need more excitement than I already have. Thankfully, my husband is the type who believes that the job of a husband is to be a calming influence in the home. That is a tremendous help."

Example: "I used to resent that my introverted wife had such a small circle of friends, as I am an extrovert and would like a more active social life. Basically, she's happy just being with her own family members or one or two childhood friends. She never reaches out to others, though she is nice when people come to visit. Now that I understand her, I am less resentful."

INTUITIVE V. SENSING TYPES

Dominant "N"s usually experience a great of questioning, discontent, and a searching for meaning. They grow richer, more complex, more diversified with the years, whereas with an "S", you might now the person as well after a few days as you will ever know him.

Many NFs dislike having to deal with money, especially when

bargaining or controversy are involved. They would rather give in and avoid a fight. To some "N"s, having to deal with money is a come-down from what they see as a loftier plane of existence. That is one reason why they usually do poorly in business and are often taken advantage of by others.

Extreme "N"s may seem clumsy and uncoordinated when dealing with the "S" world.

Example: "I can almost gauge the amount of 'N' in a person by seeing how much he likes this book. The more 'S', the less he seems to relate to it."

Example: "After many years, I went to visit my parents. Right away, I started having these intense, deep discussions with my dad. Then, every time my mother would come in the room, we would both switch to 'S' realities, like food, finances, fashion, and various scheduling arrangements. As soon as she would leave, we would go back to our 'N' topics. I finally understood why, when we were small, she used to complain about feeling left out and lonely, since all her three children are various degrees of 'N'. By understanding her world, I was able to relate to her and her interests. Though we don't have the depth of contact I would like, we now get along well. I have another friend who had the exact same experience, except that his mother is the 'N', while his father is the left-out 'S'."

Example: "My husband is an extremely intelligent SJ who learns full time. He is very dedicated and devoted to learning and a real *masmid* [diligent student]. However, he is frustrated at not having that special NT brilliance. All I can do is remind him that many great Torah giants were extremely intelligent SJs who accomplished a great deal even though they were not brilliant NTs. As an 'S', I'm not big on complexities. I like to keep things simple and practical. I prefer that my husband be the way he is."

Example: "I am an 'S' and learning full time. But my 'N' wife really wanted an NT scholar. When she would come home from a class marveling about the depth of wisdom of the teacher, I would feel very jealous. Finally, I just told her straight out that her comments hurt me. Then we were able to talk about our disappointments in each other and in ourselves. Just being able to talk openly like this was very helpful."

Example: "I never thought my 11 year old would get into learning. He is an SP without mechanical or artistic skills, but with a lot of interest in money and sports. I had just about given up on him, but then he went to camp, and got so turned on by the fun, competition and prizes that he memorized 120 *mishnayot* in one month and hoped to reach 240 by the end of camp! I never thought he had it in him!"

Example: "My 'N' friend said that it was 'unspiritual' to want to look nice. I reminded her that the Holy Temple was a physical entity full of gold and silver and objects of beauty. The important thing is to dedicate this beauty to a G-dly purpose."

Example: "Every time I have to change the film in my camera, I take it to the local photo shop. Each time, the man patiently goes through the steps with me. But two or three months later, I have to come back again for him to show me once more because I always forget in the interim. I thought I was the only 'N' to be such a klutz with mechanical devices. But since I've been talking about it, other 'N's have told me similar stories, which makes me feel like I'm not such a dunce after all."

Even if this "N" sat down and sweated over those instructions until she understood them, it would not be the same as an "S" who "just knows" how these mechanisms work.

FEELING TYPES

True empathy requires that one be able to imagine how it would feel to be in another person's shoes. Since imagination is an "N" quality, do not expect an "S" to have the same degree of empathy as an NF, unless the "S" has a good deal of "N" imaginative skills.

Just as SPs do a lot of "verbal doodling" about the changes they would like to make, and SJs "doodle" about the need for more order in the external environment, "F"s do a lot of "emotional doodling." That is, they often get very dramatic and over-emotional with a lot of "I can't take it! I can't stand it!" "I'm going nuts!" "It's a catastrophe," "It's too much for me." A lot of the time, this is merely "emotional doodling," which can be avoided by having the "F" go into "T" mode and consider choices. (Obviously, if the "F" really is breaking down, a professional should be consulted immediately.)

Example: "I'm such a strong 'F' that I sometimes find myself buying an item just not to make the salesperson feel bad. In addition, I'm a 'P', so I tend to buy impulsively. Now that I understand how disastrous that combination can be, I stop myself when I sense that I am being too sympathetic toward a salesperson or getting impulsive. Now, I am more careful about purchases and other decisions, even though my strong impulsive nature is the same."

Example: "I am a strong NF and so concerned about not hurting people's feelings that I often don't ask for people to return books or money or other items that they have borrowed. I also agree to do things I don't really want to do. Recently, I even signed my children up for lessons that we do not have the money to pay for, just because a neighbor is giving the classes and I didn't want to say 'No' when she asked me. But now that I recognize this syndrome, I'm beginning to be more honest with people."

Example: "It took me years to make the connection between one tiny critical remark and my wife being cold for days or weeks. It astounds me how sensitive she is."

PARENTS: If you see that a child is a strong "T", it is very important to spend extra time developing "F" abilities, especially if the child is a boy.

JUDGING V. PERCEIVING TYPES

Example: "My 'ENFP' son was considering a *shidduch* [marriage proposal] with an extreme 'ISTJ' girl. When I asked if he really liked her, he would say things like, 'She'll be good for me because she'll keep me in line.' When I pointed out that she is very strict and has no sense of humor, he said he would teach her to be less up tight. But after he read about the types, he realized that such a person might not be amenable to change. Did he want to take that chance? I explained that he's the one who has to keep his own self in line. If it comes from an outside source, he'll hate it and will rebel. Also, he has a very creative and pioneering 'P' spirit, which I don't think she would appreciate. He came to the conclusion that he would like a more affectionate but stable 'J' with a strong 'P' side."

Example: "I had no trouble classifying myself until it came to the 'J'-'P' preference. On one hand, I see myself as a 'J' teacher of *halacha*, someone who is extremely upset by others' deviation from it or from my concept of justice. On the other hand, I love learning new things and refuse to be bound by convention. I am often the 'odd man out,' because I like doing things my own way. So perhaps I am 50-50."

Example: "My SP son came home from the first day of school and said that he had the best seat in the class. To me, an NF who loves ideas and contact with the teacher, 'best seat' would mean being in the first row next to the teacher's desk. But he said, 'No, the best seat is in the last row where I can move around and play with my gadgets without the teacher noticing.' If nothing else, I did thank him for his honesty."

Example: "I use every possible opportunity to overcome my 'P' impulsivity, even on small things like taking the time to screw the caps back tightly on bottles. My biggest victory is not responding so quickly when my children say something disrespectful. I used to tell myself all the time that, 'They make me crazy,' and 'They make me angry.' By taking responsibility for my own responses, I am ridding myself of this attitude of 'They make me....' I now feel more in control, instead of thinking that people and events control me. The more I talk about the need for responsible choices, the calmer our home atmosphere is."

Example: "I try to use every possible opportunity to overcome my 'J' rigidity. Like, this morning, I was standing in line at the supermarket. I noticed that the line next to me was going more quickly. But I felt that since I had already chosen the line I was in, that meant it was the *right* line and that it was *wrong* to change. By recognizing my tendency to think in terms of rigid rights and wrongs on non-essential matters, I was able to have the courage to move to the other line. It may sound silly to most people, but it was a real victory for me."

We often do not realize that what may be easy for us, because of our particular dominance, may seem like a Hurculean effort for someone of a different dominance. This is why it is so important to express joy over our victories, no matter how minor they may seem, as this positive attitude will encourage further growth.

Example: "I was trying to get myself and four children packed and ready for a trip. As a rather unintegrated 'P', this seemed overwhelming at first and I was getting very edgy and starting to lash out at them a lot. Then I starting using 'J' language to calm myself down. I kept saying statements like, 'Children, this is the procedure for getting lunch on the table.' 'This is the schedule for the next hour.' These are the rules for using that toy.' I walked around saying to myself, 'Stay focused.' 'Concentrate on one thing at a time. Make lists.' This all helped tremendously to keep me from feeling like I was breaking down. I keep telling myself that I'm not bad or inferior because I'm not as organized as I would like to be."

Example: "After reading this book, I am less hostile toward my 'P' children's difficulty with remembering and internalizing rules. For example, when I saw my son putting an unscraped dish in the dishwasher, I was going to explode at him. Then I thought that just because I've been telling him for months to scrape the dishes before putting them in does not mean that that rule has been internalized. 'P's don't see such patterns as quickly. So I simply reminded him in a non-hostile voice. And I see with my younger 'P's that whether it's saying their blessings before eating, going to bed at a certain time, or putting their dirty clothing in the hamper, it takes a hundred reminders. Now I just state the rule without hostility. I accept that it may take far more time for them to internalize rules than the 'J' children since the natural tendency of the 'P' is to break out of any and all boundaries. I could make charts and give stars and do these positive reinforcement tricks, but I'm not 'J' enough myself to stick to these plans! I hope to get to that level some day."

Example: "A 'J' friend asked what hour we have dinner each night. At first I felt so inferior because we have dinner whenever it comes together, and that usually means different hours for each child, since they all get home at different times and want to eat right away. I now realize that as a 'P', my life is more in flux and my schedules more flexible, and that does not mean that I am bad or incompetent."

Too much discipline, and the personality never has an opportunity to develop. However, too little discipline, and the personality disintegrates in a tumult of conflicting options and over-powering impulses.

PERCEIVING TYPES AND DECISIONS

Option-oriented "P"s do not fit into the kind of established mold which closure-seeking "J"s crave. This can cause them, and often their parents as well, a great deal of anguish unless their drive for independence and individuality is validated. Force a 'P' into a strict mold and he will either rebel or his spirit will die.

NPs (Intuitive-Perceiving) tend to be eclectic religiously, and may seek Torah wisdom from a broad variety of sources, often combining seemingly contradictory outlooks.

Example: "When I first looked at the types, I thought that I was more 'J' than 'P' because I am so organized and meticulous. But then I thought about all the times I was sent to the principal's office for misbehaving in class, and how I never really fit in anywhere. So I must have a strong 'P' part."

Someone offered a twenty-five year old NFP a *shidduch* [marriage proposal]. She replied, "I don't see how I can get married when I've only been Observant for a few years. I'm not sure of my *hashkafah* [religious outlook]. I don't yet know exactly what I want to do with my life. In fact, I don't even know *who* I'll be tomorrow! I want to be more settled first."

(The above young woman was encouraged to seek a compatible mate anyway. Being a "P", waiting to be "settled" takes a lifetime.)

Example: "Even though my spouse is a wonderful person, every once in a while, I start feeling dissatisfied with my marriage, and angry at myself for marrying so young. Now I realize that this is just part of my 'P' syndrome, and my craving for change and excitement. Before I understood myself, I might have taken these thoughts seriously. Now I stop myself from going off on these destructive tangents and focus on being grateful for what I have and how to bring some positive excitement into our lives."

The problem is that "P"s may always be in flux to some extent, and they have to dig in somewhere and make decisions despite it. However, NPs, in particular will never fit into any pre-determined mold. They are pioneers and innovators in the world of ideas. The SPs are pioneers and innovators in the world of concrete things, such as fashions, engineering, business, machines and other practical matters.

An NFP in her late 30's went to a very "J" therapist because she was having trouble deciding whether or not to marry a certain man. She also experienced herself as having a great deal of inner turmoil. She was a poetic, innovative teacher who had designed a special program to encourage teachers to alter their teaching methods in order to appeal to students who did not learn well in a traditional manner. For example, she taught teachers to alter their teaching methods in order to appeal to children who were dominant in the right as well as the left hemispheres of the brain, and how to stimulate children who were visual, auditory or kinesthetic learners.

Despite her successes and the fact that she had been teaching for 15 years, the "J" therapist saw her as unstable and disturbed because of her inner turmoil. She said that her client should continue therapy until she felt comfortable making decisions and no longer experienced herself in flux. Neither the "J" therapist nor the "P" client understood the "P" component in her personaltiy. After a year of such therapy, the "P" was very depressed and convinced that she was really, fundamentally disturbed. It was only after understanding the types that she began to feel better about herself. She found a more compatible therapist and changed her unrealistic goal of turning herself into a "J". A few months later, she was happy to report that, "My therapist is really helping me to like all the pieces of myself and enjoy my inner symphony."

It is important to realize that:

a. "P"s often fear making decisions because every decision involves a loss of those options which were not chosen. However, if the decision involves an increase in freedom or excitement they may have no difficulty at all in making up their minds!

b. "P"s may have trouble making decisions because they see both sides of the issue so clearly; both may seem equally attractive or "right." Ambivalence is normal for "P"s. They should expect that the process of acceptance, (e.g., "This is where I will live," "This is my job," "This is my spouse for life.") will be more difficult for them than for most "J"s..

c. "P"s think that because they *feel* bad when they make a decision, that the decision must *be* bad. This is a wrong attitude. "P"s should not wait until they have full certitude about a decision before taking action. They should not think that their inner discomfort implies that they should procrastinate or that they are wrong. They need to ignore the discomfort, have the courage to make a firm decision anyway, and not torture themselves with regret over their choice, whether it has to do with buying an item or choosing a mate. Usually, it is only *after* the decision has been made, that they know for sure if it was right or wrong.

The fact that the lives of "P"s are in flux and that they do not conform to any mold is, as with all modes, either a blessing or a curse. The blessing is their open-mindedness, courage to take risks and try new things, and innovative spirit. However, if they do not act responsibly and morally, that attitude is destructive.

PATIENCE

Each type must have patience for the other. For example, the children of NFs often sense that their parents are different from other parents and may be ashamed of them during their early teenage years. In a loving atmosphere, they eventually learn to appreciate your specialness.

"F"s often have to tell "T"s over and over what words and actions hurt or please them. The "T"s aren't forgetting on purpose. F"s should expect that "T"s may scoff at their feelings, invalidate them or ridicule them for their seriousness. If it would be helpful to speak up about this, it is best to do so in a serious, "reporting" tone of voice or, when appropriate, with humor.

Example: "While I was away on a trip, I called my husband who is a very restrained and unemotional 'T'. I very much wanted him to say that he missed me, or something loving like that. But he didn't. Just before I hung up, I had the courage to say, 'I know that you have words of endearment to tell me.' There was silence at the other end. Then he said that he missed me! I was thrilled! I have to get used to the fact that he does not like displays of affection and that if I get what seems to me like a five percent show of warmth from him, it might seem like a hundred percent in his mind. I'm hopeful that if I praise these little sprouts of love, they will grow stronger in time."

Reassurance is essential. Reassure "F"s that these minor upsets are not as bad as they feel at first. Reassure "J"s that nothing catastrophic will happen if they deviate from established procedures, consider new material, or change their schedules. Reassure the "P" that he won't regret his decision. All this should be done in a loving manner or you will alienate the other person and perhaps polarize him even further.

When talking to an "F" and trying to get the person to think more logically, first allow time for his emotions to cool off and the solution-oriented attitude to be aroused. If you are talking to a "T" and want to arouse feelings, allow extra time for the person to "engage" his feeling centers.

QUESTIONS

Since most people do not like to have their inadequacies pointed out to them, it might be better to ask questions. For example:

To a "J": "Is that your opinion or is it *halacha*?" "What terrible punishment do you think you will suffer if you make this change?"

To a "F": "I know you're upset. But what are your options?"

To a "T": "What would I have to do or say in order for you to take my feelings seriously?" "Do you realize that what you said was very hurtful?"

To the "P": "I know you want to rush into this. What would you lose if you waited a day or two? "What are the pros and cons of each side in this decision?"

TYPE AND PERCEPTION

Our perceptions are greatly colored by our type. For example, what an "N" might consider to be totally unimportant and insignificant details, the "S" might consider to be absolutely essential. What may seem like pretty good organization and order to a 'P' may look like a mess to a 'J'. What seems like "pampering" to a "T" may seem like legitimate loving-kindness to the "F".

Example: "My SF father was always doing for other people. My mother *perceived* him as being taken advantage of, but to him, helping people was the joy of his life."

Example: "My SJ doctor husband is the kind of person who must have all the shirts in his closet facing in the same direction and the top three buttons buttoned. He actually *enjoys* vacuuming and helping with household chores! As a 'P', I don't even *see* what he perceives as a mess."

Example: "I am an NF teacher. In a number of schools where I have taught, other teachers have sometimes complained that I do too much, like preparing too much material and spending my free time and lunch hours talking to troubled children. Now I realize that what is normal for an NF in terms of giving is seen as abnormal to many others."

Example: "My married son thinks he does a lot for me by just calling once a week. What seems like a small favor to me may seem like an enormous act of self-sacrifice in his mind."

Example: "My SJ daughter-in-law considers nothing less than a three-course meal to be a sign of love. If she doesn't do it for others or doesn't get one herself, she considers this to be a great slight to her honor or the honor of others. I just can't see putting all that time, effort and money into food, but this is her means of expression and her means of judging others' love for her, and I must avoid judging her for her attitude."

Lack of integration also alters perceptions. Unintegrated people can never be satisfied. They will always complain that others lack enough respect and love for them. Arguing won't help. Instead, validate the feeling by saying, 'I'm sorry you feel that way." Then try, "Let's focus on solutions. Tell me specifically how much time you want and how you want me to show that I care." The answer often has to do with food and housework. However, because they see themselves as impoverished, no matter how much you give, it always seems like nothing. No matter how little you spend, it will always seem like an outrageous amount. You can bend over backwards to try to please them and win their approval, but they will never be satisfied. Be as caring as possible without stifling your own needs.

TALK THE OTHER PERSON'S LANGUAGE

Example: "I needed more shelves in the living room. But my husband, a very oppositional ST, disagreed with me, as usual. As an NF, I was always so worried about not hurting his feelings and making peace, that I was going to give in, albeit resentfully. Then I realized, that as an ST, he actually *enjoyed* a good argument. That was a realization to me. So I started debating the subject and decided to be assertive until we came to some agreement. I saw that having a little fight really *energized* him, whereas it used to deplete me. Now that I understand that he doesn't oppose me to hurt me, I'm able to negotiate with him when I feel the issue is really important, instead of giving in passively and resentfully. He likes to talk the language of bargaining and negotiating."

Example: "It was only after reading about the types that I understood why my NF child is so different from the SJ. Like other 'N's, she learned to read very early, and still reads voraciously. She loves to be surrounded by books. She reads everything she can get, and on a very wide variety of subjects. She also kept a diary, on her own, from the age of eight. It was amazing to me. At the same time, she also has a very big SP side, and loves animals, sports and nature. She was also much more resistant to accepting outside authority. Through the years, my SJ has been much more predictable. She never had the same passion as the NF for books and ideas and new information. The SJ was excited and energized by activities and ideas which bored the NF. As an SJ, I did not understand the NF's needs. We used to mock her. I thought her teenage talk about death, for example, was just drama. Thankfully, I encouraged her to find people who could talk her language. As she got older, she saw how important it was to be able to switch and talk other people's language, and make compromises in order to be sensitive to other people's needs. I thought the reason these two didn't get along together and had so many fights when they shared the same room was because I wasn't a good enough mother. Now I realize that there were other forces at work."

Just as a fish cannot learn to "adapt" and live without water, the "N" cannot "adapt" for long to an environment or people lacking in inspiration. This is especially true for the NF, whose needs for contact and communion are so often mocked or invalidated by others. In such a situation, the NF's emotional discomfort often becomes manifest as a painful physical reality as well.

Remember, talking another person's language is a temporary mechanism, not a fulfilling source of inner satisfaction for any length of time.

THE SHADOW

Psychologists who deal with this personality system refer to the non-dominant side of the personality as the "shadow". The shadow may manifest itself unexpectedly, in a sudden expression which is uncharacteristic of the person, or in a profound change due to various circumstances.

Example: "I used to be a much more fun-loving 'P', but my husband was an even stronger 'P'. I had to develop my 'J' side and become very organized and responsible about financial matters just so someone would be 'manning the ship' around here."

Excessive pressure to develop one's shadow side can have detrimental effects:

Example: "Before marriage, I was slightly introverted. But my 'F' need for affection and 'P' desire to perform made me enjoy being around people. Then I married a much more introverted STJ with almost no need for affection or socializing. Over the years, I became much more inhibited and introverted to the point where I now find it difficult to reach out to people or be spontaneously affectionate because I am so certain of her disapproval. One highly 'P' child is quite a nervous wreck because he had so much disapproval from her for that side of himself."

The "P" is happiest when discharging energy, whether it be in sports, writing, talking to people, using a tool or instrument or just moving around. "P"s are going to march to their own inner drummer no matter how upset others are with their behvaior. Instead of trying to break their spirits, they should be encouraged to find positive outlets for their energies and praised for developing their shadow side, i.e., self-restraint, long-range planning, and on-going commitment.

Example: "Whenever I would express my need for closeness, certain people would tell me that it was because of the early influence of television and Western values. So I tried to suppressing my needs. But it didn't really work. I was only fooling myself. Now I realize that even if I had been brought up on a desert island or never heard the word TV, I would have this craving. It is not something to be ashamed of.

"It seems to me that the reason men are required to pray so often is because we need to awaken in ourselves this ability to express love and appreciation for G-d so that we can do the same for the people around us. Does G-d need our praise, or are we the ones who need to praise, for our own inner spiritual development? I think prayer is for us basically. We pray three times a day to get us used to expressing love. If we don't transfer that expression to others, our prayers have no real meaning. G-d does not command us to pray once a week or once a year, but every day, at least three times a day, to keep us in the habit of expressing love, paise and appreciation for others. If we don't do it, if we fail to nurture the people around us and ourselves, we become emotionally crippled."

Even if people have been crippled by early childhood deprivation, they can learn to make at least a minimal emotional investment in relationships if they really want to do so. But the realization that something is missing may take years to develop, and afterwards, it takes constant perseverence on the part of both partners to make sure that time is set aside for sharing.

NFs are the ones most likely to feel a profound, existential loneliness. They are the ones most likely to talk about universal brotherhood and humanitarian ideals. They are likely to read and re-read literature on the holocaust, to agonize over man's inhumanity and insensitivity to man, and constantly ask, "How can people be so uncaring?"

"S"s are not intellectual agonizers. It is the "N"s who tend to agonize over profound philosophical and psychological questions.

People often ask if they, or those around them, can change. Hope lies in the existence of the shadow self, and one's desire to develop it. However, be aware, that the dominant side will take precedence in the long run.

A FINAL REMINDER

The ability to love is like the ability to play an instrument. A lot of people "play" very poorly or not at all. There are very few Reb Aryeh Levins who have so much warmth, understanding and sensitivity for their fellowman. Be forgiving and understanding of yourself and all those who have not yet polished their "loving" skills or who may not even know what these skills consist of.

Our Holy Temple required the combined talents of scholars and ritual slaughterers, mystics and bakers, engineers and poets, musicians and common laborers, artists and artisans of all kinds.

Every person had a unique contribution, which was his particular way of serving G-d.

The same is true in terms of different personality types, all of which are equally important and necessary. Within the framework of Torah values, we must develop respect for others, each with his or her individual talents, needs and drives. Each person is created in the image of G-d, and, as such, is equal to every other in terms of intrinsic value. Each of us wants to be loved, accepted and understood as we are. Perhaps the re-building of the third Holy Temple will come about only when we recapture this spirit of respect for each individual.

In *Brachoth* 58a, our Sages teach us that when a person sees a multitude of Jews gathered together, he should say a special blessing: "Baruch chacham ha'razim." (Blessed is the Wise One of the hidden). They explain this blessing as showing appreciation for G-d's greatness for the extraordinary feat of having created such an infinite variety of human beings. Just as He created no two people with the same physical features, so too, "ain da'atam zeh l'zeh," (no two people are at the exact same level of awareness and understanding.)

A Torah outlook requires that we see every person as a being of infinite value. No matter how much we know about ourselves or each other, we have only scratched the surface. There will always be a world of "hidden truths" within us which remains to be revealed.

By showing appreciation for our unique, individual differences, we show our appreciation to G-d for His wondrous ability to create such variety in man. When we focus on gratefulness, we are less likely to feel resentment and annoyance towards others, or despair about ourselves. May our ability to feel such gratefulness grow with the years, and bring us to a heartfelt love of others as ourselves.

INDEX

GLOSSARY
bitachon: confidence in G-d
Chazal: our wisest Torah scholars
chevra kadisha: the group which takes care of preparing the dead
for burial
chiddushim: new insights into Torah
dan l'chaf zchuth: give the benefit of the doubt
Dayanim: Rabbinical judges
emunah: faith in G-d
gabbai: the caretaker of a synagogue
Gadol: A great Torah scholar
halacha: Torah law
kiddush: Sabbath prayer over wine
lashon hara: gossip
middah: a good character trait
milchig and fleishig: milk and meat
nisayon: a difficult test which becomes a learning experience
Poskim: Rabbinical scholars who give decisions regarding Torah
law
shtender: a small lectern
shivah: the seven-day mourning period
simcha: joy
Talmid chacham: A Torah scholar
traife: non-kosher food
Yiddishkeit: Judaism